ISBN: 978129002730

Published by:
HardPress Publishing
8345 NW 66TH ST #2561
MIAMI FL 33166-2626

Email: info@hardpress.net
Web: http://www.hardpress.net

WILD CAT

LLOYD'S NATURAL HISTORY.

EDITED BY R. BOWDLER SHARPE, LL.D., F.L.S., &c.

A HAND-BOOK

TO THE

BRITISH MAMMALIA.

BY

RICHARD LYDEKKER, B.A., F.R.S.,

Vice-President of the Geological Society, etc., etc., etc.

LONDON:

EDWARD LLOYD, LIMITED,

12, SALISBURY SQUARE, FLEET STREET.

1896.

PRINTED BY
WYMAN AND SONS, LIMITED.

PREFACE.

THE Author, in his Preface, has exhausted the material for an introductory notice to this little work, for the scope of which I must refer the reader to Mr. Lydekker's own words. It is a significant fact that in the present day no author pretends to write a complete account of his subject, who does not take some notice of its Palæontological aspect, and I feel myself very fortunate in having secured the assistance of such a well-known Palæontologist as my friend Mr. Lydekker for this record of our British Mammalia, past and present.

Mr. Lydekker is not an advocate for the adoption of the *Scomber scomber* principle in zoological nomenclature. I feel convinced, however, that the absolute justice of retaining every specific name given by Linnæus will some day be recognised. Thus, in my opinion, the correct title of the Badger should be *Meles meles* (L.); of the Otter, *Lutra lutra* (L.); of the Roe-deer, *Capreolus capreolus* (L.); of the Common Porpoise, *Phocæna phocæna* (L.); of the Killer, *Orca orca* (L.).

R. BOWDLER SHARPE.

AUTHOR'S PREFACE.

ALTHOUGH memoirs relating to particular groups have from time to time made their appearance, no Monograph of the British Mammals as a whole has been published since the second edition of Bell's "British Quadrupeds" in 1874. Since that date considerable advances have been made with regard to our knowledge of the geographical distribution of our Native Mammals, while the careful study of nomenclature instituted of late years, has rendered it necessary that many of our Mammals should be known by scientific names different from those by which they have been commonly designated in the older works on Natural History. These two circumstances would alone justify the issue of the present volume; but there is a further justification for its appearance, in that it contains, for the first time in a work of this nature, brief notices of the species exterminated within the historic period, with a further section devoted to the fossil forms.

The Author makes no claim to being an observer of the habits of British Mammals; and he has accordingly drawn largely from Macgillivray's excellent "Manual," published in the original issue of the "Naturalist's Library." Indeed, the present volume may be regarded almost as a new edition of that excellent, although now somewhat antiquated, work. When necessary, Macgillivray's observations have, however, been added to or modified; and the Author's best thanks are due to Mr. A. Trevor-Battye and Mr. W. E. de Winton for many original observations on the subject of habits. Thanks are also due to Mr. J. E. Harting, from whose numerous papers on British Mammals, especially his volume on the species recently exterminated from our islands, and also his Report on the "Vole-Plague," a large amount of matter has been culled. My acknowledgments must likewise be tendered to Mr. A. G. More, of the Dublin Museum, for much important information kindly communicated by letter on the subject of Irish Mammals.

Although attention has been especially directed to the subject of distribution, it has not been deemed necessary to give the name of every county from which the more uncommon species have been recorded.

RICHARD LYDEKKER.

SYSTEMATIC INDEX.

LIST OF PLATES.

BRITISH MAMMALS.

INTRODUCTION.

ACCORDING to the admirable classification proposed by Dr. A. R. Wallace, the British Islands come under the category of "Continental" Islands; that is to say, they are islands of large size, composed to a great extent of sedimentary rocks, and situated near to a continent, with the fauna and flora of which their own animals and plants agree to a greater or less extent. Many islands of this class have evidently been united to the continents to which they are adjacent, at no very remote epoch; and this is attested in our own case not only by the shallowness of the English Channel and the North Sea, but likewise by the similarity of the geological formations on the two sides of the Channel, as well as by the fact that there is not a single indigenous species of British Mammal that is not likewise met with on the Continent. That there are certain continental Mammals now unknown in a living condition in our islands is, indeed, true, but of this we have an adequate and sufficient explanation. Before discussing this point it may, however, be well to mention that the second group of islands in Dr. Wallace's classification are termed "Oceanic" Islands. These are generally of small size, situated either in mid-ocean, where they rise abruptly from great depths, or, if near to a continent, separated therefrom by exceedingly deep water. Instead of largely consisting of ordinary sedimentary rocks, formed in seas of moderate depth, they are in most or all cases composed of coral or igneous rocks ; and as their fauna and flora are of a totally different type from that of the continents to which they are nearest, it is evident that they have always existed as islands.

To unite the whole of the British Islands to the Continent would require an elevation of one hundred fathoms at the most; and that these islands formerly stood at a much higher elevation than is at present the case, we have abundant evidence. There occur, for instance, on many parts of our coasts, submerged forests belonging to a comparatively late period, which are now only partially exposed at very low spring-tides after stormy weather, when they are seen to contain stumps of trees rooted in their natural position in the soil, mixed with deposits, containing remains of existing kinds of plants and animals. Such submerged forests occur near Torquay in Devonshire, and Falmouth in Cornwall, as well as on various parts of the coast of Wales, and in Holyhead Harbour. In the case of Falmouth it is estimated that the submergence has been close on seventy feet. Again, on the east coast of England, at Cromer in Norfolk, we have another submerged forest of older date, which belongs either to the base of the Pleistocene, or the upper part of the Pliocene period, and is known as the "forest-bed." Moreover, the occurrence of thousands of teeth of the Mammoth, as well as remains of other Mammals which lived during the Pleistocene epoch, or the one immediately preceding our own, on the Dogger Bank, in the North Sea, affords further testimony that this area formed at no very distant epoch a connecting land-link between Britain and the Continent.

If we need further evidence of this subsidence, we have it

In the numerous ancient valleys and river-channels which are met with in various parts of the country, running at depths of from one hundred to more than two hundred feet below the present level, and frequently cutting right across the present lines of drainage, and connecting valleys now completely separate. Completely choked with deposits of sand and mud, and showing no evidence of their existence in the present configuration of the country, these ancient drainage channels have been revealed to us by the borer, and afford incontestable evidence of a very extensive subsidence. The evidence of this submergence indicates, therefore, that at no very distant epoch portions, at least, of the land must have stood at least two hundred and fifty feet higher above the sea than they do at present, and probably considerably more; and such an elevation would, in the opinion of Dr. Wallace, have been amply sufficient to unite England with the Continent.

We may admit, then, that during, or about, the period when the Norfolk forest-bed (which, we may state, antedates the Glacial epoch) was deposited, the British Islands were connected with the Continent, and doubtless also with one another. And it would appear from the researches of palæontologists that their Mammalian fauna was then in all probability identical, or nearly so, with that of the Continent. For instance, apart from a host of extinct species, into the consideration of which it will be unnecessary to enter on this occasion, it appears that during the forest-bed period there existed in England the Russian Desman (*Myogale moschata*), the Continental Field-Vole (*Microtus arvalis*), and the more arctic Glutton (*Gulo luscus*) and Musk-Ox (*Ovibos mo..hatus*). And there is evidence that at the later period of the caverns and brick-earths there were many other Continental forms, such as the Lemming (*Cuniculus torquatus*), two species of Suslik (*Spermophilus*), the Elk (*Alces machlis*), the Reindeer (*Rangifer tarandus*), &c., &c.

It should be added that the evidence of the non-existence of these forms during the period of the forest-bed is merely of a negative nature.

On the other hand, at the present day, Britain lacks a very large number of the species of Mammals now inhabiting the Continent, and this deficiency is much more marked in the case of Ireland than it is in England and Scotland; while if we take into consideration Reptiles and Amphibians, which are much less readily dispersed than are Mammals, the discrepancy is still more marked.

In dealing with the Mammals, we must of course omit all the purely aquatic forms, such as Seals, Whales, Porpoises, Dolphins, &c., and confine our attention to those which pass the whole or a large portion of their time on land. On the other hand, it is obvious that we have no right to exclude species like the Wolf and Wild-Boar, which have been exterminated by human agency, during the historic period ; and we accordingly reckon all such as part and parcel of the present British fauna.

The following list includes the various species of terrestrial Mammals which are known to have inhabited the British Islands during the historic period, the writer being indebted to Mr. A. G. More, of Dublin, for those found in Ireland.

1. Greater Horse-shoe Bat (*Rhinolophus ferrum-equinum*).
2. Lesser Horse-shoe Bat (*Rhinolophus hipposiderus*).   I.
3. Long-eared Bat (*Plecotus auritus*).   I.
4. Barbastelle Bat (*Synotus barbastellus*).
5. Serotine Bat (*Vesperugo serotinus*).
6. Noctule Bat (*Vesperugo noctula*).
7. Hairy-armed Bat (*Vesperugo leisleri*).   I.
8. Pipistrelle Bat (*Vesperugo pipistrellus*).   I.
9. Daubenton's Bat (*Vespertilio daubentoni*).   I
10. Reddish-grey Bat (*Vespertilio nattereri*).   I.
11. Bechstein's Bat (*Vespertilio bechsteini*).

12. Whiskered Bat (*Vespertilio mystacinus*). I.
13. Hedge-hog (*Erinaceus europæus*). I.
14. Mole (*Talpa europæa*).
15. Common Shrew (*Sorex vulgaris*).
16. Lesser Shrew (*Sorex pygmæus*). I.
17. Water-Shrew (*Crossopus fodicus*).
18. Wild Cat (*Felis catus*).
19.*Wolf (*Canis lupus*). I.
20. Fox (*Canis vulpes*). I.
21. Pine-Marten (*Mustela martes*). I.
22. Polecat (*Mustela putorius*).
23. Stoat (*Mustela erminea*). I.
24. Weasel (*Mustela vulgaris*).
25. Badger (*Meles taxus*). I.
26. Otter (*Lutra vulgaris*). I.
27.*Brown Bear (*Ursus arctus*). I.
28. Squirrel (*Sciurus vulgaris*). I. (? introduced.)
29.*Beaver (*Castor fiber*).
30. Dormouse (*Muscardinus avellanarius*).
31. Harvest-Mouse (*Mus minutus*).
32. Wood-Mouse (*Mus sylvaticus*). I.
33. Yellow-necked Mouse (*Mus flavicollis*).
34. Common Mouse (*Mus musculus*). I.
35.†Black Rat (*Mus rattus*). I.
36.†Brown Rat (*Mus decumanus*). I.
37. Common Field-Vole (*Microtus agrestis*).
38. Bank-Vole (*Microtus glareolus*).
39. Water-Vole (*Microtus amphibius*).
40. Common Hare (*Lepus europæus*).
41. Mountain-Hare (*Lepus timidus*). I.
42.†Rabbit (*Lepus cuniculus*). I.
43. Wild Cattle (*Bos taurus*).
44. Red Deer (*Cervus elaphus*). I.
45.†Fallow Deer (*Cervus dama*). I.

46. Roe Deer (*Capreolus caprea*).
47.*Wild Boar (*Sus scrofa*).   I.

In this list No. 11 has but little right to a place, having only
been taken once in Britain.   Three other Bats, namely *Vesperugo discolor*, *Vespertilio dasycneme*, and *Vespertilio murinus*,
which have been recorded from England, are altogether omitted,
since the first was almost certainly introduced, while the other
two have no claim to be regarded as habitual denizens of our
area.   The four species marked with a * are extinct, and perhaps Wild Cattle should be included under the same heading.
The Reindeer is not mentioned, since its existence within the
limits of the British Islands during the historic period is very
doubtful.   Those species which have been introduced have a
† prefixed to their names ; while such as occur in Ireland have
the affix ."I."   It is not improbable that the Common Mouse
should be included under the former heading.

Omitting the latter, together with those forms which are certainly known to have been introduced, and likewise disregard-
ing Bechstein's Bat, we thus have a total of forty-one terrestrial
Mammals which can be regarded as indigenous inhabitants of
Britain during the historic period ; five, or perhaps six, of these
being extinct.   Out of these only twenty-three are found in Ireland ; and since the Squirrel was probably introduced into that
island, while three species are now exterminated, the list of
truly indigenous living Hibernian terrestrial Mammals is reduced to nineteen.   On the other hand, it is stated by Dr.
Wallace that Germany possesses nearly ninety species, and
even Scandinavia as many as sixty ; although it is probable
that these numbers include the introduced species mentioned
above.

We have now to account for this discrepancy between the
British and Continental Faunas ; and here we may state that
the Glacial period, during which the greater part of Britain

appears to have been covered with an ice-sheet similar to that now enveloping Greenland, occurred subsequently to the deposition of the Norfolk forest-bed, but attained its maximum before that of the brick-earths of the Thames Valley and the loam filling our caves. The relations of these later deposits are, however, far from being fully understood; and it is quite probable that some of the beds indicating a comparatively mild climate were laid down during warm interludes in the Glacial period, which would account for the curious oscillations of southern and northern forms of Mammals met with in our later deposits.

With regard to the date when the last union of Britain with the Continent took place, Dr. Wallace, in his "Island Life," writes that this "was comparatively recent, as shown by the identity of the shells [found in the later deposits] with living species, and the fact that the buried river-channels are all covered with clays and gravels of the Glacial period, of such a character as to indicate that most of them were deposited above the sea-level. From these and various other indications geologists are all agreed that the last continental period, as it is called, was subsequent to the greatest development of the ice, but probably before the cold period had wholly passed away."

In referring to the poverty of Britain as compared with the Continent in species, the same author observes that "the former union of our islands with the Continent is not, however, the only recent change they have undergone. There is equally good evidence that a considerable portion, if not the entire area, has been submerged to a depth of nearly two thousand feet, at which time only what are now the highest mountains would remain as groups of rocky islets. This submersion must have destroyed the greater part of the life of our country; and as it certainly occurred during the latter part of the Glacial

epoch, the subsequent elevation and union with the Continent
cannot have been of very long duration, and this fact must have
had an important bearing on the character of the existing
fauna and flora of Britain. We know that just before and
during the Glacial period we possessed a fauna almost, or quite,
identical with that of adjacent parts of the Continent and
equally rich in species. The submergence destroyed this
fauna ; and the permanent change of climate on the passing
away of the Glacial conditions appears to have led to the extinction or migration of many species in the adjacent continental areas, where they were succeeded by the assemblage of animals now occupying Central Europe. When England became
continental, these entered our country; but sufficient time
does not seem to have elapsed for the migration to have been
completed before subsidence again occurred, cutting off the
further influx of purely terrestrial animals, and leaving us without the number of species which our favourable climate and
varied surface entitle us to. . . . . The depth of the
Irish Sea being somewhat greater than that of the German
Ocean, the connecting land would there probably be of small
extent and of less duration, thus offering an additional barrier
to migration, whence has arisen the comparative zoological
poverty of Ireland."

It will be apparent from this that Dr. Wallace attributes the
clean sweep, which he considers to have been made of the ancient British fauna, not to the ice-sheet at the epoch of maximum glaciation, but to a submergence of much later date.
It does not appear, however, that the evidence that the submergence in question took place at such a late date is by any
means decisive; and other geologists attribute the disappearance of the greater part of the fauna to the ice-sheet itself, a
view with which we ourselves are more inclined to agree. On
the other hand, as we shall presently see, another writer disputes

the clean sweep of the fauna altogether, and thinks it may have survived in the southern part of England, whence it again spread northwards with the return of more favourable conditions; although with the loss of such forms as were unable to withstand a considerable amount of cold. On this latter view it is considered that Britain was never connected with the Continent after the passing away of the Glacial period.

To make matters more intelligible, we may give a summary (taken from Mr. Horace Woodward's "Geology of England") of what Prof. James Geikie considers to have been the sequence of physical changes in Britain subsequent to the deposition of the Norfolk forest-bed, arranged in chronological order.

1. Deposition of Norfolk forest-bed, and indications of approaching cold.

2. "Till" deposits of Cromer, and the lowest Boulder Clay (an ice-formation) of other parts; this being a period of elevation of land, accompanied by severe glacial conditions.

3. Period of considerable submergence, during which marine sands and gravels were deposited in many parts, reaching nearly to the summit of Moel Tryfaen; this epoch being apparently equivalent to Dr. Wallace's great period of submergence.

4. Period of elevation of land, during which a large portion of Britain was covered with sheet-ice, and the greater part of the Boulder Clay was deposited; this being the period when, according to the more general view, the country was uninhabited by the greater part of the Mammals with which it is now populated.

5. A period of less severe climatic conditions, during which the brick-earths and cavern deposits were laid down, and the climate gradually changed from intense cold to temperate and genial; Arctic and Southern animals visiting Britain, according

as the conditions were the more favourable to the one or the other.

6. A period of severe glacial conditions, with glaciers and coast-ice, chiefly affecting Scotland, and the north of England and Wales.

7. Period of the retreat of the ice, when a few mountain-glaciers alone remained, and Britain was probably insulated.

8. Britain again continental; summer and winter temperatures more excessive than now; great forests largely prevalent. Incoming and spreading of the existing fauna.

9. Period of final insulation of Britain; the climate being moist, the great forests tending to disappear, and peat-mosses prevalent.

10. The present condition of things.

Whether, therefore, the disappearance of the continental fauna in Britain be attributed to submergence or to the direct action of the ice-sheet, it will be apparent that both Mr. Wallace and Professor Geikie are at one in considering that Britain has been connected with the Continent at two distinct epochs, and that the present fauna did not make its appearance till the second continental period.

While admitting that both these high authorities are right in regard to the disappearance of the original continental fauna from the greater part of the islands, Mr. G. W. Bulman, however, in a paper contributed to *Natural Science* for October, 1893, disputes the contention that its disappearance was total, and consequently urges that there is no need for a second connection with the Continent after the first severance.

This writer bases his contention of the survival in our islands of a part of the original fauna from the southern extent of the ice during the period of maximum intensity of the

Glacial epoch, apparently agreeing with Professor Geikie in regarding the subsidence that has taken place in Britain as not being sufficient to have exterminated either the fauna or flora, and consequently attributing such extermination as he admits to have taken place, solely to the ice-sheet. He is of opinion that during the Glacial period the ice-sheet did not, at most, extend further south than the latitude of London, and that it very possibly stopped short of this. Taking the former view, he remarks that "this would leave the counties of Kent, Surrey, Sussex, Hants, Dorset, Somerset, Devon, Cornwall, and part of Wiltshire free from ice. As far as space, then, is concerned, we have an area capable of affording an asylum to a considerable number of our plants and animals. If, however, the Boulder Clay was not formed beneath the ice, then the latter probably did not extend so far south as the latitude of London, and the area fitted to form an asylum for our pre-glacial flora and fauna increased."

After going into the consideration of the nature of the climate of countries lying on the borders of ice-sheets, and also noting that the limit of the ice-sheet marked by the Boulder Clay would be the extreme winter extension of the ice, which must have receded to a certain extent during the summer, while mention is made of the circumstance that the Gulf-stream probably then, as now, warmed our western and southern shores, Mr. Bulman adds that during the greatest glaciation of Britain there may have been areas fitted to preserve temperate forms of life besides the southern counties already mentioned.

After referring to certain instances in our flora and fauna which are considered to prove survival from the pre-glacial epoch, the author proceeds to argue that, had the alleged second continental connection been a fact, it must in all probability have been of such duration as would have permitted the whole of the post-glacial continental Mammals to have reached Britain. And he adds that if it can be shown that the continental forms missing from our present fauna are those most likely to have been exterminated by the cold, or least likely to cross the separating sea—and if, in addition, they are species calculated to migrate as quickly as those which are common to this country—then there will be a further argument against the second continental period.

Without offering a definite opinion on a question so bristling with difficulties as the above, we may say that, so far as Mammals are concerned, we do not think that anything decisive one way or the other can be deduced from the considerations referred to in the last sentence. If the ancestors of our present Mammals did survive the whole Glacial period in the south of England, there would of course be no difficulty in regarding them as having repopulated England and Scotland at its close. The case is, however, more difficult with regard to Ireland, which, on this hypothesis, must at the same time have been separated from the sister-island, since here, too, we must have had an area in which the present Irish Mammals survived the cold period. If, however, those that now exist there then survived, why did not at least as many persist there as in England, seeing that the Irish climate was probably then, as now, milder than that of England? It can hardly be urged that the area free of ice in Ireland was too small for all the species, seeing that animals of the size of the Red Deer and the extinct Irish Deer are known to have lived in Ireland within the recent period, and must, consequently, on the hypothesis under consideration, have been among the survivors; it being evident that an area of land sufficiently large to have supported such creatures would perfectly well have also maintained such existing English Mammals as are unrepresented in the Irish fauna.

The great objection that Mr. Bulman seems to have to the alleged post-glacial connection of Britain with the Continent is the amount of earth-movements which it must necessarily have entailed. Although we are averse to calling in such movements unnecessarily, we confess that, in our opinion, his theory does not account for the poverty of the Mammalian fauna of Ireland as compared with that of the rest of Britain in the perfect manner in which that of Mr. Wallace does; and until this is done we prefer to incline towards the latter, which, it must be remembered, is to a considerable extent supported by the submerged forests and ancient deserted river-channels of England.

Whether, however, the one theory or the other of the re-population of England be adopted, we have to remember that the present impoverished Mammalian fauna of Britain, as compared with the Continent, is due to the direct or indirect action of the Glacial period, the effects of which have been so far-reaching both on inanimate and animate nature in the Northern Hemisphere.

THE BATS. ORDER CHIROPTERA.

The special modification of the bones of the fore-limb for the purpose of flight, coupled with the presence of a leathery flying-membrane extending from the front of the fore-limb, connecting together the toes, or fingers, of the same, then joining the hind-limbs, and likewise connecting together the two latter, with or without the intervention of the tail, at once serves to distinguish sharply the Bats from all other members of the Mammalian class. They are likewise the only Mammals endowed with the power of true flight, like birds; the long flying leaps of the Flying Squirrels and the Flying Phalangers being nothing more than a prolongation of an ordinary leap by the aid of a parachute-like expansion of the skin of the flanks, without any special modification or elongation of the bones of the fore-limbs.

Referring in some detail to the structure of the fore-limb,

which in this group it will be convenient to designate as the
arm, and its extremities as fingers, it will be seen from the
accompanying figure of the skeleton of the same that all the
bones are characterised by their slenderness and elongation.
The first finger, or thumb, remains, however, comparatively
short, and is furnished with a well-developed claw; but the
remaining four fingers are greatly elongated, so that the third,
fourth, and fifth, which are devoid of any trace of a claw, are

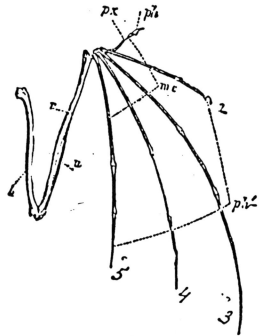

Skeleton of the Right Fore-limb of a Bat. *h*, bone of upper arm, or
humerus; *r.u.*, bones of the fore-arm, or radius and ulna; *px.*, thumb; *ph.*,
claw of same; *mc.*, metacarpus; *ph. ph'.*, bones of second and fifth fingers.

absolutely longer than the fore-arm; the elongation attaining
its maximum in the third, or middle, finger. Between these
long spider-like fingers the wing-membrane is tightly stretched
when the limb is expanded; while when at rest the whole
structure can be compactly folded along the sides of the body.
Apart from the total absence of feathers, those who have even
the most elementary acquaintance with anatomy will not fail

to see how totally different is the structure of a Bat's wing from that of a bird.

Another peculiarity connected with these animals is that the knee is directed backwards, instead of forwards in the ordinary manner. Moreover, in the great majority of the members of the Order, a cartilaginous process or spur extends from the inner side of the ankle to aid, after the manner of a yard-arm, in supporting the membrane connecting the two hind-legs.

In all the Bats with which we have to deal in the present work the cheek-teeth are furnished with sharp cusps, admirably adapted to seize and pierce the insect-prey on which these little animals subsist ; these cusps being generally arranged on the crowns of the upper molars in the form of the letter W. As the number of the teeth is of considerable importance in the systematic arrangement of the members of the order, it may be well to mention here that the maximum number of teeth present in the Order is thirty-eight. When the whole of these thirty-eight teeth are present there are always two pairs of incisors in the upper, and three in the lower jaw ; while in each jaw there is a single pair of canines, three pairs of pre-molars, and three of molars.*

All Bats are nocturnal and crepuscular in their habits, the majority of the insect-eating species (to which group all the British forms pertain) spending the greater portion of the time during which they are active on the wing, in search of their prey; and crawling slowly and with apparent difficulty. During their flight they are aided in finding their way in the dark by the peculiarly sensitive nature of the wing-membranes, or of certain leaf-like appendages growing from the upper surface of the nose. Throughout the day-time they usually hang suspended

---

* It may be well to mention here that the pie-molars are those teeth of the cheek-series (that is those situated behind the tusks, or canines) which have deciduous predecessors, or baby-teeth, while the molars are not so preceded. The incisor teeth are those in the front of the jaws in advance of the tusks.

head-downwards from the claws of the hind feet in dark and sequestered situations, although they are also capable of hanging in an upright position suspended by the claws of the thumbs. In the winter, the whole of the British species hibernate, generally in the former posture, although they occasionally venture out on warm evenings.

Since Bats are essentially animals characteristic of the warmer regions of the globe (where the great group of Fruit-Bats is alone represented), it is not surprising to find the number of British species comparatively small. As a matter of fact, there are fifteen species of Bats reputed to occur in the British Islands, but several of these are of rare occurrence, while of two, only single examples (which in one case may have been accidentally imported) have been taken within our limits. Only twelve species can therefore be regarded as in any sense thoroughly British. Out of the whole fifteen, thirteen belong to the large and widely-distributed Family *Vespertilionidæ*, while the remaining two are referable to the *Rhinolophidæ*.

As regards their reproduction, Bats are slow-breeding ani mals, the female producing, at most, two young at a birth. These are carried about by their parent, tightly clinging to the fur of the body, and protected during the periods of quiescence by the enfolded wings, until they are able to fly about by themselves in search of their own nutriment.

Since Bats are, on the whole, less interesting than many other British Mammals, our notices of the various species will be comparatively brief.

THE LEAF-NOSED BATS. FAMILY RHINOLOPHIDÆ.

The Bats of this family derive both their scientific and popular names from the presence on the muzzle of a number of leaf-like processes of skin around the nostrils, which form their most characteristic feature, and one by which they can be distinguished at a glance from all the other British representatives of the Order. It may be added that the ears are large and generally separated from one another, while they are devoid of an inner earlet, or tragus. There are several other peculiar features connected with these Bats, but since these are not required to distinguish them from their British cousins of the next family, we shall content ourselves by observing that the two pairs of upper incisors are quite rudimentary, while the anterior pre-molar tooth in the upper jaw is reduced to an extremely minute size.

From the great development of the nose-leaf (which must be regarded as a highly sensitive organ of perception), coupled with other features in their organisation, the Leaf-nosed Bats must be considered as the most highly organised and specialised members of the insect-eating division of the Order. Unknown in the New World, as well as in a large part of Oceania, these Bats are distributed over the temperate and tropical regions of the Eastern Hemisphere, where they are represented by several genera, and a large number of species. The two British members of the family belong to the under-mentioned and typical genus.

GENUS RHINOLOPHUS.

Rhinolophus, Desmarest, Nouv. Dict. d'Hist. Nat. vol. xix. p. 383 (1803).

First hind-toe with two joints, and each of the others with three; a distinct anti-tragus (or secondary earlet) separated by a notch from the outer margin of the ear.

These two features serve to distinguish the members of this genus from all the other representatives of the Family, but a few additional peculiarities may be noticed.

The incisors comprise two upper and three lower pairs, and

5   C

the same numbers hold good for the pre-molars; the molars being three pairs in each jaw. The nose-leaf consists of three portions, of which the anterior is horse-shoe shaped, usually with a deep median incision in front, the posterior is erect and pointed, while the middle one, which is situated between and behind the nostrils, is flat in front, and bent up behind into an erect process, usually consisting of two flat moieties, of which the front one is placed transversely, and the hinder one longitudinally. The ears are lateral and free; and the tail (which, as in all British Bats, is enclosed in the membrane connecting the hind-limbs) is relatively short.

The members of the genus have a distribution co-extensive with that of the family.

1. GREATER HORSE-SHOE BAT. RHINOLOPHUS FERRUM-EQUINUM.

Vespertilio ferrum-equinum, Schreber, Säugethiere, vol. i. p. 174 (1775).

Rhinolophus ferrum-equinum, Leach, Zool. Miscell. vol. iii. p. 2 (1817); Bell, British Quadrupeds 2nd ed. p. 12 (1874); Dobson, Cat. Chiroptera Brit. Mus. p. 119 (1878).

(*Plate I.*)

Characters.— Size medium; second upper pre-molar tooth placed close to the canine, and the minute anterior upper pre-molar placed externally to the line of the two teeth just mentioned; second lower pre-molar very minute, and placed externally to the line of the other teeth. Ears acutely pointed, and rather shorter than the head; posterior nose-leaf without a large internal hollow; lower lip with a single median vertical groove. General colour reddish-brown with a greyish tinge; under-parts pale grey, approaching white. Length of head and body about 2$\frac{1}{2}$ inches; of tail 1$\frac{1}{2}$ inch.

Although there is no difficulty in distinguishing this species

PLATE 1.

GREATER HORSE-SHOE BAT.

by its superior size from the other British representative of the genus, the above-mentioned minute characteristics are necessary to differentiate it from its foreign allies, some of which approach it very closely.

Distribution.—This species has a very wide geographical distribution, ranging over the greater part of Europe, Africa, and Asia north of the Himalaya. Its northern range is, however, not so extensive as that of the next species. In Britain it appears to be essentially a southern form, being seemingly very rare even in the midland counties, and quite unrepresented in the north, as well as in Scotland. First discovered as a British species at Dartmouth, it has been taken in many localities in the south and west of England, such as Bristol, Colchester, Rochester, and the Isle of Wight. Its favourite haunts are old stone buildings, such as castles and churches, and caves ; and it is especially common in the well-known cave of Kent's Hole, near Torquay, of which it has probably been an inhabitant ever since the age of the Mammoth, since its fossilised remains have been found there in association with those of the latter and other extinct animals. It may be mentioned that, on the Continent, this Bat is also very generally found in caves, sometimes in enormous numbers, and, what is more remarkable, usually in colonies composed entirely of either male or female individuals. This Bat is not recorded by Thompson from Ireland, and is probably unknown there.

Habits.—The Greater Horse-shoe Bat makes its appearance rather late in the evening ; and when on the wing shows a preference for the neighbourhood of trees, and flies high in the air, though its flight is not so powerful as that of its smaller cousin. Its favourite food is said to be fern-chafers. On the wing this Bat appears nearly, or quite, as large as the under-mentioned Noctule, but it is said to be easily distinguished from the latter by the relatively wider wings.

C 2

II. LESSER HORSE-SHOE BAT. RHINOLOPHUS HIPPOSIDERUS.

Noctilio hipposideros, Bechstein, Naturgeschicte Deutschland's
     p. 1194 (1801).
Rhinolophus hipposideros, Leach, Zool. Miscell. vol. iii. p. 2
     (1817); Bell, British Quadrupeds 2nd ed. p. 96 (1874);
     Dobson, Cat. Chiroptera Brit. Mus. p. 117 (1878).
Rhinolophus hipposiderus, Blanford, Faun. Brit. Ind. Mamm.
     p. 277 (1891).

Characters.—Size small; second upper pre-molar tooth separated from the canine by a distinct interval, in the middle of
which is the minute anterior pre-molar; second lower pre-molar
placed nearly in the line of the other teeth, in the angle
between the two adjacent teeth. Ears rather shorter than the
head, sharply pointed, with the outer margin deeply excavated,
and separated from the large anti-tragus by a deep angular
notch; posterior nose-leaf longer than broad, with the sides
slightly emarginate, and the extremity blunt; lower lip with a
single median vertical groove. General colour light brown,
with the under-parts light greyish-brown; young individuals
being frequently darker than the adult. Length of head and
body about 1½ inch; of tail, 1⅛ inch.

Distribution.—The range of this species is not quite so extensive as that of the last, since in Africa it appears to be only
known from the north-eastern regions; in Europe it extends,
however, somewhat more to the north, reaching as far as the
Baltic. First recognised as an English species in Wiltshire,
this Bat resembles the last in being mainly confined to the
southern counties. Unlike the last, however, it has been
taken in Ireland, where it occurs in the counties of Galway
and Clare. In the latter county it was found hibernating in
caves among plantations, the entrances to which were more or
less thickly hung with plants; and in all cases the two sexes
occurred in separate colonies.

Inhabiting caves and buildings in the daytime, this species is so similar in its mode of life to the last, that scarcely any observations on this point are necessary. It is, however, stated to fly stronger and at a higher elevation, and not to be so partial to the neighbourhood of trees.

THE TYPICAL BATS. FAMILY VESPERTILIONIDÆ.

The members of this, the largest family in the whole Order, are readily distinguished from the *Rhinolophidæ* by the absence of a leaf-like expansion on the nose, and by the presence of an earlet or tragus in the ear. These characters suffice, therefore, to distinguish them from the other British Bats, and likewise to differentiate them from the allied family of the *Nycteridæ*, in which both the appendages in question are present. Since they fail, however, to distinguish them from the other two families of insect-eating Bats, we have to add certain other characteristics. These are that the tail is either contained completely within the membrane connecting the hind legs, or is produced but a very short distance beyond its free margin; while, when the wings are folded and at rest, the first joint of the third or middle finger is extended in the line of the arm, instead of being folded back upon its metacarpal bone.

All these Bats have comparatively long tails, and minute bead-like eyes, while their ears take origin from the sides of the head, and not from the forehead. Although there are always three pairs of lower incisor teeth, in the upper jaw there may be either one or two pairs of these teeth, which are in either case widely separated from one another in the middle line. As regards the pre-molars, the number of pairs of these teeth in the upper jaw varies from one to three, the anterior ones being always small, and in some instances situated internally to the general line of the teeth; in the lower jaw there may be either two or three pairs of these teeth.

The typical Bats have a cosmopolitan distribution, so far as the temperate and tropical regions of the world are concerned. The majority of the species are included in the two genera, *Vespertilio* and *Vesperugo*, and although the more typical representatives of each of these are markedly distinct from one another, yet there are certain intermediate forms which connect them so closely, that their definition is a matter of some difficulty. Under these circumstances, the obvious course would be to unite the two genera, were it not that the number of species is so great that, if this plan were adopted, each genus would be inconveniently large and unwieldy.

THE LONG-EARED BATS. GENUS PLECOTUS.

Plecotus, Geoffr., Descript. de l'Egypt. p. 112 (1812).

Crown of the head flat, or only slightly elevated above the line of the face; upper incisor teeth closely approximated to the canines, and thus widely separated in the middle line. Ears very large, with the inner margins united at the base, and the outer borders severally terminating behind the angles of the mouth; earlet, or tragus, very long, narrow, and tapering. Nostrils placed at the extremity of the muzzle, in form elongate, narrow, and crescentic; upper surface of muzzle hairy, flat and depressed in the middle line, but swollen and elevated at the sides—sometimes to such a degree as to form a roof behind the nostrils over the middle region; no grooves in the front of the muzzle below the nostrils. Two pairs of both incisor and pre-molar teeth in the upper jaw; and three of the latter in the lower.

There are but two species of Long-eared Bats, one of which is an Old World, and the other a North American form.

THE LONG-EARED BAT. PLECOTUS AURITUS.

Vespertilio auritus, Linn., Syst. Nat. ed. 12 vol. i. p. 47 (1766).

LONG-EARED BAT

Plecotus auritus, Geoffr. Descript. de l'Egypte p. 118 (1812);
Bell, British Quadrupeds 2nd ed. p. 72 (1874).

(Plate II.)

Characters.—Ears enormous, not greatly inferior in length to the head and body, sub-oval, with the tips broadly rounded, and their inner margins joined near the base, above which is a prominent rounded lobe.   Wings arising from the base of the toes ; feet slender ; tail as long as the head and body, with its tip just projecting beyond the margin of the membrane ;* fur soft.   General colour brown, usually becoming fawn-coloured or light brown above, and whitish beneath ; at least the basal halves of the hairs being black.   Length of head and body about 1¾ inch ; of tail slightly less, or the same.

Distribution.—This species has a very wide geographical distribution, extending from Ireland through Europe and Northern Africa to the Himalaya, and probably inhabiting the greater portion of temperate Asia.   In the British Islands it is one of the most common and widely-distributed members of the Order, ranging over the greater part of Scotland, and reported to occur through the Inner Hebrides, where it has been taken, at least, in Mull and Islay.   It has been doubtfully recorded from Lochabar, and has been once taken at Torcastle.   In Ireland it appears to be distributed in suitable localities throughout the island.   A specimen obtained many years ago by the late Leonard Jenyns (afterwards Blomefield) in the Isle of Ely, was described as a distinct species under the name of *Plecotus brevimanus*, on account of certain differences in the relative proportions of the limbs and coloration ; it is now known to be nothing more than an individual variety.

Habits.—Essentially an inhabitant of the open country, and

* In the relative length of the ears and tail, the illustration is not quite true to nature.

not resorting to the neighbourhood of trees and plantations, this Bat, writes Macgillivray, in the original issue of the " Naturalists' Library," flies, like the Pipistrelle, " but it possesses considerable agility, and turns with ease in every direction. It rises with facility from the ground, or even from the bottom of the box in which it may be kept. When it alights, it clings by the hooks of its fore-limbs and by its hind-claws. In climbing it moves the fore-feet alternately, advancing slowly, and in an awkward manner, which is still more apparent when it crawls on a level surface. It adheres to the slightest asperities, and retires to the corners of the deserted apartments of old buildings, steeples, and the crevices of rocks, where it suspends itself by the hind-feet, which are, as in other Bats, eminently adapted for the purpose, the claws being very acute, and of nearly equal length. When springing off from a wall, it raises its fore-legs first, stretches out its head, and erects its ears, which had been folded down, and it retains them erect when flying. When preparing for repose, it brings the fore-feet close to the body, the cubital- [elbow] joint projecting and in contact with the knee, incurvates the tail, folds up the lateral membranes neatly, and brings the ears backwards, curving them along the sides of the head and body, so as to resemble a ram's horn ; the tragus, or small anterior appendage, projecting forward. Its voice is a low chirping squeak ; and when teased or frightened, it utters a querulous note, like the wailing of a very young child."

To this it may be added, that when the great ears are laid back in the manner described, the upstanding earlets look exactly as though they were the real ears. On the Continent this species is described as frequenting hollow trees for repose fully as much as buildings ; and everywhere its long winter sleep generally seems to be continuous and unbroken, so that it is only seen abroad from the late spring to the early autumn.

Thompson states, however, that a specimen he once obtained from an uninhabited house in the month of January did not exhibit any symptoms of torpidity, flying readily in the room in which it was placed. The same writer observes that "when the roofs of old houses are being repaired or taken down in the north of Ireland, numbers of these Bats are often discovered. The Pipistrelle frequents similar places, but is probably less gregarious, as I have not known it to be found so plentifully under similar circumstances, although it is more frequently seen flying about."

In connection with the shrill cry of this species, it may be mentioned that many persons, whose ears are not attuned to receive such high-pitched sounds as those of others, are totally unable to hear them. It may, therefore, be that when a number of Bats are on the wing, while the air will be rent with their piercing cries to one person, to another absolute silence will reign.

GENUS SYNOTUS.

Synotus, Keyserling and Blasius, Wirbelthiere Europ. p. 55 (1840).

Ears united by their inner margins on the forehead, rather large, and with their outer margins also carried forward in front of the eyes to terminate on the upper lips, so that the eyes are enclosed within the bases of the ears; earlet triangular above and narrowed towards the tip; nostrils opening on the upper surface of the extremity of the muzzle, in front of a naked space, margined by the raised edges of the face; upper lip divided on each side by a deep vertical groove passing down from each nostril; the space between these grooves being swollen. Feet slender, with long toes; tail nearly equal to, or exceeding the body in length; skull considerably elevated above the plane of the short muzzle; the upper incisor and pre-molar teeth numerically the same as in *Plecotus*; but two pairs of lower pre-molars present instead of three.

This genus, as now restricted, is represented only by the under-mentioned species and an allied Indian form, known as the Eastern Barbastelle (*Synotus darjilingensis*).

THE BARBASTELLE BAT.   SYNOTUS BARBASTELLUS.

Vespertilio barbastellus, Schreber, Säugethiere vol. i. p. 168 (1775).

Barbastellus daubentonii, Bell, British Quadrupeds p. 63 (1837); 2nd ed. p. 81 (1874).

Barbastellus communis, Gray, Ann. Mag. Nat. Hist. vol. ii. p. 494 (1838).

Synotus barbastellus, Keyserling and Blasius, Wirbelthiere Europ. p. 55 (1840).

Characters.—Ears broad, and when laid forward, extending to a point midway between the eye and the end of the muzzle, tips shortly truncated, inner margin regularly convex and slanting much backwards; outer margin concave, with a small projecting lobe at the junction of the upper with the middle third; earlet broad at the base, then narrowed opposite the middle of the straight inner margin, and thence thinning to the acute tip. Fur soft, deep black, with an indistinct greyish tinge on the tips of the hairs. Length of head and body about 1⅔ inch; of tail the same.

Distribution.—The Barbastelle ranges over Southern and Central Europe, Northern Africa, and the greater part of temperate Asia north of the Himalaya. In Britain it is a comparatively rare and local species, seemingly not known to the north of the Lake District, and unrecorded from Ireland. First discovered in our islands at Dartford, Kent, it was subsequently taken in a chalk-cave at Chiselhurst, in the same county; while it has also been recorded from Warwickshire (where it is not uncommon), Cambridgeshire, Northampton-shire, Norfolk, and Suffolk. According to Mr. Montagu Browne, a single example was taken in Leicestershire about the year 1876; and the Rev. H. A. Macpherson informs us that a few examples were captured many years ago near Carlisle, which seems to be the northern limit of its range in Britain. Their presence in Cumberland, writes the observer last mentioned, can only be accounted for on the supposition that they are summer migrants into the district; the fact that Bats do migrate, either occasionally or periodically, being well ascertained on the testimony of several trustworthy observers.

Habits.—Nearly allied to the Long-eared Bat, the Barbastelle is a species of delicate constitution, and becomes torpid very early in the autumn. It appears early in the evening, and flies higher and more rapidly than the Long-eared Bat. The Indian Barbastelle is remarkable for its habit of squeezing itself into chinks and crevices, which are so narrow as to render it a marvel how the creature gets in.

Bell states that he has seen a white and also a parti-coloured individual of this species; while a variety from Warwickshire had, when fresh, the fur of the under-parts tinged with purplish-red or rose-colour.

GENUS VESPERUGO.

Vesperugo, Keyserling and Blasius in Wiegmann's Archiv. für Naturg. 1839 p. 312 (1840).

Ears separate, never very long, and generally shorter than the head, with the outer margin ending behind the angle of the mouth, and some distance in advance of the base of the ear-let; end of outer margin usually consisting of a rounded lobe, or anti-tragus, and the inner margin turned in near its base, where its rounded edge forms another lobe; earlet or tragus generally short and obtuse, with the outer margin more or less convex, and the inner one either straight or concave. Muzzle usually short, broad, and blunted, with prominent glandular swellings between the eyes and nostrils, giving an abnormal width to the face; sides of hinder part of head and tip of muzzle sparsely haired. Tail shorter than head and body; a small additional membranous expansion behind the spur on the ankle, and the membrane connecting the hind-legs terminating in a salient angle. Number of incisor teeth generally as in the preceding genus; but the upper pre-molars sometimes reduced to a single pair, although there are always two pairs of these teeth in the lower jaw. Wings generally arising from the bases of the toes.

The numerous species of this, the largest genus of the Order, have a cosmopolitan distribution, except as regards the Polar Regions; but they are most numerous in the temperate and sub-tropical parts of the Eastern Hemisphere.

I. THE SEROTINE.   VESPERUGO SEROTINUS.

Vespertilio serotinus, Schreber, Säugethiere vol. i. p. 167
    (1775).
Scotophilus serotinus, Gray, Mag. Zool. vol. ii. p. 497 (1838);
    Bell, British Quadrupeds, 2nd ed. p. 44 (1874).
Vesperugo serotinus, Keyserling and Blasius in Wiegmann's
    Archiv. für Naturg. 1839 p. 312 (1840); Dobson, Cat.
    Chiroptera Brit. Mus. p. 191 (1878).

Characters.—Ears moderate, with broadly rounded tips, which, when laid forwards, are nearer to the nostrils than to the eyes; their inner margins slightly convex, with a rounded basal lobe; outer margins straight, or very slightly concave in the upper half, then convex, slightly emarginate opposite the base of the earle⸱, and ending in a convex lobe behind the angle of the mouth ; earlet, or tragus, broadest immediately above the base of the inner margin, thence gradually narrowing to the rounded tip, the inner margin straight or slightly concave, and the outer convex, with a small lobe at the base. Head flat ; muzzle flat and thick, with swollen glandular sides; front of face nearly naked, but a slight fringe of hairs on the upper lip. Thumb with a callosity at the base ; wings arising from the metatarsus close to the base of the toes ; extra membrane near spur very narrow. Upper inner incisor teeth, when unworn, with bifid extremities ; all the lower incisors trifid, and closely crowded together. Colour generally dark smoky-brown, with the underparts varying from yellowish-brown to yellowish-white ; but in examples from desert-regions the upper-parts are buffish-brown and the lower surface paler. Length of head and body about 2¾ inches ; of tail 2 inches.

Distribution.—This species is rare and local in the British Isles, but is one of the most widely distributed members of its Order, ranging over temperate Europe, Asia, and North America, being likewise found in North Africa, as well as in Kashmir and Yunnan. It also occurs in parts of South America. It has been said to occur in the neighbourhood of London, and has been taken at Folkestone and the Isle of Wight, and probably occurs in several of the other southern counties, although it is most likely often overlooked and mistaken for the Noctule. It is not recorded from Ireland.

Habits.—As indicated by its specific name, the Serotine is a Bat which makes its appearance late in the evening, but differs from the majority of its genus in the slowness of its flight, which is, moreover, fluttering. Then, again, whereas most of the members of the present genus differ from the majority of Bats in producing two young at a birth, the Serotine is peculiar in that but a single offspring is born at a time. A late hiberna-

tor, it is never seen abroad in cold and damp evenings, or at
such times as a strong wind is blowing, preferring for its
aerial peregrinations those nights which are warm and still;
when, in the full summer, its favourite haunts are gardens,
orchards, and the outskirts of woods. During the daytime it
generally takes up its abode in the hollow stems of trees, and
even in winter never congregates in large colonies. As its
slow and fluttering flight lacks the sharp turns and twists
characterising the members of the genus *Vesperugo* generally,
it is evident that, as regards habits, the Serotine is an altogether aberrant and peculiar species. It may be added that
it is the only truly British representative of the sub-genus *Ves-
perus*, in which the upper pre-molars are reduced to a single
pair, and the wings arise from the base of the toes; the next
species being scarcely entitled to rank as a member of the
British fauna.

II. THE PARTI-COLOURED BAT. VESPERUGO DISCOLOR.

Vespertilio discolor, Natterer in Kuhl's Deutsch. Flederm. p. 43
    (1817).
Scotophilus discolor, Gray, Mag. Zool. vol. ii. p. 297 (1838);
    Bell, British Quadrupeds 2nd ed. p. 31 (1874).
Vesperugo discolor, Keyserling and Blasius, Wirbelthiere Europ.
    p. 50 (1840); Dobson, Cat. Chiroptera Brit. Mus. p. 204
    (1878).

Belonging to the same sub-division of the genus as the
Noctule, the Parti-coloured Bat may be distinguished not only
by its inferior dimensions, but likewise by the earlet, or tragus,
being relatively shorter and expanded above, so that its greatest
width is above the margin of its inner margin. The additional
lobe of membrane near the spur on the ankle is also broader
and more distinct. Colour of upper-parts dark brown, with

the terminal fourth of the hairs shining yellowish-white; under-parts similar, with the terminal fourth ashy. Length of head and body about 2 inches ; of tail, 1¾ inch.

An inhabitant of the mountainous regions of Continental Europe and temperate Asia, as well as Northern Africa, the sole claim of this species to be recognised as British appears to rest on a single example obtained many years ago by the late Dr. W. E. Leach at Plymouth, now preserved in the British Museum. As suggested by Bell, it appears highly probable that this specimen may have been imported in the rigging of some vessel from the Continent.

III. THE NOCTULE, OR GREAT BAT. VESPERUGO NOCTULA.

Vespertilio noctula, Schreber, Säugethiere vol. i. p. 166 (1775).

Vespertilio magnus, Berkenhout, Synops. Nat. Hist. Gt. Britain p. 2 (1789).

Vespertilio altivolans, White, Nat. Hist. Selborne, letter 37 (1789).

Scotophilus noctula, Gray, Mag. Zool. vol. ii. p. 497 (1838); Bell, British Quadrupeds 2nd ed. p. 17 (1874).

Vesperugo noctula, Keyserling and Blasius in Wiegmann's Archiv. für Naturg, 1839 p. 117 (1840); Dobson, Cat. Chiroptera Brit. Mus. p. 212 (1878).

Characters.—The Noctule is our first representative of the second or typical sub-division of the genus, differing from the last in the presence of two pairs of upper pre-molar teeth, of which the front pair are very minute. This species, together with the next and two Malayan forms, is further distinguished from all other members of the genus by the wings arising from the ankle, instead of from the bases of the toes. The following are the specific characters of the Noctule, as distinct from the other members of the sub-genus.

Size large, ears thick, bluntly rounded, nearly as wide as long, and when laid forwards extending but little in front of the eyes; their outer margin convex and turned backwards, slightly notched below the base of the earlet, then forming a thick convex lobe in front of the notch, and ending behind the angle of the mouth; inner margin nearly straight above, and convex inferiorly; basal lobe somewhat rounded; earlet, or tragus, short, expanded above, curved inwards, with a broad, rounded tip; outer margin highly convex, with a small pointed projection at the base, inner margin concave. Head very broad and flat, with the swellings at the sides of the muzzle very prominent, and the projecting nostrils directed outwards and downwards, with a hollow space between them. Thumb short, with a short callosity at the base; feet thick, with short toes; origin of wings as above; only the tip of the tail projecting beyond the margin of the membrane connecting the hind-legs. General colour light yellowish-brown, only slightly paler on the under-parts, and the hairs of the back and sides becoming paler at the base; in some examples the general colour reddish-brown. Length of head and body about 3 inches; of tail, 2 inches.

Distribution.—The Noctule is spread over the greater part of temperate Europe and Asia, and likewise ranges over a considerable portion of Africa. In Britain it is mainly a southern form, being abundant in many of the southern and midland counties of England, and ranging as far west as Cornwall, but becoming gradually more scarce as we proceed northwards, and being quite unknown in Scotland. The most northern locality which Bell was able to ascertain for this species was Northallerton, in Yorkshire, but it has been recorded by the Rev. H. A. Macpherson from Carnforth, on the coast of Lancashire, and it is possible that certain large Bats observed at Bowness-on-Solway during the summer of 1888 may have pertained to the present species. In Wales the Noctule appears to be un-known; and it is not recorded by Thompson among the Mam-mals of Ireland. There is, however, reason to believe that it is an inhabitant of the latter island, as may be gathered from the following extract from a paper on Bats by Mr. Harting, who writes that in the *Zoologist* for 1874 "Mr. Barrington gave a very interesting account of the discovery, in June, 1868, of a colony of large Bats in the demesne of the Duke of Man-chester at Tandragee, county Armagh, and of the subsequent capture of several (presumably of the same species) at the same place in May, 1874. Mr. Barrington identified them as *V. leisleri*, observing 'they were all of the hairy-armed species. I have presented two specimens to the British Museum.' These two specimens were examined by Dr. Dobson in 1876, and he pronounced them to be immature examples of *V. noctula*." This seems to establish the occurrence of the latter species in Ireland, where, however, it may well be accompanied by the Hairy-armed Bat. In England it appears to be more common in some of the midland counties than elsewhere.

Habits.—The first notice of the habits of this species in Britain was from the pen ʻof Gilbert White, who remarks that in Hampshire it is a rare species, flying at a great height in the air when in pursuit of its food, and retiring early in the sum-mer. In his native village, this observer states, indeed, that he never saw the Noctule abroad before April nor after July; but subsequent observations have shown that in the same neigh-bourhood it may frequently be seen in August and September, while in Cambridgeshire it has been recorded as late as November.

With the exception of the Mouse-coloured Bat, the Noctule is the largest of the British members of the Order, and it is essentially a gregarious species, collecting in large numbers for its winter sleep. Upwards of one hundred and eighty-five

Bats, taken from beneath the roof of Queen's College, Cambridge, on a single night very many years ago, and sixty-five on the following evening, were, indeed, referred to this species; but, as Bell remarks, it is probable that these were not submitted to a careful examination, and may, therefore, have included members of other species. Generally frequenting well-wooded districts, and feeding chiefly on cockchafers and other large beetles, the Noctule usually selects a hollow tree for its diurnal resting-place in summer. Indeed, Bell states that he has never known one taken from any other situation. A later observer states, however, that he has known these Bats select thick ivy as a place of concealment; while Mr. Harting records having seen them resort to the thatched roofs of cottages in Sussex, where they crept up beneath the eaves. For their winter haunts they select indifferently either hollow trees or the roofs of buildings.

Since this Bat appears early in the evening, its title of "Noctule" is somewhat misleading, although it is too well established to be changed; the name of Great Bat being decidedly no better. In the high regions of the air, where it delights to fly, on account of the abundance of beetles to be met with there, its flight is powerful and sustained; and when on the wing it gives utterance to a sharp and harsh cry. As mentioned by White, these Bats have a strong and offensive odour, which renders a colony of them exceedingly unpleasant to have anything to do with. Although in some English examples which were kept in captivity it was found that only a single offspring was produced at a birth, the experience of continental observers shows that there is more commonly a pair. When first introduced into the world, the young are perfectly naked, as well as blind.

It is stated that when hibernating in winter, the Noctule generally associates. after the manner of many of its kindred, in separate colonies of males and females ; such, at least, being the experience of Mr. J. Gurney, who further states that the number of females is greater than that of the males. Mr. Harting mentions, however, that he knew of an instance where a solitary pair of Noctules, taken from a hollow tree in the Bishop of London's park at Fulham, proved to be male and female. The same observer also draws attention to the circumstance that during repose, while the tail of the Horse-shoe Bat is carried bent upwards and forwards over the back, in the Noctule it is carried bent downwards and backwards between the legs.

IV. THE HAIRY-ARMED BAT. VESPERUGO LEISLERI.

Vespertilio leisleri, Kuhl, Deutsch. Flederm. p. 38 (1817).

Scotophilus leisleri, Gray, Mag. Zool. vol. ii. p. 497 (1838);
    Bell, British Quadrupeds 2nd ed. p. 26 (1874).

Vesperugo leisleri, Keyserling and Blasius, Wirbelthiere Europ.
    p. 46 (1840); Dobson, Cat. Chiroptera Brit. Mus. p.
    215 (1878).

Characters.—Closely resembling in external form a small individual of the preceding species, the Hairy-armed Bat may be distinguished by the following characters. Thus, whereas in *V. noctula* the outermost pair of upper incisor teeth have their basal transverse diameters equal to only half those of the outermost lower incisors, in the present species the two dimensions are equal. Moreover, in the present species the lower incisor teeth are arranged in a regular semi-circle, with scarcely any overlapping of one over another, in place of being closely crowded. Length of head and body about $2\frac{1}{4}$ inches; of tail, $1\frac{2}{3}$ inch.

In common with the Noctule, the present species has a band of fine short hair running down the under side of the fore-arm to the wrist, and it is from this character that the Hairy-armed Bat derives its common English name.

Distribution.—Ranging over the greater part of Europe and temperate Asia, the present Bat appears to be a rare species in Britain, although this rarity is doubtless owing to its being frequently mistaken for the Noctule. In the main, it appears to be confined to the western counties of England, having been recorded from Worcester, Gloucester, and Warwick; but, according to Mr. Montagu Browne, it is unknown as far north as Leicestershire, as also in the Lake District. It has been obtained from more than one Irish locality—notably Belfast.

Habits.—Much apparently remains to be learned regarding the habits of this Bat, there being a discrepancy in the accounts given by Continental and British observers. While all are agreed that it makes its appearance early in the evening, Blasius, for instance, states that it also resembles the Noctule in frequenting the neighbourhood of trees, and flying at a considerable altitude with a similar powerful flight. On the other hand, Bell writes that its flight is totally different from that of the latter, observing that " whilst the Noctule may, throughout the whole of the summer, be seen taking its regular evening flight, night after night, near the same spot, the Leisler's Bat, on the contrary, will be seen once, perhaps for a few minutes only and then lost sight of. It appears to affect no particular altitude in its flight, any more than it preserves any regular or prescribed beat. When the weather is fine, you may see this Bat passing on in a kind of zig-zag manner, apparently uncertain where to go, generally, though not always, at a considerable elevation, and in a few minutes it is gone."

V. THE PIPISTRELLE OR COMMON BAT.   VESPERUGO PIPISTRELLUS.

Vespertilio pipistrellus, Schreber, Säugethiere vol. i. p. 167 (1775).

PLATE III

PIPISTRELLE OR COMMON BAT.

Vespertilio pygmæus, Leach, Zool. Journ. vol. i. p. 560 (1825);
  Bell, British Quadrupeds p. 31 (1837).
Scotophilus pipistrellus, Bell, British Quadrupeds 2nd ed.
  p. 34 (1874).
Vesperugo pipistrellus, Keyserling and Blasius in Wiegmann's
  Archiv. für Naturg. 1839 p. 321 (1840); Dobson, Cat.
  Chiroptera Brit. Mus. p. 223 (1878).

(Plate III.)

Characters.—Although belonging to the same sub-generic
group as the two preceding species, the Pipistrelle is at once
distinguished from both of the latter by the membrane of the
wings arising from the base of the toes, in the manner characteristic of the genus generally. The present species belongs
to a section of the typical sub-genus, characterised by the earlet
being widest at a point slightly above the base of the inner
margin. The following are its special characters.

Ears sub-triangular, with the tips rounded, and the outer
margins nearly straight for one-third the length below the tips,
and then suddenly curving out into a prominent lobe, there
being a slight concavity opposite the base of the earlet, in
front of which is a prominent convex lobe. Earlet as above,
a little inclined forwards, the tip rounded, the inner margin
very slightly concave, and the outer one convex with a small
lobe at the base, above which there is a very shallow concavity.
Muzzle blunt, with well-developed lateral glandular swellings,
behind which the face is depressed; the whole of the region
of the muzzle as far back as the eyes, sparsely haired. Feet
small, with the lobe of membrane behind the spur well developed. Inner pair of upper incisor teeth with bifid crowns, in
which the outermost cusps are smaller and more posteriorly
situated than the inner ones; the outer incisors either longer or
shorter than the external cusp of the inner pair. General
colour of fur rather deep rufous brown, becoming paler on

the under-parts, the basal half or three-fourths of every hair being black. Length of head and body, about $1\frac{3}{5}$ inch; of tail, $1\frac{2}{5}$ inch.

Distribution.—The Pipistrelle ranges from Northern Africa, over the greater part of temperate Europe and Asia, as far south as Kashmir and Gilgit; it is replaced in India and the adjacent countries by the closely allied Indian Pipistrelle (*V. abramus*), distinguished by its more completely naked muzzle and the form of the incisor teeth, which ranges eastwards as far as Northern Australia, and, in summer at least, is found in Central Europe, and even in Sweden. In the British Islands the Common Pipistrelle appears to be universally distributed, being found from one end of Ireland to the other, and ranging from the south of England to the extreme north of Scotland, in-habiting even the outer Hebrides.

It may be mentioned here that, although the Pipistrelle is the smallest of the British Bats, it was long confounded with the much larger *Vespertilio murinus*, which, as being the com-monest Bat on the Continent, was not unnaturally assumed to be the most abundant species on this side the Channel, where, however, it happens to be rare. After persisting for a long period, this error was finally rectified many years ago by the late Rev. Leonard Jenyns (Blomefield), who was one of the pioneers in British vertebrate zoology.

Habits.—Writing of the habits of the Pipistrelle, or, as it is called in many parts of the country, the "Flitter-mouse," Mac-gillivray observes that, "from the middle of spring, but earlier or later according to the warmth of the season, to the middle of October, sometimes commencing as early as March, and continuing till November, this Bat may be seen after sunset in the neighbourhood of towns and villages, over the streets of cities or the roads, in the alleys and lanes, or along the course of brooks and rivers, fluttering with an unsteady motion, and apparently undetermined course. Its flight is not rapid, like that of a bird, but rather resembles that of a large Moth or Butterfly. It turns and winds in all directions, flying at various heights from ten to twenty or more feet, and sometimes as high as the tops of the trees, but more commonly at an elevation of about fifteen feet. It is attracted by a white handkerchief, or any other body, thrown up in the air, for which reason boys are fond of tossing their caps at it. Sometimes it has been caught upon the fly-hooks of a fishing-rod hung over a bridge. It continues its flight until dark, and probably during the night, as well as in the morning twilight ; and reposes through the day in the corners and crevices of old buildings, towers, and steeples. As its food consists entirely of insects, and especially the nocturnal Lepidoptera, it is forced by the increasing cold of winter to relinquish its pursuits, and betake itself to some secure retreat in a ruined building or cavern, where it remains until the returning heat arouses it from its torpor. In this state it is found suspended by its feet in chimneys, crevices, or corners, or jammed into a hole or fissure. A frequent place of retirement is under the roofs of houses, and especially churches ; but it presents great variety in its selection, and I have obtained specimens from the hollow of a decayed tree near Duddingston."

"The Pipistrelle rises with facility from a flat surface, and is capable of advancing on the ground with considerable celerity, and ascends a vertical plane, provided it be somewhat rough, without much difficulty. In confinement it feeds on flies and raw meat."

From its hardy nature, as indicated by its northern range in Britain, the Pipistrelle is by no means continuous in its winter slumber, any unusually warm day being sufficient to awaken the little creature. During the mild winter of 1893-94, I observed on the evening of January the 20th one of these

Bats flying near my own house in Hertfordshire; and in the north of Ireland Thompson states that it may frequently be seen abroad in mid-winter.   Occasionally it may be observed fluttering about in a half-dazed state in the full sunlight.   Although, in the passage above-quoted, Macgillivray states that its chief food consists of moths, we should rather be disposed to consider that flies and gnats of various kinds form its main subsistence.

With regard to the number of young produced at a birth, there appears to be a marked difference between Continental and British examples.   Thus, while Blasius states that all the females with young examined by him on the Continent had two, British specimens seem, as a rule, to produce but one; this being confirmed by the observations of Daniell in England, and Hyndman (as quoted by Thompson) in Ireland.

Bell has noted the interesting fact that the tip of the tail in this, and certain other Bats, affords assistance in climbing. After mentioning that a small portion of the tail, in most members of the present Family, projects beyond the edge of the membrane connecting the hind-legs, he proceeds to observe that "not only does the animal employ the tail in horizontal progression—in which case it assists in throwing forward the body, by being brought into contact with the ground on either side alternately, corresponding with the action of the hinder foot on the same side,—but in ascending and descending a rough perpendicular surface, this little caudal finger holds by any projecting point, and affords an evident support.   This is particularly conspicuous when the Bat is traversing the wires of a cage, in which situation the fact was first observed."

When flies or moths are offered to a captive Pipistrelle, these are seized by the mouth alone without any aid from the wings.   The creature, after seizing its prey, bends down its head upon the chest as if for the purpose of preventing their escape. Every portion of such insects, including even the wings, is consumed.

GENUS VESPERTILIO.

Vespertilio, Linn., Syst. Nat. ed. 12 vol. i. p. 47 (1766).

This genus, in which are included the whole of the six remaining British Bats, may be at once distinguished from *Vesperugo* by the presence of three pairs of pre-molar teeth in the upper jaw, the number of teeth on each side behind the canine being thus six, in place of five or four. Together with certain allied genera, it is further distinguished from *Vesperugo* and its allies by the outer margin of the conch of the ear commencing abruptly nearly opposite the inner margin of the earlet, or tragus, instead of near the angle of the mouth. The thin and narrow ears are also, generally at least, as long as the head, instead of being triangular or rhomboidal, and shorter than the latter ; while the long and narrow tragus, if curved at all, is inclined outwards instead of inwards. Then, again, the muzzle is narrow and hairy in front, instead of being nearly naked, with lateral glandular swellings. From its nearest allies of the same group, *Vespertilio* is distinguished by the simple and scarcely projecting nostrils, the aperture of which is crescentic, as well as by the small size of the two anterior pre-molar teeth, as compared with the last tooth of the same series.

Although containing fewer species than the last, the present genus has a wider geographical distribution than any other in the entire Order, its range including the whole of the temperate and tropical regions of both hemispheres. From their close similarity to one another, the majority of the species are exceedingly difficult to distinguish. The Old World species may, however, be thrown into two groups, or sub-genera, according as to whether the feet are relatively large or of moderate size; two of the British species belonging to the former, and four to the latter group.

I. THE ROUGH-LEGGED BAT.   VESPERTILIO DASYCNEME.

Vespertilio dasycneme, Boie, Isis 1825 p. 1200; Dobson, Cat. Chiroptera Brit. Mus. p. 295 (1878).

Vespertilio limnophilus, Temminck, Monogr. Mamm. vol. ii. p. 176 (1839).

Characters.—Belongs to the group in which the feet are relatively large, measuring from the wrist to the end of the claws more than one-fourth the length of the fore-arm, and the heel-spur also long, extending fully three-quarters the distance from the ankle to the tail. This species is also readily distinguished from the other members of the same group by the form of the earlet, which has a blunt rounded tip, the inner margin slightly concave, and the outer convex, thus resembling the same appendage in the typical sub-genus of *Vesperugo*. The ears also are shorter than the head, and the face less hairy than in other species,—characters which again recall the last-named genus. On the upper surface, the fur is dark at the base and light brown at the tips of the hairs; while beneath, the hairs are black at the base and white at the tips. Length of head and body about 2⅔ inches; of tail, 2 inches.

Distribution.—The Rough-legged Bat has long been known as an inhabitant of Continental Europe, whence it extends eastwards through temperate Asia, and has often been stated to be a visitor to the south of England, although it is not mentioned in the second edition of Bell's "British Quadrupeds." Its right to be regarded as a British species appears to rest on the evidence of a specimen captured on the banks of the Stour, which was noticed by Backton in the "Proceedings" of the Linnean Society, for 1853, p. 260, and regarded as a variety of *V. daubentoni*, although subsequently referred by

Tomes (*Zoologist*, 1854, p. 361) to the present species. It is probably this example which is entered in Dr. Dobson's " Catalogue of Chiroptera in the British Museum," as being of British origin.

II. DAUBENTON'S BAT.   VESPERTILIO DAUBENTONI.

Vespertilio daubentonii, Leisler, in Kuhl's Deutsch. Flederm. p. 51 (1817); Bell, British Quadrupeds 2nd. ed. p. 60 (1874); Dobson, Cat. Chiroptera Brit. Mus. p. 297 (1878).

Vespertilio emarginatus (nec Geoffr.), Jenyns, Brit. Vert. p. 26 (1835).

Vespertilio ædilis, Jenyns, Ann. Nat. Hist. 1839 p. 73.

Vespertilio daubentoni, Blanford, Mamm. Brit. India p. 331 (1891).

Characters.—This, the second representative of the long-footed group, has the wings arising from the sides cf the feet just below the ankle, while the ears when laid forward extend to the tip of the nose.   Ears with the tips rounded, but not very broadly, and the inner margin regularly convex, and the outer straight or slightly concave for nearly the upper half of its length, below which it becomes suddenly convex.   Earlet moderately pointed, about half the length of the ear, its inner margin straight, and the outer slightly convex, with a rounded lobe projecting just above the base.   Face in front of eyes partially naked, and a rather tumid area between the eyes and nostrils.   Upper incisor teeth nearly equal in size, with widely divergent cusps; middle upper pre-molar clearly visible externally, and about one-third the height of the first.   Colour, brown above and dirty white beneath; at least the basal half of all the hairs being dark brown.   Length of head and body about $1\frac{9}{10}$ inch; of tail, $1\frac{3}{4}$ inch.

Distribution.—Daubenton's Bat is an inhabitant of Northern

Africa and the greater part of temperate Europe and Asia.   It
appears to have been first recognised as a British species by
the late Rev. Leonard Jenyns (Blomefield), who provisionally
identified it with the *Vespertilio emarginatus* of Geoffroy—an
identification which was subsequently corrected by Bell.   In
Britain it appears to be pretty widely distributed, although
more common in the southern and midland counties than
further north, and very variable in this respect, even in the
former districts.   Thus, whereas Bell speaks of it as being
very common in some parts of Warwickshire, Mr. Montagu
Browne records only one specimen known to him from
Leicestershire.   Only a single example appears to have been
recorded from Yorkshire (*Zoologist*, 1891, p. 395).   At an
early period of its British history it was obtained from near
Winchester; and Bell records it from Durham, while the Rev.
H. A. Macpherson notices one specimen captured on the
Carlisle canal in 1852, and a second near Ulswater, eleven
years later.   Although somewhat rare even in the Lake District,
this Bat extends into Scotland, having been long known from
Aberdeenshire, and recently recorded from the extreme north-
east of Banffshire.   Some years ago, as the writer is informed by
Mr. Harvie-Brown, great numbers of these Bats were discovered
in an old vault in the castle of Gight, in Aberdeenshire, but
immediately after their discovery and disturbance they forsook
their old quarters, and their new habitation has not been
discovered.   Since this species is not mentioned by Messrs.
Harvie-Brown and Buckley as occurring either in Sutherland,
Caithness, Argyllshire, or the Hebrides, it may be presumed
that its range does not include the extreme north of Scotland.
In Ireland it has been recorded from Kildare, Derry, and
Donegal, and probably occurs elsewhere, although it is rare.

Habits.—The essential peculiarity in the habits of Daubenton's Bat is its extreme partiality for water, on the surface of

PLATE IV.

REDDISH-GREY BAT.

which it skims in the evening in a manner not unlike that of a Swallow by day. Thus, in describing the appearance of some Bats which he believed referable to this species, the Rev. H. A. Macpherson writes that "they flew actively over the water, frequently dipping, sometimes two or three times in succession, apparently feeding, their shadows being reflected as they hovered over the water, and the motion of their wings recalling the flight of the Common Sandpiper. They flew uniformly low over the water. Sometimes one would approach the margin of the lake, but they seemed to obtain most of their prey in the centre of the latter." Generally making its appearance soon after sun-set, this Bat, after hawking for a short time for flies and gnats, usually returns to the shore to rest for a time before con-tinuing its flight in quest of food. During the period of its active life, its favourite haunts for repose are trees; but, as we have seen above, it may retire for its winter torpor to under-ground or deserted chambers of old buildings.

III. THE REDDISH-GREY BAT. VESPERTILIO NATTERERI.

Vespertilio nattereri, Kuhl, Deutsch. Flederm. p. 33 (1817); Bell, British Quadrupeds 2nd ed. p. 54 (1874); Dobson, Cat. Chiroptera Brit. Mus. p. 307 (1878).

(*Plate IV.*)

Characters.—This species brings us to the second or short-footed group of the genus, in which the foot is of moderate size, measuring less than one-fourth the length of the fore-arm, while the spur on the foot extends only about one-half the dis-tance from the ankle to the tail. The present species may be characterised as follows.—Earlet narrowing above, sharply pointed, and curved outwards; wings arising from the base of the toes; fur of neck and shoulders scarcely longer than that of head and body; ears longer than the head; membrane connecting the hind-legs with its posterior margin fringed with stiff hairs; tail as long as the head and body. Fur very long and dense, on the upper-parts dark brown with light reddish tips; on the under surface, darker at the base, with the terminal third of the hairs white. Length of head and body about 1$\frac{4}{5}$ inch; of the tail the same.

The fringed inter-femoral membrane serves to distinguish the Reddish-grey Bat not only from all the other British species, but likewise from all other members of the genus, with the exception of the West African Welwitsch's Bat, which is remarkable for its orange-and-black wings.

Distribution.—The Reddish-grey Bat seems to be an exclusively European species, ranging from Ireland in the west to the Ural Mountains in the east, and from the southern districts of Sweden in the north to the Alps in the south. In England, although somewhat local, it appears to be not uncommon in several of the southern and midland counties, but seems to get scarcer as we go north. It is recorded by Bell from near London, Essex, Cambridgeshire, Hampshire, Kent, and Norfolk; Mr. Montagu Browne notes its presence in Leicestershire; and in the Lake District a colony was discovered, according to the Rev. H. A. Macpherson, in the summer of 1886, in an old outhouse at Castletown. In the second edition of Bell's "British Quadrupeds," this species was said to be unknown in Scotland, but there is a specimen in the British Museum from Inverary, Argyllshire, presented by the Duke of Argyll, showing that the statement in question is incorrect. In Ireland it has been taken at least in the counties of Dublin, Cork, Longford, and Wicklow, but is very rare.

Habits.—When on the wing above the observer's head, this Bat may be easily recognised by the light colour of its underparts; its whole coloration being, indeed, of a lighter shade

than in any other British member of the order. This characteristic is noticed by Mr. Montagu Browne, who captured one
of these Bats among a colony of Pipistrelles in a church in
Leicestershire. Thus he writes that "the flight of the two
species varied much, the Pipistrelles flying quicker, and constantly changing the direction of their flight in a zig-zag kind
of manner, whereas the flight of Natterer's Bat was more fully
sustained, and much more direct, though somewhat slower.
A marked difference between the flight of the two species was
not so much the greater spread of wing as the evident breadth
of the wing-membrane. Most noticeable, however, was the
greyish-white tint of the under-part of the body ; and this was
readily observed, not only when flying in the light of the
lamps, but when the animal was high up, or in the darkest
parts of the church—so much so, indeed, that the people who
were assisting constantly exclaimed 'Here comes a white-
waistcoated one.'" Essentially a gregarious species, the
Reddish-grey Bat seems invariably to select either buildings—
and preferably their roofs—or caverns for its retreat. Bell
records the discovery of an enormous colony in the year 1848
between the ceiling and roof of Arrow Church, near Alcester.
"Here," he writes, "the Bats were seen adhering, by all their
extremities, to the under surface of the row of tiles which
forms the crest or ridge of the roof, and others clinging to them
until a mass was made up three or four inches thick, six or
seven wide, and about four feet in length." Instead of the
repose which ordinarily characterises such an assemblage,
these Bats were in a constant state of unrest and turmoil, those
on the outskirts of the mass striving (probably for the sake of
warmth) to make their way into the interior, which was as
strenuously resisted by the occupants of the inside places.
Numbers of dead and dried young ones, which had probably
fallen from their mothers, strewed the floor of the chamber.

IV. BECHSTEIN'S BAT.   VESPERTILIO BECHSTEINI.

Vespertilio bechsteinii, Leisler, in Kuhl's Deutsch. Flederm. p. 30 (1817); Bell, British Quadrupeds 2nd ed. p. 52 (1874); Dobson, Cat. Chiroptera Brit. Mus. p. 308 (1878).

Characters.—From the preceding species, Bechstein's Bat may be readily distinguished by the posterior margin of the membrane connecting the hind-legs being naked; and by the length of the tail being less than that of the head and body. Ears oval, and considerably longer than the head. Fur light reddish on the upper-parts, and greyish-white beneath; the bases of the hairs, both above and below, being dark brown. Length of head and body about 2 inches; of tail, 1½ inch.

Dobson remarks that in general form this species resembles *Vespertilio murinus*, "but is readily distinguished from that species by the proportionately much longer ears, by the very different form of the tragus, by the wing-membrane extending quite to the base of the toes, and also by its considerably smaller size."

Distribution.—Like the last species, this Bat appears to be confined to Europe, its range extending in one direction from the south of England to the south of Russia, and in the other from Sweden to the Alps.   So far as we are aware, this species is only known as British upon the evidence of some specimens captured many years ago in the New Forest, and now preserved in the British Museum, and it has therefore a very doubtful claim to rank in our fauna.

Habits.—In marked distinction to the Reddish-grey Bat, this species is described as being an exclusively forest-haunting form, taking up its winter quarters in hollow trees, and never resorting to buildings or caves. Never associating with other members of its order, it generally flies about in small parties, which seldom exceed a dozen in number.

V. THE MOUSE-COLOURED BAT. VESPERTILIO MURINUS.

Vespertilio murinus, Linn., Syst. Nat. ed. 12, vol. i. p. 47
(1766; *in parte*) ; Bell, British Quadrupeds 2nd ed. p. 48
(1874); Dobson, Cat. Chiroptera Brit. Mus. p. 309
(1878).

Vespertilio myotis, Kuhl, Deutsch. Flederm. p. 36 (1817).

Vespertilio blythii, Tomes, Proc. Zool. Soc. 1857 p. 53.

Vespertilio africanus, Dobson, Ann. Mag. Nat. Hist. ser. 4
vol. xvi. p. 260 (1875); id. Cat. Chiroptera Brit. Mus.
p. 310 (1878).

Characters.—Although, as already mentioned, the Mouse-
coloured Bat closely resembles the preceding species in general
external characters, it belongs to a sub-group distinguished by
having the earlet or tragus straight, and sharply or bluntly
pointed, instead of being sharply pointed and curving outwards. The following are the essential characteristics of the
present species :—

Crown of head slightly elevated ; muzzle blunt; a somewhat
swollen area between the eye and the nostril, and the sides of
the face and the end of the upper surface of the nose nearly
naked, although the upper lip carries some long hairs. Ears
large, generally reaching, when laid forwards, just beyond the
end of the muzzle; their tips bluntly pointed; the inner
margin moderately convex to the base, where it is joined at a
right angle to the basal lobe ; outer margin concave below the
tip, with a shallow notch opposite the base of the earlet, succeeded by a convex lobe, terminating opposite the base of the
inner margin. Earlet of moderate length, narrowed above, and
sub-acutely pointed, with the inner margin more or less nearly
straight, and the outer with a small convex basal lobe, then convex for about half its length, and finally straight. Wings arising
from the metatarsus ; only the extreme tip of the tail projecting
beyond the edge of the membrane connecting the hind legs,

5   E

the basal part of which is well haired on its upper surface. Anterior upper pre-molar tooth about half the height of the last ; and the middle one small and generally placed somewhat internally to the line of the other teeth. General colour varying from greyish- to reddish-brown, the under-parts being pale brown, with a suffusion of white, and the bases of all the hairs dark. Length of head and body about 2½ inches ; of tail 2⅛ inches.

Distribution.—The Mouse-coloured Bat—the largest representative of the Order recorded from Britain—is an inhabitant of the greater portion of temperate Europe and Asia, as well as northern Africa. Eastwards it ranges as far as the northwestern Himalaya and Kashmir, the variety from the latter region being distinguished by its shorter ears ; while its northern range includes Denmark and the southern districts of England. The claim to rank as a British species originally rested upon the evidence of certain specimens captured in the gardens of the British Museum in Bloomsbury, some time previously to the year 1835. It is suggested, indeed, in the second edition of Bell's "British Quadrupeds" that, owing to the confusion which, as remarked above, formerly existed between the Mouse-coloured Bat and the Pipistrelle, the specimens in question did not pertain to the present species at all. If, however, a skin in the British Museum entered in Dr. Dobson's "Catalogue of Chiroptera" as of English origin, be, as is most probably the case, one of the specimens in question, and if there be no doubt as to the *bonâ-fide* British origin of the latter, then we cannot refuse to admit the right of the Mouse-coloured Bat to a place in the English fauna. The alleged occurrence of the species in Dorsetshire was subsequently contradicted (*Zoologist*, 1887, p. 234). It has indeed been subsequently recorded by Mr. A. G. More, from Freshwater, in the Isle of Wight, on the evidence of certain large Bats shot there by Mr. F. Bond, which have been referred to the present species ; but in a " Guide to the Isle of Wight," published in 1876, Mr. More pointed out that the identification was incorrect, and that the Bats in question were really Noctules.

Habits.—On the Continent, where this Bat is one of the most abundant species, it appears abroad late in the evening, and flies at a low elevation. Never associating with other species, it congregates by hundreds in the roofs of churches and other buildings, as well as in caves; and is reported to be extremely quarrelsome in disposition—so much so, indeed, that many individuals in a colony are often found with the membranes of their wings torn to rags, and some of the bones broken. Although its proper food is insects, specimens kept in confinement in India have been known to kill some of their fellows and eat a portion of their flesh. But a single offspring is produced at a birth, and the little one may be found clinging to the body of the female from the latter part of May till about the middle of July, after which it is able to shift for itself.

VI. THE WHISKERED BAT. VESPERTILIO MYSTACINUS.

Vespertilio mystacinus, Leisler, in Kuhl's Deutsch. Flederm. p. 58 (1817); Bell, British Quadrupeds 2nd ed. p. 67 (1874); Dobson, Cat. Chiroptera Brit. Mus. p. 314 (1878).

Vespertilio siligorensis, Hodgson; Horsfield, Ann. Mag. Nat. Hist. ser. 2 vol. xvi. p. 102 (1853).

Characters.—Whereas in the preceding species the wings arise from the metatarsus, or sides of the feet between the ankle and the toes, in the Whiskered Bat they take origin from the base of the outer toe. This feature, coupled with the absence of any accessory lobe of membrane near the spur on

E 2

the ankle, and the presence of a number of long hairs on the face, extending down to and covering the upper lip, will suffice to distinguish the present species from all the other British Bats.   The ears are as long as the head, and their outer margins strongly convex in the lower half.   In colour the fur is brown, with a more or less rufescent tinge above, and greyish on the under-parts; the bases of all the hairs being dark brown or black.   Length of head and body usually about $1\frac{1}{2}$ inch; of tail, $1\frac{2}{8}$ inch.

Distribution.—This Bat ranges over the greater part of Europe, extending from Ireland in the west, to Central Russia in the east, and from Finland in the north to Spain in the south; it is likewise found over a large portion of Asia, having been recorded from Syria, Nipal, Sikhim, and Pekin.   It likewise inhabits Africa north of the Sahara.   In England, although local, it does not appear to be rare, having been recorded by Jenyns from Cambridgeshire and Northamptonshire, by Yarrell from Colchester, by Bell from Chiselhurst in Kent and from Warwickshire, by Montagu Browne from Leicestershire, and by Macpherson from the Lake District; while in Dobson's "Catalogue of Chiroptera" examples are mentioned from the Isle of Wight and Hastings.   Although not included by Thompson in his account of Irish Mammals, it is stated by Kinahan to have been obtained from county Clare; but it appears to be unknown in Scotland.

Habits.—Essentially a solitary species, although occasionally seen in small companies attracted by an abundance of food, the Whiskered Bat appears to frequent, for the purposes of hibernation, either hollow trees, the roofs of buildings, or caverns; the specimens alluded to above from Colchester and Chiselhurst having been taken in chalk-caves.   It makes its appearance early in the evening, and flies swiftly in a manner very similar to the Pipistrelle; it often exhibits a preference for the neighbourhood of water, over the surface of which it skims. Towards the latter part of June, or the commencement of July, the female produces a single young one.

THE INSECTIVORES. ORDER INSECTIVORA.

Closely allied in the structure of their teeth and many other portions of their organisation to the Bats, the small and mostly terrestrial Mammals, commonly known as Insectivores, may be distinguished from the Chiroptera on the one hand, by the absence of wings and the normal conformation of the fore limb, and from the land Carnivora on the other by the circumstance that a pair of teeth in each jaw are not specially modified to act one against each other with a scissor-like action. Their feet, which are always more or less nearly plantigrade, are generally furnished with five toes, carrying claws, and, with the exception of an aberrant West African genus, collar-bones, or clavicles, are invariably present. As a rule, the distinction between incisor, canine, pre-molar, and molar teeth is less well marked than in the majority of Mammals ; but such distinctions do exist. The number of incisor teeth in the lower jaw is never reduced to a single pair, and the molar teeth have well-developed roots and short crowns—the latter surmounted with sharp cusps, which may be arranged either in the form of the letter W (as in all the British representatives of the Order), or in a V.

Although there is a remarkable difference in the external form of the various members of the Insectivora, some being robust, while others are slim, and some, again, having a coat of softest velvet, and others a covering of hard spines, yet nearly all are characterised by the elongation of the muzzle, which projects considerably beyond the extremity of the lower jaw. Unlike the Bats, where they are situated on the breast, the Insectivores invariably have their numerous teats placed on the abdomen; and the number of young is always large. Their low degree of organisation is indicated by the circumstance that the main lobes, or hemispheres, of the brain are perfectly smooth, and do not extend backwards so as to cover the hinder portion of the brain, or cerebellum. Indeed, it appears that the Insectivores are the most lowly organised of all the placental Mammals, exhibiting many signs of affinity with the Marsupials, of which they may prove to be the direct descendants. It may be added that their structural resemblances to the Bats point to the conclusion that the latter are the highly modified descendants of some very primitive and at present unknown members of the Order.

With the exception of the Tree-Shrews of India, the whole of the Insectivores are nocturnal creatures, skulking during the day in obscure corners or holes, or even, as in the case of the Mole, being entirely subterranean in their habits. Save for the so-called Flying-Lemur of the Malayan region, which is but doubtfully included in the Order, Insectivores, as their name implies, feed exclusively on insects, worms, molluscs, and suchlike creatures. The majority are purely terrestrial in their habits, although a few, like the British Water-Shrew, are aquatic, while the Oriental Tree-Shrews are arboreal, and the Flying-Lemur takes flying leaps from tree to tree in the manner of a Flying-Squirrel.

Their geographical distribution is somewhat peculiar, from the fact that while they are abundant in Africa, and still more so in Madagascar, both of which are well-known harbours of refuge for creatures of a low type, yet they are totally unknown in South America, which is another haven for such feeble animals. Although unknown in Australia, they are otherwise fairly well distributed over the remaining regions of the globe.

The British representatives of the Order, all of which, as

already mentioned, belong to the group characterised by the W-like arrangement of the cusps of the upper molar teeth, are classified under three families, of which the first is

THE HEDGE-HOGS AND THEIR ALLIES.   FAMILY ERINACEIDÆ.

Although the well-known spiny covering of the Hedge-hogs would, by non-zoological readers, be regarded as the most characteristic feature of the Family to which these creatures belong, yet, as a matter of fact, it is of no real importance. Thus, for instance, while similar spines occur in the Tenrecs of Madagascar, which belong to another family of the Order (pertaining to the group with a V-like arrangement of the cusps on the upper molars), in the so called " Gymnuras " of the Oriental region, which are included in the present Family, such spines are totally wanting.   Under these circumstances naturalists have to resort to other characters by which to define the Family.   Since, however, these are somewhat technical, and require a certain amount of anatomical knowledge for their proper comprehension, we shall not allude to them here, as it is sufficient for the purposes of this work to state that in Britain the Family is represented solely by the Hedge-hog, which cannot possibly be confounded with any other of our native animals.

THE HEDGE-HOGS.   GENUS ERINACEUS.

Erinaceus, Linn., Syst. Nat. ed. 12 vol. i. p. 75 (1766).

The genus may be shortly defined as including those members of the family in which the back and sides are covered with short spines, and the tail is short and rudimentary.

Hedge-hogs have a total of thirty-six teeth, there being ten pairs in the upper and eight in the lower jaw.   Of these, there are three pairs of incisors, one of canines, three of pre-molars, and three of molars. In the lower jaw, while the number of canines and molars is the same, there are but two pairs both of incisors and pre-molars. In the upper jaw, the inner pair of incisors are conical and vertically-placed teeth, widely separated from one another in the middle line, while the lower incisors incline almost horizontally forwards.

The spines clothing the bodies and sides of the Hedge-hogs, which are generally marked with fine longitudinal grooves, are inserted in a layer of tissue beneath the skin by small knob-like terminations resembling pins' heads, and may thus be likened to pins stuck through a piece of soft leather. Beneath the skin lies a thick layer of muscle—the *panniculus carnosus*—which is much more developed than in any other Mammal, and by its contraction enables the creatures to roll themselves up into the well-known ball-like form, when the head and limbs are completely concealed from view, and only a uniformly formidable array of radiating spines exposed.

Hedge-hogs are exclusively Old World animals, and are distributed over the main portion of the three great continents, although they are unknown in Madagascar, Ceylon, Burma, and the Malayan region. As a rule, the numerous species are exceedingly like one another, both as regards external appearance and their general structure, although, somewhat curiously, the European species differs in certain respects from the whole of the rest.

I. THE COMMON HEDGE-HOG. ERINACEUS EUROPŒUS.

Erinaceus europœus, Linn., Syst. Nat. ed. 12 vol. i. p. 75 (1766); Bell, British Quadrupeds 2nd ed. p. 102 (1874).

(Plate V.)

Characters.—Both the third upper incisor and the canine inserted by single roots; the fur usually long and coarse.

COMMON HEDGE - HOG.

Length of head and body, about 10 inches ; of tail, 1½ inches.

The two characters above-mentioned at once serve to distinguish this species from the whole of the other members of the genus, in all of which the third upper incisor and canine teeth each present the rare and remarkable peculiarity of being inserted by two distinct roots ; while the fur is shorter and much less coarse.

Differing from all other British Mammals by its coat of spines, the Hedge-hog is the largest indigenous representative of the Order to which it belongs. The muzzle is conical, and the body oblong and convex above, while the legs are so short and the feet so completely plantigrade, that the abdomen almost touches the ground when the creature is walking. The short, broad, and rounded ears are less than half the length of the head ; the eyes are of moderate size ; and while the whole of the back and sides are protected by spines, the face and under-parts are clad with stiff and brittle fur, the tip of the muzzle being naked and black. In colour the spines are dirty white, with a brown or blackish ring somewhat above the middle, while the hair on the face and under-parts is yellowish-white. The rather long claws are moderately curved, and much compressed, but are evidently not adapted for burrowing. The female has six pairs of teats.

Distribution.—The common Hedge-hog ranges over the greater part of Europe, and extends eastwards through Asia as far as Amurland. In England it is generally distributed, although in many parts the fashion so prevalent of grubbing up hedgerows to make large fields has resulted in a considerable diminution in its numbers. Abundant in the Lake District, it crosses the border into Scotland, where it is mainly characteristic of the southern and central counties, and some years ago it seemed to be chiefly confined to Clackmannan, Stirling, Dumbarton,

and Perth, in the counties north of the Firths of Forth and
Clyde. Now, however, according to Messrs. Harvie-Brown
and Buckley, its range seems to be extending somewhat, probably owing to artificial introduction ; but it is quite unknown
in the Isles—that is to say, at least, as an indigenous animal.
In Sutherland and Caithness it is, according to the testimony
of the same writers, "still unknown in the west, and, so far as
known to us, in all other parts of the counties. Though pet
specimens have been introduced, and have escaped, there is
no evidence that they have established themselves in a wild
state." In Ireland, Thompson says that the Hedge-hog is found
everywhere in suitable localities.

Habits.—Like nearly all the members of the Order to which
it belongs, a purely nocturnal animal, the Hedge-hog, or Urchin,
as it is termed in many parts of England, reposes during the
day in some snug and safe retreat, generally situated beneath
the roots of some old tree or stub, in a hedge-bank, thicket, or
a crevice in a rock or wall. During the winter the Hedge-hog
passes its time in a state of complete torpor, apparently never
awakening, and therefore requiring no store of food, which in
the case of an animal subsisting on insects and other creatures
it would be impossible to accumulate. Although insects com-
pose a considerable portion of its diet, the Hedge-hog by no
means subsists entirely on them, nor, indeed, on invertebrates
generally, since almost all animals that it is able to kill, appear
to be equally acceptable as food. As Mr. Harting remarks, while
the animal under consideration exhibits a partiality for slugs,
snails, worms, and beetles, it has been ascertained that it likewise consumes eggs, chickens, young landrails and game-birds,
mice, young rabbits and hares, frogs and snakes, not even
the noxious viper being safe from its attack. With regard to
their depredations on young game-birds a recent writer in
Land and Water states that a few years ago he lifted some

pheasants' eggs from the road-side and put them under a hen.
The coop was placed outside the poultry-yard and near an old
summer-house which stood among shrubs, and was thickly
covered with creepers. The birds came out in due time, but
soon began to disappear. Rats were at first blamed, but as no
traces of their presence could be detected, the keeper was set
to watch, with the result that Hedge-hogs were proved to be
the delinquents.

A writer in the *Field* bears testimony to the egg-stealing propensities of these animals. He states that on a certain date there
was a duck's nest near his house containing five eggs. "On the
following morning," he writes, "there were only two. On the
following night I put down a common rabbit-trap at the nest,
let into the ground, and covered over. About ten p.m. I heard
something crying out (similar to the noise made by a hare
when in distress). Upon going there I found a very large
Hedge-hog in the trap. I took it out, killed it, and set the
trap again. About eleven there was another large Hedge-hog in
the same trap, which I killed, and set the trap again. I went
again the next morning at five and found another Hedge-hog
in the trap, making three Hedge-hogs caught the same night in
the same trap. Since then the duck has been sitting in the
same nest undisturbed by anything." This evidence, although
circumstantial, appears to be pretty conclusive, and it is confirmed by another instance narrated by the same writer. In
this second case a pheasant's nest with fifteen eggs was found
to have nine destroyed ; each of the damaged eggs having been
apparently bitten half through. The six remaining sound eggs
were taken home and a small quantity of strychnine inserted
into each through a small perforation, after which they were
sealed up and returned to the nest. The next morning two of
the eggs were partially eaten, while near by lay a Hedge-hog.
stone dead.

In attacking a snake a Hedge-hog proceeds with extreme caution, seizing a favourable opportunity to give the reptile a bite, and then immediately rolling itself up into a ball till it is enabled to repeat the attack, and so on till the snake finally succumbs. "If the snake happens to be a viper," writes Mr. Harting, "still more caution is displayed; for the latter invariably strikes at the Hedge-hog on being bitten, and it requires a remarkably quick 'shut up' to avoid the viper's fangs. The result in this case is very different; the viper repeatedly strikes against the sharp spines of the Hedge-hog, and in so doing becomes lacerated to such an extent that it eventually succumbs to its self-inflicted injuries." Frogs, according to the same observer, are boldly attacked at once without the slightest hesitation, and torn almost limb from limb.

In gardens frequented by Hedge-hogs, these animals may often be observed on the paths and lawns in the dusk of a summer's evening in search of beetles or worms. The latter are seized as they issue from their holes, and are eaten in a methodical manner, the Hedge-hog commencing at one end and working steadily on till he reaches the other.

It is not often that the observations of Gilbert White on the habits of British animals are incorrect, although this is the case with regard to one on the food of the Hedge-hog. He states that these animals were in the habit of eating the roots of the plantains growing in his garden at Selborne; and the statement has been admitted into the works of other writers on British animals, although it has been shown that the destruction of the plants in question is due to a nocturnal caterpillar.

Although generally a silent creature, the Hedge-hog gives vent to a peculiar sound, which has been described as something between a grunt and a squeak; and the cry of these animals when trapped has been already incidentally mentioned.

In regard to its senses, it appears from the observations of the late Colonel J. Whyte that although the power of vision is not very highly developed, hearing and smell are extremely acute. From observations made by the same gentleman on a captive specimen, it would seem that these animals keep on the move throughout the night, travelling the whole time at the rate of some six miles an hour in search of their prey, except of course during those intervals in which they are engaged in devouring the latter.

With regard to the breeding-habits of Hedge-hogs, some difference of opinion has prevailed among naturalists. Writing from observations made on continental specimens, Blasius states that the number of young produced at a birth varies from four to eight, and that these are usually born during the months of July or August. On the other hand, Bell writes that "the female produces from two to four young ones early in the summer, though the difference in their size in the autumn, when they are often found by sporting dogs, would seem to point out a somewhat variable period of birth." The latter discrepancy was explained by Dr. Dobson, who ascertained that a second litter is often produced in the autumn; and the same observer further came to the conclusion that the number of young in a litter does not exceed four, in which respect he is in accord with Bell. Mr. Harting, however, in an interesting paper published in the *Journal of the Royal Agricultural Society* for 1892, under the title of "Vermin of the Farm," states that the number of young in a litter is more frequently five or six, and that he has known two instances where seven were produced. The period of gestation does not exceed a month. At birth the young are blind, and covered with soft and flexible white spines, which, however, soon harden and assume their adult coloration. The young are born in a comfortable, well-roofed nest of dried leaves, grasses, and occasionally moss; the same or a similar nest being used for the winter-slumber

In conclusion, it may be mentioned that, in spite of its spiny armour, the Hedge-hog has two deadly enemies in the persons of the Fox and the Badger; and where those two animals abound, the number of Hedge-hogs, as Mr. Harting observes, will be small.

THE MOLES AND DESMANS. FAMILY TALPIDÆ.

Since the sole British representative of this Family is the Common Mole, we shall not spend much time in pointing out the distinctive Family characters, merely stating that all the *Talpidæ* may be distinguished from the *Erinaceidæ* by the absence of the central fifth cusp found on the two anterior molars of the latter; while from the *Soricidæ* they differ in that the first pair of lower incisor teeth are not hook-like and directed forwards; and likewise by the presence of zygomatic arches, or cheek-bones, to the skull.

Although the Desmans, which formerly inhabited England, but are now confined to the Continent, are aquatic in their habits, the great majority of the members of the Family have their fore-limbs more or less specially modified for digging in the ground. This modification shows itself especially in the very forward position of the fore-limbs, which in the most specialised types are extremely short, and furnished with very wide and powerful feet. Their forward position is brought about by the shortness of the collar-bones and the anterior extension of the breast-bone; while the shortness of the limbs is due to the extraordinary form of the arm-bone, or humerus, which, in place of being long and slender, in the True Moles is almost square, and about as unlike its representative in ordinary Mammals as can well be conceived. The

Desmans, it should be observed, which depart from the typical Mole type, may be regarded as connecting links between the Moles and Shrews.

THE TRUE MOLES. GENUS TALPA.

Talpa, Linn., Syst. Nat. ed. 12 vol. i. p. 73 (1766).

Body almost cylindrical, and passing imperceptibly into the head without any well-defined neck; limbs, especially the front pair, completely modified for digging; fore-feet normally turned outwards, instead of downwards, very broad and flat, and furnished with large, nail-like claws, their breadth being increased by a large sickle-like bone on the inner side. All the bones of the fore-limb very short; and the collar-bones frequently as broad as long. Tail short; no external ears; eyes very minute and entirely hidden by the fur, which is short, soft, and velvety, with its component hairs set vertically in the skin, and not directed backwards. Usually forty-four teeth,* of which in each jaw three pairs are incisors, one canines, four pre-molars, and three molars; incisors chisel-like and set in a semi-circular row; upper canines long, conical, and inserted in the jaw by double roots; the lower canines similar in character to the incisors.

Moles are among the few existing placental Mammals which retain the typical number of forty-four teeth, though this feature was not uncommon among their extinct ancestors of the early portion of the Tertiary period.

The True Moles are an exclusively Old World group, where they are represented by eight species, which are confined to Europe and Asia. In addition to the Common Mole, a second species is found in Europe to the south of the Alps; while of the Asiatic forms only two occur to the southward of the Himalaya.

* In some species the first pair of upper pre-molars is absent, thus reducing the number of teeth to forty-two.

THE COMMON MOLE.   TALPA EUROPŒA.

Talpa europœa, Linn., Syst. Nat. ed. 12 vol. i. p. 73 (1766);
   Bell, British Quadrupeds 2nd ed. p. 115 (1874).
Talpa vulgaris, Owen, Brit. Foss. Mamm. p. 19 (1846).

Characters.—Tail about one-fourth or one-fifth the length of the head and body, slender, nearly of equal diameter throughout, and haired; upper surface of hind feet thinly clothed with fur; eyelids open. Fourth upper pre-molar tooth without distal internal basal process, and the corresponding lower tooth smaller than the first of the same series. General colour some shade of black, varying from bluish-black to sooty-black, but occasionally grey, cream-colour, or even white. Length of head and body about $5\frac{1}{2}$ inches; of tail, $1\frac{2}{5}$ inch.

It may be noted that as the European Hedge-hog differs from all its congeners in the characters of its teeth, so the Common Mole is distinguished from all the other members of its genus in that its minute eyes are not covered with a continuous membrane; and it is, therefore, capable of receiving impressions of light. In this respect it is accordingly a rather less specialised creature than its kindred; and the existence of these perfect, although useless, eyes, is of itself a sufficient proof that Moles are descended from animals which lived on the surface of the earth, and that their completely subterranean habits have been gradually acquired.

Although some shade of black, generally with a more or less well-marked greyish sheen, is the normal colour of the Mole, variations from this are by no means uncommon; and Bell records grey, dark olive-brown, pied, yellowish-white, and wholly or partially orange Moles, while he notes some specimens with an orange patch on the chest, although elsewhere of the normal hue. Albino specimens are also from time to time met with; while there is almost every transition between the colours mentioned above. Piebald specimens appear to be the most uncommon of the normal variations. A white Mole with a red throat is on record; and Mr. Harting mentions a specimen captured in Fifeshire in 1880, which had a white head, while elsewhere it was of the normal colour.

Distribution.—Although unknown in Ireland, the Mole ranges over the greater part of Europe and Asia north of the Himalaya, occurring as far eastwards as Japan, and it is also found in the Altai mountains. In England it is so universally distributed as to require no special mention; and it probably occurs in most or all parts of Wales, being common even in the extreme west of Anglesea. Always more or less abundant in the Scottish lowlands, the Mole appears to have been formerly very rare or unknown in the more northern districts, but during the latter decades of the present century has been gradually extending its northward range. In Sutherlandshire, according to Messrs. Harvie-Brown and Buckley, it is still steadily on the increase, having been very rare about 1840 in Durness, where it is now common, as it is, in suitable localities, throughout Caithness. Although unknown in 1791 in the Lismore district, it subsequently made its way into the Kintyre isthmus of Argyllshire, and is now found in many parts of that county. The writer last mentioned further states that "the Mole is said to have been accidentally introduced into Mull—where it is now quite common—about eighty years ago—say about 1808—in a boat-load of earth brought from Morven. The earth was a peculiarly fine loam, intended for making the floor of a cottage when mixed with clay and smithy ashes." Quite recently it has made its appearance in the adjacent island of Ulva. It appears, however, still to be absent from the other islands. Similar testimony might be adduced as to the gradual spread of this animal in other northern counties of Scotland, but the foregoing is sufficient to show that ere long it will probably be found everywhere on the mainland, where suitable conditions for its peculiar mode of life exist. The increase of cultivation and of communication between remote districts will probably account for this widening distribution of the Mole; for it is almost impossible to believe that its introduction into certain districts can be due, as in the case of Mull, to accidental importation by human agency.

In Ireland, as already mentioned, the Mole is quite unknown.

Geologically, the Mole is a comparatively ancient animal, dating at least from the period of the so-called forest-bed of the Norfolk coast, which is assigned by some geologists to the top of the Pliocene, and by others to the base of the succeeding Pleistocene epoch.

Habits.—Every writer who has described the organisation and habits of the Mole has commented on the admirable adaptation of the creature to the necessities of its surroundings. Passing nearly the whole of its time beneath the ground, the Mole leads an existence of continuous labour—an existence to our ideas which appears dull enough, but which nevertheless may not be devoid of enjoyment of a certain kind. So swift and rapid, when in suitable soil, are its subterranean movements, that the creature has been not inaptly said to swim through the earth. Such rapidity of movement through such a resisting medium necessarily entails, however, an enormous drain on the Mole's vital powers, to sustain which a vast and almost continuous supply of food is essential to its well-being. Hence even a very short period of deprivation of food speedily results in death.

As special instances of adaptation we may note the following structural peculiarities in the Mole. In the first place, the cylindrical body, sharp muzzle, and short limbs, present the least possible impediments to the creature's subterranean progress ; while the absence of external ears, and the rudimentary condition of the eyes, are likewise subservient to the same purpose. Not less important is the vertical position of the hairs of the fur, which admits of either backward or forward progress in the tunnel with equal facility. Then, again, the broad, shovel-like fore-paws, armed with strong claws and turned outwards, are the very best instruments we could possibly conceive for tunnelling and shovelling backwards the earth ; these being worked by muscles of immense power, attached to bones which, by their shortness and width, are calculated to afford the maximum development of strength. Lastly, we must not omit to mention the long, pointed, and mobile snout, furnished with an extra bone at its tip, and the large series of small but sharp teeth, which are equally well adapted for seizing and retaining the worms and grubs which form its food.

Regarding the general mode of life of the species, we may quote from the summary given by Macgillivray in the original edition of the " Naturalist's Library." He says that its food consists mainly of earth-worms, "in quest of which it burrows its way in the soil, extending its subterranean excursions in proportion as its prey diminishes in number ; but the excessive and unremitting labour required in this pursuit, were it carried on at random, is rendered unnecessary by an instinct which compels it to excavate a series of runs or galleries, along which it can walk without inconvenience, and from different points of which it proceeds, forcing its way into the hitherto unperforated soil. In forming its subterranean paths, it works with its fore-feet, which, as has been seen, are admirably adapted for scraping away the earth and throwing it backwards, propelling itself forward by its hind-feet, which are disposed in the usual manner. When it has thus excavated an extended series of walks, it can run along them to any point without difficulty, and finds security in them from the pursuit of many enemies, although man employs them as a sure means for entrapping it." *

After mentioning that we are mainly indebted to the observations made many years ago by Le Court for our knowledge of the construction of the Mole's runs and habitation, the author proceeds to say that "each individual appropriates to himself a district, or space of ground, in which he forms a kind of fortress under a hillock in some secure place, as beneath a bank or near the roots of a tree.   In this eminence, of which the earth is rendered very compact, is formed a circular gallery, communicating with a smaller gallery, placed above it, by several passages.   On the level of the lower, or larger, gallery is a roundish cavity, or chamber, communicating with the upper by three passages.   From the outer gallery branch off a number of passages, which run out to a variable extent, and, forming an irregular curve, terminate in what may be called the high-road, which is a long passage proceeding from the outer circular gallery, and at the same time communicating directly with the central cavity.   It extends to the farthest limit of the domain, is of somewhat greater diameter than the body of the animal, has its walls comparatively compact, and communicates with the numerous passages by which the domain is intersected.   By this principal passage the Mole visits the various parts of its hunting-ground, burrowing to either side, and throwing out the earth here and there, so as to form heaps or mole-hills.   As it traverses this path several

---

* I am indebted to Mr. Aubyn Trevor-Battye for some observations on British Animals, which will be read with interest.   Concerning the present species he writes as follows :—" With regard to the question of vision, I can state that a Mole which I kept for some time in captivity would take worms from my fingers.   When I swung a worm about in front of his face he would—nose in air—follow it backward and forward with his head. Whether he saw it or only smelt it (in which case his quickness of scent was simply marvellous), I am unable to say."

times daily, it is in it that snares are laid for its capture. The excavations vary in their distance from the surface according to the nature of the soil and other circumstances. In deep, rich earth they are sometimes nearly a foot in depth, while in gravelly or clayey ground, covered with a thin layer of soil, they are often scarcely an inch. Often, also, the Mole burrows quite close to the surface of rich, loose soil which has been ploughed, and sometimes runs along it, forming merely a groove or trench. The principal object of its pursuit is the earth-worm, but it also feeds on larvæ, and occasionally devours frogs, lizards, and even birds.* Its voracity is excessive, insomuch that hunger urges it to exhibit a kind of fury, and it is found to perish in a very short time if deprived of food. It drinks frequently, and forms passages to brooks or ponds in the vicinity of its residence. During winter, when the cold forces the worms deeper into the ground, it follows them in their retreats, driving its galleries and alleys to a corresponding depth."

On the above notes Mr. Trevor-Battye observes :—" Macgillivray's remarks require some modification. It is not strictly true that ' each individual appropriates to itself a district,' for Moles have often, I think generally, a common system of runs used by various individuals from many different points. Thus I have known as many as twenty-four full-grown Moles to be taken in a single trap in one position, in a single run through a gateway." As to its feeding on larvæ, he says :—" A curious case came under my notice where some Moles had made a raid on the larvæ of cockchafers. Here they had been working half their time above ground, driving short shafts down into the roots of the sward, so that a friend thought at first that Rooks had been at work."

* We have ventured to make a verbal alteration in this and a subsequen sentence, where statements given hypothetically are now known to be certain.

It may be mentioned here that, as a general rule, the Mole exhibits a marked preference for light soils, such as old pastures, warrens, downs, or recently manured ploughed lands, in all of which the earth can be tunnelled with comparative facility. Occasionally, however, it frequents clayey or barren districts. A peculiarity in its habits is that it works during the day at certain regular hours, which are observed with extraordinary punctuality. Continuing his account, Macgillivray observes that during the winter the Mole " retires at intervals to its fortress, in which it has formed a bed of dry leaves or grass, to enjoy a profound repose; but in spring it quits this habitation, and rests during the warm season in a mole-hill.

" On the surface, to which it sometimes makes its way, it can run with considerable speed, but, if not in the immediate vicinity of its hole, is easily overtaken. It is more especially in the early part of the day that it is thus occasionally met with. When a meadow which it has frequented has been inundated, the Mole has been seen to swim with great vigour; and instances are known of its making its way to islands in lakes and rivers.

" The males are more numerous than the females, and the former sometimes engage in desperate combats. The number of young produced at a birth varies from three to seven, and the period of parturition is from April to the end of summer; but whether more than one litter has been produced in a year has not been ascertained. The nest is generally found beneath a large mole-hill, and is formed of a mass of leaves, grass, fibrous roots, and other vegetable substances."

With regard to the appearance of the Mole above ground, Mr. Trevor-Battye sends me a note :—" This often happens in the evening, especially in July and August, when the animals are searching for white slugs and larvæ of *Tipulæ*, &c., in damp places, and this always occurs when the season is dry. Moles pair as early as February and commonly in March, and any mole-catcher will tell you that the latter month is the best time for Moles to run."

In reference to the number of young produced at a birth, it may be added that four or five is the most usual complement, as few as three or as many as six being rare ; and we are not aware whether more than one instance of the occurrence of as many as seven is on record. The period of gestation is given by Bell at two months or more, while by Jesse it is set down at one month only. Naked, and of course blind, at birth, the young are able to follow their parents in about five weeks, when they have attained nearly three-fourths their full dimensions.

The voracity of Moles almost surpasses belief, their stomachs being frequently found absolutely crammed full of worms, some of which show every appearance of having been swallowed whole. Writing of a captive specimen, Alston states that it would devour an amount of food which he estimated as exceeding its own weight in the course of a single day. During the first three days of its captivity it consumed three or four dozen earth-worms, a large frog, a quantity of raw beef, the body of a turkey-poult, and part of a second, as well as one or two black slugs.

From the testimony of more than one person well acquainted with their habits, it has been thought that, in some cases at least, Moles will accumulate a store of worms for use during those portions of the winter when the ground is too hard for tunnelling, except at great depths. These are said to be kept in a basin-shaped cavity in clayey soil, with the bottom beaten hard so as to prevent the worms from making their escape by boring; while according to one statement the worms themselves are partially disabled by a bite from the teeth of their captor. More information is, however, required as to these stores of worms, and when they are consumed. In regard to the latter point, Mr. Harting observes that it seems doubtful whether the worms could live long in such a state of confinement, for if unable to make their escape they themselves would die for lack of nourishment. There is, moreover, another circumstance connected with the winter-life of a Mole. Thus, if it be true that during a frost the animal descends lower down in the soil until it comes to the level where worms are to be found, we should like to know how it disposes of the soil dug out in making its tunnels, as it would be clearly impossible to throw up the ordinary mole-hills through the frozen earth above.

Concerning these worm-basins, Mr. Trevor-Battye writes to me :—" I strongly doubt this statement. I think it has arisen from the fact that during the winter the Mole does drive down tunnels almost, and sometimes quite, perpendicularly. These are frequently found to end (sometimes at depths of four feet) in a circular expansion, of which the inside is certainly smooth. I have always supposed that Moles lay up for the winter in these ; but the whole question of their hibernation wants making clear. As you dig down to these chambers with a spade, you will notice that all the earth is not removed from the shaft, nor is this necessary. A Mole can work backwards and forwards underground quite easily, without removing earth in the form of a mole-hill. There are numerous questions regarding the history of the Mole still to be settled. Why, for instance, should this species and a Badger die from a slight tap on the nose ? "

Some difference of opinion has long obtained as to whether the Mole is injurious or beneficial to the agriculturist, although it is pretty generally admitted that to the gardener it is an unmitigated nuisance. On this subject Macgillivray writes that "by destroying vast quantities of worms and grubs, the Mole may be considered as conferring a benefit on the agriculturist; and by perforating the soil, and throwing up the earth, it has been by some alleged to improve the natural pastures, especially in hilly districts, but in the cultivated grounds, and particularly in gardens and nurseries, the injury which it inflicts by its incessant labour is more obvious than any benefit that is derived from them, and, in fact, sometimes very great." This was written in pre-Darwinian days, when the importance of worms in improving and renovating the soil was quite unrecognised, and it is therefore perhaps more than an open question whether their destruction is an advantage. On the other hand, the quantity of grubs and other noxious creatures which the Mole consumes undoubtedly renders the creature serviceable to the farmer. On the whole, some of those best entitled to give an opinion on the subject, are in favour of not destroying the Moles on agricultural land. It is, however, essential that on pasture land the mole-hills should be knocked about and spread in the early spring, before the grass is allowed to stand for hay, when the fine earth of which they are composed forms an excellent top-dressing.

The Mole has several enemies which do not reflect whether or not it is valuable to man, and kill it ruthlessly whenever they have the opportunity, the chief of these being Weasels, Owls, and Buzzards. That Weasels kill Moles has been demonstrated on more than one occasion, when they have been seen carrying off the bodies of their victims; while in the case of Owls the occurrence of the remains of Moles among their castings affords decisive evidence. In the case of the Buzzard, Mr. Harting remarks that the bird, "in the vicinity of mole-hills will take up a position on some tree and watch until it sees a Mole working near the surface, when it will instantly drop down and seize it. In this way (*i.e.*, by watching and jumping down) Buzzards destroy numbers of Rats and other vermin, for which good service they deserve to be protected, instead of being shot and trapped at every opportunity."

In conclusion, it may be mentioned that in the north of England the Mole is still very often designated by its Saxon name of *Mouldiwarp* (or earth-turner), while in the west it is more commonly known as the *Want*, and in the midland counties as the *Hoont*, or *Woont;* these names being doubtless synonyms derived from the old Danish designation *Wand*.

THE SHREWS. FAMILY SORICIDÆ.

Different as is the appearance of the Moles from the Shrews, the two groups, as already stated, are so closely connected by the Desmans, that we have to resort to details of structure to differentiate them. The Shrews may, however, be distinguished by the circumstance that the skull has no bony zygomatic arches, or cheek-bones, and that its auditory bulla, at the base of the region of the internal ear, is imperfectly, instead of fully, ossified. A more ready means of recognising a member of the present Family is afforded by the characters of the first pair of incisor teeth, which, in both jaws are very much larger than any of the others. In the upper jaw these teeth are curved and hook-like, with a more or less strongly marked basal cusp on the hinder edge; while in the lower jaw they are elongated and project nearly horizontally forwards, sometimes with a slight upward curvature at the tip. Canine teeth are totally wanting in the lower jaw, and in the upper they are similar in character to the outer incisors and anterior pre-molars, so that a Shrew has no tooth which can be termed a tusk. In the lower jaw there are invariably six pairs of teeth, of which the first two are incisors, the third a pre-molar, and

PLATE VI.

COMMON SHREW

the remaining three molars. On the other hand, in the upper jaw the number is variable, ranging from seven to ten pairs.

The Family, which contains a large number of representatives, has a wider geographical distribution than any other of the Order, ranging over the temperate regions of Europe, Asia, Africa and North America, as well as many of their islands. In habits, most of the Shrews are terrestrial, although a few, and among them one British species, are aquatic.

In popular estimation these animals (as their common designation of Shrew-Mice indicates) are often confounded with Mice, although the two groups have not the most remote affinity with one another. A glance at the dentition will, of course, at once serve to decide to which group any given specimen pertains.

THE TRUE SHREWS. GENUS SOREX.

Sorex, Linn., Syst. Nat. ed. 12 vol. i. p. 73 (1766).

Teeth thirty-two in number, with their tips coloured reddish-brown; ear well-developed; tail long, and covered with more or less nearly equal hairs; limbs normal, and adapted for walking. Habits terrestrial.

The genus is represented by a large number of species, ranging over Northern Africa, Europe, Asia north of the Himalaya, and North America, but unknown in India and the adjacent regions.

I. THE COMMON SHREW. SOREX VULGARIS.

Sorex vulgaris, Linn., Syst. Nat. ed. 12 vol. i. p. 73 (1766); Bell, British Quadrupeds 2nd ed. p. 141 (1874).

Sorex araneus, Bell, British Quadrupeds p. 109 (1837, nec Linn.).

Sorex tetragonurus, Herman, Obs. Zool. p. 48 (1870).

(*Plate VI.*)

Characters.—Ear small, rounded, and scarcely projecting

above the level of the fur; tail, although somewhat variable in length, always shorter than the body, four-sided, with the angles rounded off, its width nearly equal throughout, and its whole length clothed with short, close, and somewhat stiff hairs.   Fur usually of a reddish mouse-colour on the upper-parts, and greyish beneath.   Length of head and body, 2¾ inches; of tail, 1½ inch, or rather more.

In common with the other members of the genus to which it belongs, the Shrew is an elegant little creature, with thick, soft fur, a long, slender and pointed muzzle, and a short body —the latter being more or less arched when the animal is at rest, though capable of being depressed when in motion.   Although the term "reddish mouse-colour" perhaps best expresses the more usual tint of the fur of the upper-parts, there is a considerable amount of individual variation in respect of colour, some examples tending to a more decidedly rufous hue, while others incline to blackish.   The grey of the under-parts is likewise variable in shade, being in some cases darker, and in others lighter than usual, while it has been known to show a yellowish tinge.   Not very uncommonly the fur has a faint suspicion of white, giving a somewhat speckled appear-ance; and spotted or pied Shrews have been met with.

In the older works on British zoology the common Shrew was described under the name of *Sorex araneus*, under the impression that it was the same as the so-called Spider-Shrew of the Continent.   The latter, as was pointed out by the late Rev. Leonard Jenyns (Blomefield), who contributed so largely to our knowledge of British vertebrated animals, is, however, a totally different creature, and is now assigned by zoologists to a distinct genus.

In size the common Shrew may be roughly compared to an ordinary Mouse, although in build it is more slender and delicate.   On each side of the body is situated a gland covered by two rows of coarse hairs, which secretes the well-known odour so characteristic of Shrews in general, and which, in one Indian species, is so strongly developed as to render uneatable any article of food with which the creature may have come in contact.

Distribution.—The common Shrew is one of the comparatively few Mammals which have an almost circumpolar distribution, its range extending from England across Europe and Asia, north of the Himalaya into North America. It is, however, not a little remarkable that an animal with such an exceedingly wide geographical range should be totally unknown in Ireland. In England and Wales it appears to be universally distributed, and it likewise ranges throughout the mainland of Scotland. Although it has been recorded from Iona, it now appears that throughout the Hebrides the genus is represented only by the Lesser Shrew. Fossil remains, originally assigned to the Water-Shrew, appear to indicate the existence of the present and perhaps also the next species in the Norfolk forest-bed, which, as we have seen, is at least as old as the early part of the Pleistocene epoch.

Habits.—Nocturnal and retiring in its habits, the Shrew is but seldom seen in a living state, although in summer evenings its shrill squeaking cry may often be heard in woods, hedgerows, and dry meadows, which are its favourite haunts. We say in a living state advisedly, since, in the autumn, numbers of dead Shrews are often to be seen on garden-paths and lanes, which have succumbed to a mortality, the cause of which is by no means clear. During the summer months these little creatures form well-marked runs among the stalks of grass of meadows ; and, although they are generally found in those in which the soil is dry, they are by no means wanting in damp and marshy situations. During the winter they retire beneath the roots of trees or bushes, to the deserted holes of other small Mammals, or other secure nooks, where they pass the cold months in a state of profound torpor. Although their chief food consists of worms, insects, and grubs, they also consume many of the smaller slugs and snails, while Jesse states that they will occasionally kill and eat young frogs. In the spring the female Shrew (perhaps with the aid of her mate) constructs of grass, leaves, and other herbage, a dome-shaped nest, with an entrance on one side, which is generally placed in a hedge-bank or some hollow in the grass. Here in due course she usually brings forth from five to seven naked and blind young, although occasionally there may be as many as ten in a litter. The breeding-season extends from the end of April to early in August. In disposition the Shrew is one of the most combative and pugnacious of animals; and many fights, probably between rival males, terminate fatally; while, if two or more of these animals be confined in a cage or box, they invariably fight to the bitter end.

It might be supposed that to such combats are due the number of dead Shrews so often encountered in autumn, although it is pretty evident that their death is due to some other cause. It has been suggested that Owls and Cats, which are supposed to kill, but not to eat, Shrews, are the cause of the destruction; but it is now ascertained that Shrews are eaten by the former, while from the situation in which their bodies are frequently found, it is scarcely likely that Cats are the murderers. In addition to those destroyed by Owls, it is said that a certain number of Shrews fall victims to the voracity of their cousin the Mole.

Perfectly harmless to man, both as regards his person, his cattle, and his crops, the Shrew was long the victim of a curious superstition, as is illustrated in a well-known passage from the writings of Gilbert White, which will bear one more repetition. Writing of his native village of Selborne, this

charming and quaint chronicler observes :—" At the south
corner of the plestor, or area, near the church, there stood,
about twenty years ago a very old, grotesque, hollow pollard
ash, which for ages had been looked upon with no small
veneration as a Shrew-ash. Now a Shrew-ash is one whose
twigs or branches, when applied to the limbs of cattle, will
immediately relieve the pains which a beast suffers from the
running of a Shrew-Mouse over the part afflicted ; for it is
supposed that a Shrew-Mouse is of so baneful and deleterious
a nature, that wherever it creeps over a beast, be it Horse, Cow,
or Sheep, the suffering animal is afflicted with cruel anguish,
and threatened with the loss of the limb. Against this
accident, to which they were continually liable, our provident
forefathers always kept a Shrew-ash at hand, which, when once
medicated, would maintain its virtue for ever. A Shrew-ash
was made thus : Into the body of the tree a deep hole was
bored with an auger, and a poor devoted Shrew-Mouse was
thrust in alive, and plugged in, no doubt with several quaint
incantations long since forgotten." One touch from the twig
of such an ash was sufficient to restore an afflicted animal to
health.

II. THE LESSER SHREW. SOREX MINUTUS.

Sorex minutus, Linn., Syst. Nat. ed. 12 vol. i. p. 73 (1766).

Sorex pygmæus, Pallas, Zoog. Rosso-Asiat. vol. i. p. 134
(1831) ; Bell, British Quadrupeds 2nd ed. p. 148a
(1874).

Sorex rusticus, Jenyns, Ann. Nat. Hist. 1838 p. 417.

Characters.—Size smaller than that of the last species, from
which it may be distinguished by the following characters : The
third upper incisor is not longer than the canine,* and by the
proportionately shorter fore-arm and foot. Tail usually shorter

---

* It should be noted that the Shrews are now considered to differ from
other placental Mammals in having four pairs of upper incisors, the outermost being the one here reckoned as the canine.

than the head and body, with a thick covering of hairs.   General colour brown above, and white on the under-parts.   Length of head and body about 2 inches ; of tail, 1⅓ inch.*

Distribution.—Although far less abundant in England than the common Shrew, the Lesser Shrew has a wider distribution in the British Islands, being found not only in Ireland, but likewise in the Hebrides, in both of which localities it is the sole representative of the genus.   Elsewhere it extends through Europe and Northern Asia as far eastward as the island of Saghalin, although unknown in North America.   In the north of England it appears to be even more uncommon than in the south.

This Shrew is the smallest British Mammal, and indeed, with the exception of another member of the same genus, the smallest Mammal in Europe.   In habits it appears to agree in all respects with its larger relative.

THE WATER-SHREWS.   GENUS CROSSOPUS.

Crossopus, Wagler, Isis 1832 p. 275.

Teeth thirty in number, with their summits stained brownish-red.   Ears small, but not truncated ; tail with a fringe of long hairs on its lower surface, and the feet also fringed.   Habits aquatic.

The genus is represented solely by the under-mentioned species.

THE WATER-SHREW.   CROSSOPUS FODIENS.

Sorex fodiens, Pallas, in Schreber's Säugethiere, vol. iii. p. 571
     (1778) ; Bell, British Quadrupeds p. 115 (1837).
Sorex remifer, Geoffr. Ann. Mus. vol. xvii. p. 182 (1811);
     Bell, British Quadrupeds p. 119 (1837).
Sorex daubentonii, Geoffroy, *loc. cit.*

* Mr. De Winton says that the best distinctive character for recognising the species is the extremely small size of the teeth, which require a lens to detect them.

PLATE VII

WATER - SHREW

Sorex bicolor, Shaw, Nat. Miscell. vol. ii. pl. 55 (1791).

Sorex ciliatus, Sowerby, Brit. Miscell. p. 103 pl. xlix. (1805).

Crossopus fodiens, Wagler, Isis 1832, p. 275; Bell, British
    Quadrupeds 2nd ed. p. 149 (1874).

Crossopus remifer, Wagler, *tom. cit.*

Amphisorex pennanti et *A. linneanus*, Gray, Ann. Mag. Nat.
    Hist. vol. ii. p. 287 (1838).

(*Plate VII.*)

Characters.—Larger than either of the British species of *Sorex*,
with the tail about two-thirds the length of the head and body.
In colour, typically black above and white beneath, with a
sharp division between the two, but frequently with the black
of the back extending to a portion or the whole of the inferior
surface, while in some cases the latter may be tinged with
rusty. The stiff fringing hairs of the tail and feet white.
Length of head and body about $3\frac{1}{4}$ inches; of tail, $2\frac{1}{10}$ inches.

The great variation in the colouring of the Water-Shrew gave
rise to the idea that there were two British representatives of
the genus, although it is now well ascertained that such variations are merely individual.

Distribution.—The Water-Shrew is met with in suitable
localities in many parts of Europe, whence it extends eastwards
through Northern Asia as far as the Altai Mountains. Throughout most districts in England and Wales it is far from uncommon
in the neighbourhood of brooks and streams, although, from the
nature of its habits, it is not often seen, unless special search be
made. According to the Rev. H. A. Macpherson, although
they seem to be rare in the Lake district, yet the number of
specimens killed by Cats, together with the presence of their
remains among the *débris* rejected by Owls, shows that this is
not really the case. Both the dark and pied varieties are met
with in this part of the country. In Scotland, as a whole, the
Water-Shrew appears to be a less common animal than in

5

England. In Sutherland it is, however, said to be far from rare, although the dark variety appears to be less common there than in other parts of the country. Hitherto its presence has not been detected in the Hebrides or any of the other Scotch islands; and it is quite unknown in Ireland.

Habits.—Residing in long winding burrows excavated by itself in the banks of rivulets, brooks, ditches, or ponds, the Water-Shrew is fully as active in the water as a Water-Vole or Otter. In search of food, writes Macgillivray, "it makes excursions upon the water, and dives with ease to the bottom. In swimming, it presents a singular appearance, its sides being apparently expanded, its body lying so lightly as to be two-thirds out of the water, its tail extended along the surface ; and it paddles away seemingly with little effort, scarcely causing a ripple, although its speed is considerable. I have seen it sporting as it were in the water, several individuals swimming about in different directions, sometimes shooting along in curves at an accelerated rate. It is a very timorous animal, and on the least apprehension of danger, dives and gets close to the bank, or swims directly to its hole."

An earlier writer, Dovaston, describes the graceful movements of this Shrew as follows. Lying close to the bank of the pool in which one of these creatures was disporting itself, he writes :—"I repeatedly marked it glide from the bank, under water, and bury itself in the mass of leaves at the bottom ;— I mean the leaves that had fallen off the trees in autumn, and which lay very thick over the mud. It very shortly returned, and entered the bank, occasionally putting its long sharp nose out of the water, and paddling close to the edge. This it repeated at very frequent intervals, from place to place, seldom going more than two yards from the side, and always returning in about half a minute. I presume it sought and obtained some insect or food among the rubbish and leaves, and retired to consume it. Sometimes it would run a little on the surface, and sometimes timidly and hastily come ashore, but with the greatest caution, and instantly plunge in again. . . . . When under water, it looks grey, on account of the pearly clusters of minute air-bubbles that adhere to its fur, and bespangle it all over. It swims very rapidly; and, though it appears to dart, its very nimble wriggle is clearly discernible."

The food of the Water-Shrew consists mainly of various kinds of water-insects, their larvæ, crustaceans, and fresh-water snails. In the spring it appears to be specially fond of the larvæ of the Caddis-fly; and in searching for fresh-water Shrimps the animal is in the habit of turning over the stones at the bottom of clear streamlets. It will also prey at times on the fry of fish, one of the Duke of Sutherland's gamekeepers having watched one of these Shrews attack a shoal of young Salmon which had just been liberated from the hatching-house into a small brook. This fish-eating propensity is likewise proved from the observations of Mr. Buckley; while there is also evidence that this Shrew will at times eat the flesh of dead mammals or birds. Mr. Trevor-Battye tells me that a colony of these animals, which he found in Kent, inhabited a garden-pond for a great number of years, where they showed a great partiality for frog-spawn.

The long, winding burrow already alluded to, which is expanded at its extremity into a rounded chamber, serves not only as a dwelling-place, but likewise as a nursery. In this grass-lined chamber the female, early in May, gives birth to from five to ten young ones; five or six being apparently the most usual number. When able to run about, the young are described as most sportive and amusing little creatures, chasing one another up and down the small paths radiating from the entrance to the burrow.

It is said that at times the Water-Shrew will seek its food, which probably then consists mainly of terrestrial insects, at a considerable distance from the water. That it cannot long exist without its favourite element is, however, evident from a statement quoted by the Rev. H. A. Macpherson, that in the Lake district during the droughts of 1859 and 1863 these animals suffered severely.

Although the Water-Shrew was not definitely recorded by naturalists as a native of Caithness till the year 1872, yet there seems a strong probability that it was long known to the inhabitants of that county under the somewhat remarkable name of *Lavellan*. What was really the animal thus designated was long a disputed point, although Pennant inclined to the opinion that it was the one under consideration, his view being confirmed by Messrs. Harvie-Brown and Buckley. Other writers have, however, assigned the name to a Lizard. That the Water-Shrew does inhabit Caithness was proved during a flood in the autumn of 1872, when several were seen carried down the river near Wick on bundles of corn and hay.

THE CARNIVORES.—ORDER CARNIVORA.

Formerly included in the same order as the Insectivores, the Carnivora form a very well-defined natural group, which, so far as existing forms are concerned, may be distinguished from the preceding Order by the following characters. In the case of the more typical representatives of the Order, a pair of cheek-teeth is specially modified to act one against the other with a scissor-like action, at least the anterior outer portion of both the upper and lower tooth being converted into a cutting blade ; this blade in some cases, as in the Cats, forming the whole of the tooth, while in others, as among the Bears, it constitutes but a small moiety thereof. On the other hand, in those members of the Order such as the Seals and Walruses, which do not possess these specially modified and so-called flesh-teeth, and are aquatic and mainly marine in their habits, the limbs are converted into paddle-like flippers. Accordingly, we may define the Order as including Carnivorous Mammals having either a pair of specially modified flesh-teeth in each jaw, or with both pairs of limbs converted into flippers.

In connection with these flesh-teeth, it may be observed that while in the upper jaw the pair thus named form the last of the pre-molar series, that is to say, they are preceded by milk-teeth, in the lower jaw they form the first of the molar series, or those which have no such predecessors.

Mentioning a few of the leading characteristics of the Order generally, it may be observed that the feet frequently have five toes each, and never less than four; such toes (except in the case of some of the Seals, where they are reduced to more or less well-developed nails) being furnished with claws. In no case is the first toe of either the fore- or hind-limbs capable of being opposed to the other. The teeth are always divided into incisors, canines, pre-molars, and molars; the incisors almost always comprising three pairs in each jaw, of which the outermost are larger than either of the others, and the canines being well-developed and assuming the form of distinct tusks. The pre-molars always have sharply-pointed crowns, and in some cases, as in the Seals, the whole of the cheek-teeth are thus acuminate. Among the Bears and Badgers, however, the molar teeth (with the exception of the first, or flesh-tooth, in the lower jaw) have the crowns broad and flattened, and more or less adapted for grinding; although in such cases they never have folds of enamel penetrating the crown. Owing to the fact that the lower jaw is articulated to the skull by means of a half-cylindrical hinge, or condyle, the motions of the jaws are limited to a vertical plane, and they are thus incapable of a lateral grinding action. In all Carnivores the stomach is simple; and the teats are placed on the abdomen. Unlike the Insectivora, the collar-bones, or clavicles, are never complete, that is to say, they never articulate with both the shoulder-blade and the breast-bone, while they are frequently altogether wanting. In place of the smooth brains of the Insectivora, the Carnivora have the cerebral hemispheres indented by complex convolutions.

The typical, or terrestrial, Carnivores (inclusive of the Otters), have an almost cosmopolitan distribution, although unknown in New Guinea, and represented in Australia only by the Dingo. The members of the group now living in Britain belong mostly to the *Mustelidæ ;* other families being represented only by the Fox and Wild Cat. The Seals and their allies are mainly characteristic of the colder seas.

THE CATS. FAMILY FELIDÆ.

With the exception of Australasia and Madagascar, the Cats are cosmopolitan in their distribution, and are distinguished from other Carnivores by the following collective characters.

In the skull the hollow bone found at the base of the hinder region below the entrance into the internal ear is bladder-like, rounded, and divided into two chambers by a vertical internal partition, while the tube leading into the chamber of the internal ear is very short. The head is characterised by its short and rounded form, and the small number and specialised character of the cheek-teeth, of which there are only three or four pairs in the upper jaw, and three in the lower. Of these, the flesh-teeth are the most characteristic ; that of the upper jaw consisting of a large three-lobed external blade, and a rather small inner tubercle situated at the internal front angle of the tooth, while the opposing lower tooth is simply a cutting two-lobed blade, without any tubercular heel or ledge at its hinder extremity, or any trace of a cusp on its inner border. Behind the upper flesh-tooth, which is the last of the pre-molar series, there is a minute transversely-elongated molar, which appears to be quite functionless; while in the lower jaw the flesh-tooth, which is here a molar, forms the last of the whole series. The toes, of which there are five in the front, and four in the hind, limb, are provided with long, sharp, and curved claws, capable, except in the Hunting-Leopard, of being completely retracted within protecting

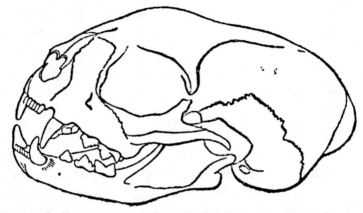

Skull of Wild Cat.

sheaths. In the intestine the blind appendage, or cæcum, is short.

In walking, these animals tread solely on their toes, which are provided on the soles with soft pads, and they are accordingly described as digitigrade.

In habits they differ from the Dogs and Foxes in that they never combine in packs for the purpose of hunting their prey, while thay are mostly expert climbers.

THE TRUE CATS. GENUS FELIS.

Felis, Linn., Syst. Nat. ed. 12 vol. i. p. 60 (1766).

Including the whole of the representatives of the family, with the exception of the Hunting-Leopard (*Cynælurus*), this genus is characterised by the complete retractibility of the claws, and the full development of the tubercle on the inner side of the upper flesh-tooth.

THE WILD CAT. FELIS CATUS.

Felis catus, Linn., Syst. Nat. ed. 12 vol. 1. p. 62 (1766); Bell's British Quadrupeds 2nd ed. p. 220 (1874).

(*Plate VIII.*)

Characters.—General colour yellowish-grey, with an interrupted longitudinal dark stripe down the back, two dusky bands on the cheeks, and numerous obscure transverse stripes of the same colour on the body and limbs ; tail of uniform thickness throughout, equal in length to less than half the head and body, and ringed and tipped with black. Length of head and body of male about 34 inches ; of tail, 11¼ inches.

In general aspect, form, and coloration, the Wild Cat resembles large "Tabbies" of the domestic breed; many specimens of the latter which have escaped from captivity and taken to a roving life in the woods, being frequently mistaken by the inexperienced for true Wild Cats. From the domestic species, the Wild Cat differs, however, by the proportionately longer body and limbs, and the shorter and thicker tail ; the fur being also more abundant than in the old original English breed, when not crossed with the Persian. Conforming in general external configuration and appearance to the type characteristic of the great majority of the members of the Family to which it belongs, the Wild Cat has the general ground-colour of the soft and long fur yellowish-grey, tending in some individuals to pale reddish-brown. In addition to some black spots near the muzzle, the face is marked with two black stripes, commencing between the eyes, and gradually increasing in width, and diverging as they pass backwards between the ears to the hinder part of the neck. Commencing between the shoulder-blades, a broad, irregular black or blackish longitudinal stripe traverses the whole length of the back, from which diverge numerous paler transverse bands, gradually becoming lighter in tint as they descend the flanks, until they are finally lost in the nearly white area of the under-parts. Usually the tail is ringed with nine black bands upon a grey ground; the first five of these bands being the narrower, and not meeting below, while the terminal black area is the largest of all, being often as much as two inches in length; it is at the same time the deepest in tint. Barred externally with horizontal bands of black, the limbs have their inner surface yellowish-grey, like the upper surfaces of the feet, while the soles of the latter are black. The claws are yellowish-grey.

Writing in the volume on British Mammals in the original issue of the "Naturalist's Library" of the coloration of the hairs themselves, Macgillivray states that in the Wild Cat "the softer hairs or fur are, in general, of a pale purplish tint, and pale reddish at the extremity; the longer hairs white at the base, then black, afterwards yellowish-red, with the tip black. Others, however, are first white, then black, yellowish-black, and finally reddish. There are a few very long white hairs on the loins inferiorly and laterally. On the white parts the hairs are of that colour from the base; on the bright red inter-crural part they are for a short space at the base bluish. The terminal rings of the tail have the hairs entirely black, but the black hairs of the feet have their base paler."

In addition to her considerably smaller dimensions, the female Wild Cat may be distinguished from the male by her generally paler coloration.

Distribution.—Ranging over a considerable portion of Continental Europe, namely, France, Germany, Poland, Switzerland, Hungary, Southern Russia, Spain, Dalmatia, Greece, and part of Turkey, and thence extending eastwards into the forest regions of Northern Asia, the Wild Cat was formerly widely distributed in Britain, although it appears never to have been a native of Ireland. At the present day it is restricted only to the northern districts of our islands, and is there becoming year by year more rare. This sole British representative of the feline family is proved, both by tradition and by the discovery of its fossilised remains in cavern and superficial deposits, to have originally ranged over the whole of such parts of England as were suited to its habits. Such remains have been discovered in the Pleistocene brick-earths of Grays, in Essex, in company with the remains of Mammoths, Hippopotami, Rhinoceroses, and other Mammals now either totally extinct, or long since banished from Britain to warmer climates. They also occur, in association with similar creatures, in the caves of Bleadon (in the Mendips), Cresswell Crags (Derbyshire), Kent's Hole (near Torquay), Ravenscliff (Glamorganshire), Uphill (in the Mendips), and the Vale of Clywd, while quite recently they have been discovered in a fissure in the Wealden rocks near Ightham, in Kent.

When the Wild Cat disappeared from the south and midland counties of England, appears to be quite unknown; but there is evidence that it lingered till a comparatively late date in the wooded parts of the Lake district, although it does not seem ever to have been numerous there during the historical period. According to the Rev. H. A. Macpherson, there is historical evidence of the existence of this animal in the Lake district in the year 1629, and again as late as 1754; while in the intervening period there are to be found in the parish records numerous entries of the sums disbursed for the destruction of these marauders. At a still later date, Gilpin, when describing a tour made through the district in 1772, says that the mountains around Helvellyn, "and indeed many other parts of the country are frequented by the Wild Cat, which Mr. Pennant calls the British Tiger, and says it is the fiercest and most destructive beast we have. He speaks of it as being three or four times as large as a common Cat. We saw one dead, which had been hunted on the day we saw it; and it seemed very little inferior, if at all, to the size he mentions." By 1795 Wild Cats seem to have become very scarce in the mountains of Cumberland and Westmoreland; and the last authentic occurrence of one of these animals in the district appears to have been in 1843, when a fine specimen is stated to have been killed near Loweswater. It is true that the occurrence of the Wild Cat has been recorded in these districts in quite recent years — even as late as 1871—but all such records appear to have been based on large feral specimens of the Domestic Cat.

In Scotland, though still lingering, the Wild Cat is rapidly decreasing in numbers. According to Messrs. Harvie-Brown and Buckley, while it has become extremely rare in Assynt during the last few years, it is still not uncommon in the Reay Forest, where it is preserved by the Duke of Westminster. These authors write that "one keeper in Assynt killed no less than twenty-six Wild Cats between 1869 and 1880, but of these only three during the last six years. Another keeper killed ten between 1870 and 1873, but no more until the winter of 1879-80, when he killed four, one of which is described as a monster." In Caithness the Wild Cat is still more rare, only four having been recorded as being killed during some ten years before 1880. Writing in 1882 of its present limits in Scotland, the former of the two authors just quoted said that the Wild Cat is "extinct all south and east of a line commencing, roughly speaking, at Oban, in Argyllshire, passing up the Brander Pass to Dalmally, following the boundary of Perthshire, and including Rannoch Moor. Thence continued north-eastward to the junction of the three counties of Perth, Forfar, and Aberdeen; thence across the sources of the Dee northward to Tomintoul in Banffshire; and lastly from Tomintoul to the city of Inverness. Northwards and westwards of this line the animal still keeps a footing." In Argyll at this date it had receded to the more mountainous districts, where, however, it was not very uncommon. In the Hebrides the Wild Cat is unknown.

Although existing in North Wales till a comparatively late period, it does not appear that the animal is now found within the limits of the Principality.

In spite of many assertions to the contrary, it may now, owing to the careful investigations undertaken by Dr. Hamilton, be taken as certain that the Wild Cat was never an inhabitant of Ireland; all the records of its occurrence there being based on specimens of the Common Cat which had reverted to a wild state, the latest of such supposed instances of the occurrence there of the true Wild Cat having been published in 1885. The first writer to dispute the existence of the Wild Cat in Ireland was the late William Thompson, of Belfast, who, in his "Natural History of Ireland," published in 1856, wrote that the creature in question "cannot be given with certainty as a native animal." Nevertheless, in the second edition of Bell's "British Quadrupeds," which appeared in 1874, the statement from the first edition that the Wild Cat exists in "some parts of Ireland" was allowed to reappear without note or comment; and it was not till the appearance of Dr. Hamilton's paper in the "Proceedings" of the Zoological Society for 1885 that the Wild Cat can be said to have been authoritatively removed from the list of Irish Mammals.

Habits.—Like the rest of its family, truculent and savage in its disposition, and endowed with, in proportion to its size, singular strength and activity of body, the Wild Cat is now the only really formidable wild animal to be met with in the

British Islands, where it always inhabits wooded, and generally mountainous, districts. In the most secluded and inaccessible parts of such regions the Wild Cat makes its lair, which may be situated either in some dense thicket, in the hollow stem of a decayed tree, or in a cleft or crevice of the rocks, and there it rears its young. Sometimes, however, the female selects in preference the deserted hole of a Badger or Fox in which to litter; and we have heard of the nest of one of the larger birds being chosen as a nursery. The young, which are born during the early summer, are usually five or six in number, and closely resemble ordinary domestic kittens. After being suckled by the female till such a period as milk no longer satisfies the needs of their appetites, they are fed by her on mice and small birds till such time as they are capable of taking care of themselves and capturing larger prey, when they are freed from parental control.

All who have had any experience of game and game-preserving are well acquainted with the enormous amount of damage that an ordinary Domestic Cat, which has taken either to occasional poaching or to a thoroughly wild life, will inflict on the denizens of their coverts, moors, or warrens. From its larger size and more powerful build, the Wild Cat is a still more serious enemy to game of all kinds; while in the neighbourhood of human habitations it is likewise a foe to poultry and pigeons. No wonder, therefore, that game-keepers wage incessant war against the Wild Cat, shooting and trapping it whenever the opportunity presents itself; indeed, the wonder is that the creature has managed to survive as long as it has. From the extreme boldness and ferocity of its disposition, an angry and wounded Wild Cat, when brought to bay, is no mean antagonist, even for an armed man; and several instances are on record where these creatures have inflicted considerable harm on their assailants before finally succumbing.

Relation to Domestic Cats.—It has long been a question whether the Domestic Cat is a descendant of the Wild Cat, or whether its origin is to be traced to some other species of the *Felidæ*. On the whole, the available evidence is in favour of the latter view ; and it is probable that the Caffre or Egyptian Cat (*Felis caffra*) of Northern Africa is the real progenitor of " Pussy." It is, however, a well-ascertained fact that the various smaller wild species of Cats will interbreed with the Domestic Cats of their respective countries ; and it is accordingly highly probable that the prevalence of "tabbies' among the Domestic Cats of Europe generally, and England in particular, may be largely due to intercrossing with the Wild Cat. On the other hand, in India, where Domestic Cats are frequently spotted, it is quite likely that the whole race may have originated from a wild spotted species very markedly distinct from the striped Caffre Cat. It may be added that during the Pleistocene period the range of the latter species extended into South-western Europe, so that there were ample opportunities for its domestication, even if this did not take place in Egypt.

THE DOGS, WOLVES, AND FOXES. FAMILY CANIDÆ.

Easily distinguished therefrom externally by their long, sharp muzzles, as well as general appearance, the Dog-tribe differ from the *Felidæ* in many important structural features. In the skull, for instance, the auditory bulla, although bladder-like and rounded, is not divided into two chambers by a vertical partition ; while the teeth are much more numerous and different in form. Then, again, the blind appendage, or cæcum, of the intestine is of considerable length, and generally folded upon itself. Except in the Hunting-Dog (*Lycaon*) of the Cape, the toes are numerically the same as in the Cats ; but the claws are blunt and non-retractile, the feet being digiti-grade.

As regards the teeth, the upper flesh-tooth, or last pre-molar, differs from that of the Cats in having only two lobes to its external blade ; while the lower flesh-tooth, or first molar, has a large tubercular heel at its hinder extremity, and generally a small cusp on the inner side of the second lobe of its blade. The pre-molars (inclusive of the upper flesh-tooth) are four in number on each side of both the upper and lower jaws ; and there are two upper molars, of triangular form, and generally three lower molars, although in certain Asiatic species the hindmost of these, which is always minute, may be absent.

Comprising several genera, the Family has an even wider distribution than that of the Cats, since it is represented by a species in Australia, which may, however, have been introduced by human agency. In habits, many of the *Canidæ* differ from the *Felidæ* by hunting their prey in packs ; while none are climbers in the proper sense of the word.

GENUS CANIS.

Canis, Linn., Syst. Nat. ed. 12 vol. i. p. 58 (1766).

Although the Indian Wild Dogs are often separated as *Cycn*, while the Foxes are divided off under the title of *Vulpes*, the genus *Canis* is here taken to include the great majority of the members of the Family, with which its distribution is co-extensive. Under these circumstances it will be unnecessary in a work of the present nature to give its distinctive characters.

I. THE WOLF. CANIS LUPUS.

Canis lupus, Linn., Syst. Nat. ed. 12 vol. i. p. 58 (1766).

Characters.—Belonging to the typical group of the genus, in which the skull is characterised by the presence of air-cells in the region of the forehead, and the smooth and convex form of the triangular process marking the hinder border of the socket for the eye, while the tail is less than half the length of the head and body and is only moderately bushy, the Wolf possesses the following special features. Size large ; fur long and thick, with a woolly under-fur. General colour rufous or yellowish-grey, more or less mingled with black in some specimens ; under-parts whitish ; tail frequently tipped with black ; under-fur of back pale slaty or light brown, with coarse whitish hairs intermingled. Length of head and body, from 3½ to 3¾ feet; of tail, 18 or 19 inches, inclusive of the hair at the tip. Great individual variation obtains as regards colour, some specimens being much paler than usual, while others are nearly, or quite, black.

Extinction in Britain.—The fate which is impending over the Wild Cat in Britain has long since befallen its canine cousin the Wolf, on which account the latter species, together with the Bear and the Beaver, is generally omitted in works on the Mammals of Britain. If, however, ornithologists are right in including the Great Auk, now totally extinct, and the Caper-cailzie, which, after complete extermination, has been reintro-duced into our islands, in works on British birds, there can be no question as to the claim of the above-mentioned Mammals to a place in the British fauna, since whether the extermination took place forty or four hundred years ago is a matter of no moment.

Distributed over the greater part of Europe, and ranging eastwards through Asia north of the Himalaya, while the North American form is apparently not specifically distinct, the Wolf, during the Pleistocene period, seems to have occurred over the whole of the British Islands. The earliest horizon in which its remains occur is the so-called "forest-bed" of the Norfolk coast, which belongs to the very earliest portion of the Pleistocene

period, if, indeed, it should not be assigned to the preceding
Pliocene epoch. Lupine remains are also commonly found in
the brick-earths of the Thames Valley and other parts of the
south of England; while they likewise occur in most or all of
the British caverns, inclusive of those of the Pentland Hills in
Scotland, and of Shandon in Ireland.

Although the records of the gradual extermination of the
Wolf from Britain are unfortunately far from complete, such as
exist have been carefully examined by Mr. J. E. Harting, from
whose writings the following extracts are taken. During the
Saxon period so numerous were these animals in England, and
so terrible were their devastations during the winter, that
January was commonly designated the " Wolf-month," and the
attempts of the pre-Norman sovereigns to reduce their numbers appear to have made but comparatively small impression
upon them. During the twelfth century Wolves were still
abundant in the New Forest and other districts of Hampshire,
while in the "Book of St. Alban's," written about 1481, wolf-
hunting during the winter months is mentioned as a royal and
noble sport. Comparatively soon after this date, that is to
say, some time between the years 1485 and 1509, during the
reign of Henry the Seventh, it appears, however, that, under
the inducement of rewards for their destruction, Wolves finally
became extinct in England. In Scotland, on the other hand,
as might have been expected from the nature of the country,
they flourished to a much later date, the numbers of these
animals during the reign of James the Fourth, at the close of
the fifteenth and commencement of the sixteenth centuries
being very great, and at times increasing to an alarming extent.
By 1620, if we may judge from the price (£6 13s. 4d.) paid
for a single skin, it would appear, however, that they had become scarce, and for many years it was commonly believed
that the last Scottish Wolf was killed in the year 1680. This,

however, is now known to be incorrect, it being well ascertained that these animals survived to a much later date, not improbably, indeed, nearly to the middle of the eighteenth century in Sutherland, where tradition points to the last Wolf having been slain in the year 1743.

Much the same story is told with regard to Ireland, where in the middle of the seventeenth century, a special Order in Council was promulgated in Dublin relating to the destruction

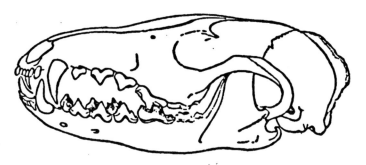

Skull of Fox.

of Wolves, on account of their apparently increasing numbers at that date. Even as late as about the year 1700 they still existed in the great forests on the borders of counties Wicklow and Carlow. When their final extermination was accomplished history telleth not, although it was probably some time between the years 1766 and 1770, inclusive.

As being no longer an inhabitant of Britain, it will be unnecessary to enter into the consideration of the habits of the Wolf.

II. THE FOX. CANIS VULPES.

Canis vulpes et *C. alopex*, Linn., Syst. Nat. ed. 12 vol. i. p. 59 (1766).

Vulpes montanus, Blyth, Journ. Asiat. Soc. Bengal vol. xi. p. 589.

THE FOX

Vulpes flavescens, Gray, Ann. Mag. Nat. Hist. vol. xi. p. 18 (1843).

Vulpes vulgaris, Bell (*ex* Brisson), British Quadrupeds p. 25? (1837); 2nd ed. p. 225 (1874).

Vulpes alopex, Blanford, Proc. Zool. Soc. 1887 p. 635; id Mammals of British India p. 153 (1888).

(*Plate IX.*)

Characters.—As the typical representative of the Vulpine group of the genus, the Fox differs from the Wolf in the absence of air-cells in the forehead of the skull, as well as in the upper surface of the triangular process defining the hinder border of the socket for the eye being concave. This group is further characterised by the more slender build of the body, the longer and more bushy tail, which always considerably exceeds half the length of the head and body, and the proportionately shorter limbs. The ears are large; the pupil of the eye, when seen in a strong light, forms a vertical ellipse, and the number of teats is only six, against ten, or more rarely eight, in the Wolf group.

The present species may be defined as a large, and in winter richly coloured, Fox, its general colour in Britain being reddish-brown above and white beneath, with the backs of the ears black, and the tip of the tail white. Length of head and body from about 27 to 34 inches; of tail, from 12 to 15 inches.

In the ordinary British Fox there is no great amount of variation in colour; the upper-parts being reddish-brown, mixed with some white hairs on the shoulders, thighs, flanks, rump, and tail. The muzzle is blackish, the inner surfaces and edges of the ears whitish, their outer surfaces black, with slight spots of white; the tail pale reddish, with the tips of the long hairs brownish-black, and the extremity white. The lower portion of the cheeks, the under part of the neck, as well as the chest and under-parts generally, together with the

H 2

inner surface of the thighs, a narrow line down the front of the hind-legs, and the hinder and inner surfaces of the fore-legs, are white. The front portion of the feet is black, that colour extending upwards nearly to the elbow and knee; the whiskers are likewise black; while the hair on the soles of the feet is deep red, the claws being light brown.

There are, however, certain racial or individual variations in the colour even of the British Fox.   Macgillivray, for instance, observes that the largest race, "or that which occurs in the Highland districts, has the fur of a stronger texture and of a greyer tint, there being a greater proportion of whitish hairs on the back and hind-quarters, while two or more inches of the end of the tail are white.   The Fox of the lower districts is considerably smaller, more slender, of a lighter red, with the tail also white at the end.   Individuals of a smaller size, having the head proportionately larger, the fur of a darker red, the lower parts dusky or dull brownish-white, and the tip of the tail either with little white or none, occur in the hilly parts of the southern division of Scotland.   The skull of the Highland Fox appears remarkably large and strong beside that of the ordinary kind, and the breadth is much greater in proportion."   Occasionally Foxes are killed in England with the tip of the tail grey or black; and a pure white Fox was killed in 1887 by the Taunton Vale Hounds, in the West Somerset country. Of more interest is the circumstance that some time previous to 1864, a young Fox was killed in Warwickshire in which the whole of the under parts were of a greyish-black hue. The coloration of this individual resembled that obtaining in the Foxes of Southern Europe; and assuming it to have been a native-bred animal, the occurrence of an individual of this southern race in England is a matter of some importance from a distributional point of view.   In Wales, as Mr. W. E. de Winton tells me, a blackish-brown form of Fox sometimes occurs.

Regarding the Warwickshire specimen, Mr. Trevor-Battye remarks :—" I agree about the interest of this specimen, but it raises a question. By this time the native blood must be pretty well diluted, and I suspect that we should find, had we proper means of enquiry, that our Foxes are now larger than they were, say, thirty years ago. The Swedish Fox, imported of late years into this country, is a decidedly larger animal than the native English Fox—larger even, I believe, and I have seen many examples of both forms, than the 'Greyhound' Fox, as the gillies call the inhabitant of the Scottish hills."

Distribution.—The ordinary variety of the Fox extends over the whole of Northern and Central Europe, being replaced in the south by the above-mentioned black-bellied race. In Central Asia we meet with a third variety, known as the Yellow Fox, and characterised by its general pale yellowish coloration, and the thickness of the tail, although it still retains the black ears and white tip to the tail of the English race. Nearly allied to the last is the handsome Himalayan variety, commonly termed the Mountain-Fox, which differs so remarkably in its winter dress from the typical form as to have been long regarded as a distinct species. In this variety the colour of the fur of the back varies from chestnut to iron-grey, and the shoulders are frequently ornamented by a dark transverse stripe, while the throat and under-parts are more or less dusky. In its black-backed ears and white-tipped tail it resembles, however, the South European race. Yet another race, commonly known as the Nile Fox, inhabits Egypt.

In North America we have other Foxes, now regarded merely as geographical races of the British species ; one of these being the well-known Cross-Fox, taking its name from the presence of a more or less well-defined dark shoulder-stripe. Lastly, the beautiful and valuable Silver Fox of the same regions is nothing more than a dark-coloured variety of the same widely-spread and variable species.

In Britain, as we learn from the evidence of its fossilised remains, the Fox is one of the oldest Mammalian inhabitants of the country, its earliest occurrence being in the sandy beds of the Red Crag of the East Coast, which belong to the upper portion of the Pliocene period. Its remains are likewise met with abundantly in the brick-earths of the Thames valley and other parts of England, as well as in nearly all the English caverns and some of those of Ireland. They do not appear, however, to have been recorded in a fossilised state from Scotland.

To a large extent, owing to its preservation for the purpose of hunting, the Fox is still a common animal throughout England; but had it not been for this artificial protection it would doubtless, in the more cultivated and open southern portions of the country, have shared the fate that has befallen the Wild Cat. In Scotland the Fox, according to Messrs. Harvie-Brown and Buckley, is almost universally distributed on the mainland; but is absent from all the islands, with the exception of Skye. There is, indeed, a statement that "the Fox was at one time common in Mull, but has been long since killed out"; even, however, if this be true, it is most probable that its occurrence there was due to accidental or intentional importation. Of its occurrence in Ireland, Thompson, writing more than forty years ago, observes that "the Fox, like the Otter, is still found in suitable localities throughout the island, wherever it can remain in spite of man. In many parts of the country this species is abundant, but in no district of which I am aware have so many been taken as on the mountains in the south of the county of Down."

It may be added that in the north of England the short-legged race inhabiting the open low grounds is commonly termed the "Terrier-Fox"; while to the larger long-legged and long-muzzled mountain race the name of "Greyhound-Fox" is applied.

Habits.—The habits and history of the Fox, or rather the British variety of the same, are so well-known as to require but brief notice ; and we shall accordingly content ourselves with extracting Macgillivray's admirable summary from the original edition of the "Naturalist's Library." The Fox, he writes, "resides in burrows, which it excavates for itself in sandy or gravelly soil, in woods or thickets, or on shady banks or the slopes of hills, remaining concealed all day, and coming abroad towards evening. Its food consists chiefly of the flesh of Mammals, birds, and reptiles. In the wilder parts it often destroys lambs, and in the more populous frequently commits great havoc among poultry ; but its favourite game are Partridges, Grouse, Rabbits, and Leverets. Insects and worms have also been found in its stomach, and in the maritime districts it has been known to frequent the shores in quest of crustaceous and molluscous animals."

"It is said to live in pairs, and the young, from three to five in number, are born towards the end of spring. The female exhibits great courage and address in defending them. The sagacity of the Fox is proverbial, and frequently enables it to escape the snares laid for it. Marvellous stories are related respecting the stratagems which it employs to elude pursuit ; and although many of these may be exaggerated, there can be little doubt that its instinctive vigilance and cunning are great. When obtained young, it may be domesticated so far as to allow a person with whom it is acquainted to handle it, but cannot be depended upon, as it exhibits no gratitude towards benefactors, forms no strong attachment, and is ever ready to embrace the opportunity of making its escape. It is said to attain the age of fourteen or fifteen years in captivity."

It may be added that the habit of burrowing is by no means universally characteristic of the species. the Himalayan variety living in thickets or on cultivated land in such shelter as it can find ready to hand.

In conclusion, it may be mentioned that there has been much discussion as to whether the Fox will interbreed with the Domestic Dog. On this point Mr. Trevor-Battye writes: " I admit that this is hard to prove. But I myself believe in such instances. I know a Dog at this moment at Pett, near Hastings, which is credited with being the offspring of such a combination. And anyone who saw him would, I will undertake to say, believe it without proof. It leans to the Fox in its habits, the texture of its hair, its brush, and its voice, which it seldom uses. It is beyond question that the North American Indians, the Crees for example, with whom I stayed for some time, are in the constant habit of tying up their dogs away in the bush, in order that they may pair with the Wolves, and the morose result of this alliance every hunter knows." On the other hand, although such interbreeding has often been asserted to have occurred, several such alleged instances having recently been recorded in the sporting papers, in the opinion of some of those best qualified to give an authoritative judgment on the subject, such unions are quite unknown. Mr. W. E. de Winton, however, writes to me on this subject: "In the pack of Otter-hounds hunted by the late Hon. Geoffrey Hill, there was one which, he told me, was a cross by a Prairie Wolf. In the Worcester Museum is an animal, killed near Ledbury about two years ago, which is undoubtedly a cross between a Fox and a Dog. It was shot wild, and can only be the result of such an union."

MARTENS, WEASELS, OTTERS, ETC. FAMILY MUSTELIDÆ.

The third great Family of Carnivores represented in the British Isles, which includes the Martens, Weasels, Badgers,

Otters, and their allies, differs widely both from the *Felidæ* and the *Canidæ* in the structure of the base of the hinder part of the skull. In place of the bladder-like and rounded auditory bulla characterising the two latter groups, in the present family this portion of the skull is depressed, with no dividing partition, its inner border being the most prominent, and thence it gradually slopes away towards the tube conducting to the internal ear, of which tube the lower lip is prolonged. The intestine is devoid of any blind appendage (cæcum); and the toes are always five in number on each foot.

The present Family is specially distinguished from others, in which the above features occur, by the following points: The upper molar teeth are reduced to a single pair, which are peculiar in that their inner border is wider than the outer; while (with the exception of the Indian and African Ratels, where they are reduced to one) there are two pairs of molar teeth, the first of which is the flesh-tooth. The number of pre-molar teeth is very variable, even within the limits of a single genus.

Having, with the exception of Australasia, a world-wide distribution, the members of this Family present none of that external similarity of form so characteristic of the representatives of the two preceding families; and they exhibit a similar diversity of habit; some, like the Martens and Weasels, being more or less fitted for climbing, while others, like the Badgers, are burrowing animals, and others, again, like the Otters, aquatic.

MARTENS, POLECATS, AND WEASELS. GENUS MUSTELA.

Mustela, Linn., Syst. Nat. ed. 12 vol. i. p. 66 (1766).

The members of this genus, together with certain allied forms which are generally separated and have no representatives in the British Isles, collectively constitute a special sub-family of the *Mustelidæ*. Terrestrial and more or less arboreal in their habits, all these animals have short and partially-webbed toes, with short, sharp, compressed, curved, and frequently partially retractile claws. The upper molar tooth is transversely elongated, and consequently wider than long. In all cases the body is much elongated, while the limbs are short.

In the genus *Mustela* the relative length of the body and limbs, like that of the tail, is subject to considerable variation; the feet are nearly or completely digitigrade; and the claws are partially retractile. Whereas in the typical forms, or Martens, the number of pre-molar teeth is four pairs in each jaw, in the Polecats and Weasels they are reduced to three.

On account of this difference in the number of their teeth, coupled with their more elongated and snake-like bodies, many naturalists separate the Polecats, Stoats, and Weasels from the Martens as a distinct genus (*Putorius*); although, to our thinking, such a sub-division is quite unnecessary.

I. PINE-MARTEN.   MUSTELA MARTES.

Mustela martes, Linn., Syst. Nat. ed. 12 vol. i. p. 67 (1766).
Martes sylvatica, Nilsson, Skand. Fauna vol. i. p. 41 (1820).
Martes abietum, Fleming, British Animals p. 14 (1828); Bell,
    British Quadrupeds 2nd ed. p. 217 (1874).

(*Plate X.*)

Characters.—Four pre-molar teeth; tail, with the hair, as long as the body; general colour rich brown; throat and chest yellow; upper flesh-tooth with its outer margin concave; upper molar (last tooth) simply rounded externally.

It was long thought that two species of Marten inhabited the British Islands, namely, the present species and the Beech-Marten (*M. foina*), the latter being distinguished by its white throat and chest, narrower skull, the convex outer border of the upper flesh-tooth, and the notch on the outer side of the upper molar. It was, however, definitely shown by Alston in

THE PINE-MARTEN.

the "Proceedings" of the Zoological Society for 1869, that the Beech-Marten is not found within our limits.

The Marten has the body of moderate elongation and slenderness, and the tail relatively long; the head being somewhat triangular in form, with the muzzle pointed, the eyes prominent, and the ears large and rounded. The body is covered, during the winter at least, with fur of two kinds, the outer fur being very long, glossy, and ash-coloured at the base, with some shade of brown at the tip, but varying in intensity on the different regions of the body, the middle of the back, the tail, and the outer surfaces of the limbs being darker than elsewhere. The throat and chest are yellow, and the remainder of the under-parts are greyish; while the edges and insides of the ears are whitish. The under-fur is yellowish-grey. The length of the head and body is about 18 inches; and that of the tail, inclusive of the hair at the tip, about 13 inches.

Distribution.—The range of the Pine-, or, as it is sometimes called, the Yellow-throated, Marten includes the whole of Northern Europe; but it is replaced in North-eastern Asia by the closely-allied Sable (*M. zibellina*), in which the fur is still longer and silkier, and consequently of greater value. On the other hand, the Beech-Marten occurs throughout the greater part of Europe, although not in the extreme north, and ranges eastwards into Western Asia, where it extends probably throughout a large portion of the higher Himalaya.

Occurring in a fossil state in the Norfolk forest-bed, as well as in the caves of Bleadon, Long Hole, Ravenscliff, and Spritsail Tor in England, and in that of Shandon in Ireland, the Pine-Marten was probably at one time a common animal throughout the forest-clad districts of the country. It has, however, now practically disappeared from the greater part of the southern and midland districts of England, although occasional stray examples are now and then met with. Even, indeed, in a county with so much wild country in it as Leicester, the Marten, according to Mr. Montagu Browne, appears to have been completely exterminated, although it was at one time exceedingly abundant there. It still lingers, however, in Suffolk and North Devon, and, it is believed, in Epping Forest, and has been lately recorded from Hampshire. In the Lake district of Cumberland the species is, however, still fairly common, and is regularly hunted during the winter with a few couples of Beagles or Foxhounds, accompanied by several Terriers. Although most numerous in Cumberland, the Marten is also found occasionally in the mountainous districts of Northumberland, Durham, Westmoreland, and around Furness in Lancashire. It is likewise found in North Wales.

In Scotland, Messrs. Harvie-Brown and Buckley write that the Marten now appears to be scarcer than the Wild Cat, "being extinct in many places frequented by the latter, but, curiously enough, it has survived over a larger area up to a later date, that is to say, that while the boundaries of the country at present inhabited by the Wild Cat are easily defined, and are gradually contracting, the occurrences of the Marten are more sporadic, often turning up in localities, far distant from one another, where no records had previously occurred for many years." Mr. W. E. de Winton tells me that there is no doubt that it existed on the islands of Lewis and Harris up to about twenty years ago.

In Thompson's time the Marten was found all over Ireland in suitable localities, but was even then becoming scarce, and its numbers have doubtless considerably diminished since that date, although it is not uncommon in Kerry.

Commenting on a note relating to the distribution of the Marten, by Mr. J. E. Harting, Mr. Barrett-Hamilton writes that " I have been for some time collecting notes on the distribution and life-history of this animal in Ireland, and

indeed of all our native Irish Mammals. I had at first contem-
plated the publication of a list of localities in Ireland where
the Marten has been found of late years, but an accumulation
of notes has convinced me that this animal is much more
common in the wooded parts of Ireland than is generally
supposed, and consequently that such an article would be
almost as unnecessary as one on the distribution in Ireland of
such common Irish Mammals as the Otter or Badger.   I think
the statement that 'at one time, in all probability, the Marten
must have been generally distributed in Ireland, but as civilisa-
tion has extended inland from the east and south, and as
woods have been cut down, and the country opened up by
railways, drainage, and cultivation, so has this animal been
gradually driven into the wilder portions of the north and west,'
needs considerable modification.   No doubt the Marten is now
being driven out from the east and south, but it is only of late
that this has been the case, and I contend that even in the
more highly-cultivated parts of the eastern counties of Ireland
it would be an impossibility to name a county in which the
animal has not occurred recently. Taking the eastern counties
from north to south, Mr. Harting's own notes establish its
occurrence more than once in Antrim in 1893, while in Down
(again quoting from the same article), ' amidst the wild and
broken ground of the Mourne Mountains,   .   .   . the Marten
will probably for some time yet to come defy the efforts of its
would-be exterminators.'   From Louth and Meath I have no
records by me, but there is little doubt that stragglers are still
occasionally found in those counties, since they lie quite close
to more favoured counties.   From the small county of Dublin
there is no recent record, but the outer parts of the county are
not so far from the woods of Wicklow, which are still one of
the strongholds of the Marten ; and even in Wexford, ' the
model county ' of Ireland, its occurrence has been noted as

late as June, 1892, a fact which is not at all surprising
when we consider that Wexford comes next to Kilkenny, a
county in some parts of which the Marten is still plentiful."

Habits.—An excellent climber, the Marten during part of the
year is a denizen of woods and plantations ; but, as we shall
see below, in some districts at least is to be found in the open
rocky country.   Occasionally it has been known to take up its
abode near a farmyard, and to wage war on the smaller denizens
thereof.   As a rule four or five young form a litter, but the
number may vary from two to seven ; and as at least two litters
are produced in a year, the Marten may be regarded as a
prolific animal, so that it is only as the result of continual
persecution that it is so rapidly becoming exterminated.   Its
usual food comprises such birds as it can kill, together with
their eggs, the smaller mammals, and reptiles.

Writing of the habits of these animals in the north of
England, Mr. F. Nicholson says that when hunted, " they
usually make at once for the rocks and crevices, going at a
great pace at first, but are soon run into unless they succeed
in reaching some hole in a crag where hounds and huntsmen
cannot follow.   They fight desperately with both claws and
feet.   When before hounds on level and snow-clad ground they
proceed with a succession of astonishing long leaps, often six
or seven feet apart.   They do not usually come down to the
wooded parts of the country except for breeding purposes, but
the greater part of the year they follow the screes and higher
fell-ground.   Though they generally come down to the woods
in the valleys in April and May to have their young ones,
selecting some old Magpie's nest or Squirrel's drey for a home,
still they sometimes breed in the rocks near the tops of the
highest hills.   It is only at such times that the Marten is
easily trapped, for, unlike the Polecat, it does not approach a
given spot by one track.   They do not seem so suspicious of

POLECAT

traps as some wild animals, or as the Polecat.   If you find
traces of, or see the latter about a building, you will most likely
find a run near by which it frequents, and a trap has only to be
set, and it will be taken ; not so with the Marten, as it is only
by accident that it is captured in this manner."   The writer
then goes on to say that, owing to their partiality for Rabbits
and their unsuspiciousness of baited traps, where the latter
animals are systematically trapped, a considerable number of
Martens are accidentally caught.

If taken at a sufficiently early age, Martens can be readily
tamed, when they display considerable attachment to their
owners ; and since they lack the disgusting odour of the Polecat and most other members of the Weasel tribe, they form
rather agreeable pets.

Although much less valuable than that of the Sable, the fur
of the Pine-Marten is of considerable commercial importance,
an average of about three thousand skins being yielded annually,
according to Mr. Poland, by Courland and Lithuania alone.
Although of late years considerably depreciated in price, good
Marten skins even now fetch about ten shillings each in the
market.

II. THE POLECAT.   MUSTELA PUTORIUS.

Mustela putorius, Linn., Syst. Nat. ed. 12 vol. i. p. 67 (1766) ;
  Bell, British Quadrupeds 2nd ed. p. 203 (1874).
Fœtorius putorius, Keyserling and Blasius, Wirbelthiere Europ.
  p. 62 (1840).
Putorius fœtidus, Gray, List Mamm. Brit. Mus. p. 64 (1843).
Putorius vulgaris, Owen, Brit. Foss. Mamm. p. 112 (1846).

(*Plate XI.*)

Character.—Size medium ; body very long and slim ; tail and
limbs relatively short ; three pairs of pre-molar teeth in each
jaw ; fur long, dark brown, with the under-fur yellowish ;
head blackish with white markings in the neighbourhood of

the ears and mouth. Length of head and body about 17 inches; of tail, including hair at the end, 7 inches.

The Polecat, Fitchet, Fitchet-Weasel, or Foumart (= Foul Marten), as it is indifferently called, is the largest British representative of the sub-genus *Putorius*, which includes the whole of the remaining species of *Mustela*. Macgillivray, in the original edition of this work, describes it as follows : " The head

Polecats and Moorhen.

is of moderate size, oblong, or oval-triangular, when viewed from above, with the muzzle rather rounded ; the ears short, and broadly rounded ; the neck of moderate length and very thick ; the body very long ; the feet short and strong. On the anterior limb the first toe is very short, the fifth or outer a little longer, the fourth next, the second a little shorter than the latter. On the hind-foot the first toe is also very short, the second longer than the fifth, the third longest, but the fourth almost equal. The eyes are small, with the iris dark brown; the claws rather long, compressed, arched, and a greyish-yellow tint. The under-fur is very soft and woolly; the pile long and rather coarse, but smooth and glossy. The general colour is dark brown, the long hairs brownish-black, the under-fur yellowish; the lower parts of the neck and body, with the feet and tail, darker than the rest, the sides yellowish-brown; the lips white, as are the ears anteriorly and along the tip behind; and between the eye and ear is a brownish-white patch.*

Distribution.—The geographical range of the Polecat includes the greater portion of Europe, its northern limits extending to the south of Sweden, and in Russia to the White Sea; it is, however, unknown in the extreme south, and its predilection for a cool climate is indicated by the circumstance that during the summer it ascends in the Alps far above the forest limit. In England, owing to the relentless persecution of gamekeepers, it is one of those species fast approaching extinction, being now but rarely met with in most of the southern and midland counties. Mr. Montagu Browne, for instance, writes that in Leicestershire and Rutlandshire it is becoming increasingly rare, and will soon be exterminated. In the Lake district, where these animals were once so abundant that in one unusually good season as many as thirty-nine were killed, we are told by the Rev. H. A. Macpherson that within the last thirty years,

* Mr. W. E. de Winton writes:—"The winter fur becomes pale and faded before it is shed in May. By the first of June the fur is entirely changed in both sexes. The female, or 'Jill,' changes her entire coat directly she has young, at the end of April or beginning of May. The male, or 'Hob,' changes his more leisurely throughout the month of May. He is then known as the 'Black Ferret,' and has a beautiful purplish-black coat. As in all *Mustelidæ*, the male is half as big again as the female. I have kept Polecats alive, and know where they are still fairly plentiful."

5 I

mainly owing to the employment of steel traps, they have become very scarce. The narrow strip of marshy and heavily-timbered country extending from Bowness is, however, still a stronghold for this much-persecuted creature, and one from which it will with difficulty be completely exterminated. Although to southern ears the idea of hunting such an insignificant animal with hounds appears absurd, yet Foumart-hunting was at one time a favourite sport of the Westmoreland dalesmen; the hunts generally taking place during the night in midwinter. Much the same story is told with regard to Scotland, in many parts of which it has become well-nigh exterminated. Messrs. Harvie-Brown and Buckley observe that the causes which have operated in the case of the Marten have likewise reduced the numbers of the Polecat. " Rabbit-trapping has proved fatal to it; for whilst the increase of Rabbits has provided abundance of food, it has been the indirect means of causing the decrease of the species by the agency of steel traps. Inland localities, formerly inhabited by Polecats, have been deserted by them, for, drawing down towards the sandy burrows to prey upon the Rabbits, they themselves became an easy prey." In the Hebrides and other islands the Polecat seems to have always been unknown.

Although Thompson had doubts of its occurrence, there appears good evidence that the Polecat, in his time at least, was an inhabitant of the woods of Kerry, Down, and other parts of Ireland.

Habits.—A dreaded enemy to all game-preservers, the Polecat possesses, for its size, a remarkable combination of strength and agility. Dwelling generally in woods and copses, or thicket-clad hills, it selects as a retreat and hiding-place either an empty Rabbit-burrow, a crevice among the rocks, or even the cavities in a heap of stones. In such a spot the female, during May or June, gives birth to from four to six young. Remaining

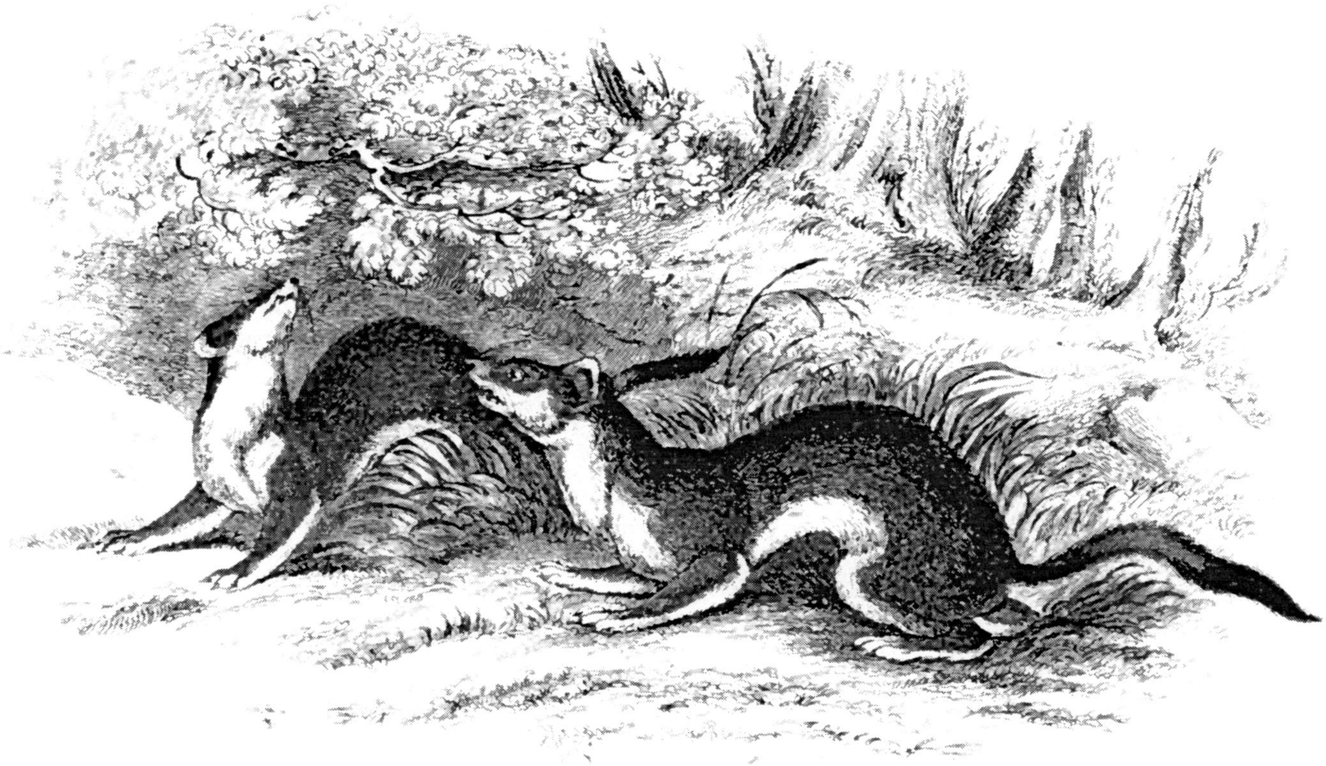

Wyman & Sons Limited

STOAT IN SUMMER DRESS

quiet during the day, and issuing forth towards evening, the Polecat, writes Macgillivray, when settled in the neighbourhood of a farm-yard, will, at times, commit "great depredations among the poultry, sucking the eggs, and killing the chickens, grown-up fowls, and even turkeys and geese. Not satisfied with obtaining enough to allay its hunger, it does not intermit its ravages until it has destroyed all within its reach, so that the havoc it makes is not less subject of surprise than of indignation to those on whom it has inflicted its unwelcome visit. It generally perforates the skull of its victim, and is said to devour the brain first, as well as to suck the blood. If undisturbed it sometimes satisfies its hunger on the spot, and in the midst of its slaughtered victims, but in general it carries its prey to some safe retreat. Its ferocity, cunning, and extreme agility, render it a great enemy to game of all kinds; and it destroys the eggs of Pheasants, Grouse, and Partridges, seizes the birds on their nests, pursues Rabbits into their burrows, and frequently seizes on young Hares. Besides birds and

Skull of Polecat.

mammals, it also feeds on fishes and frogs, which have, in some instances, been found in its nest." Our illustration, which is taken from Bewick, commemorates an instance when a Polecat was frequently seen to resort to the bank of a river for the purpose of catching Eels, which were carried off to its retreat, where no less than eleven were discovered.

Mr. Trevor-Battye writes :—"The Polecat is an expert

I 2

swimmer. Kept in captivity it shows a great fondness for water, and will not hesitate to plunge in and pick up food from the bottom of a bath full of water. Captive Polecats are frequently early overtaken by blindness."

Although both the Polecat and the Stoat are regarded—and on the whole rightly—as unmitigated vermin, to be ruthlessly destroyed whenever met with, there can be no doubt, as Mr. Harting remarks, there was a time, before the days of strict preserving, when both these animals lived among game of all kinds without causing any diminution in the numbers of the latter. Indeed, it is by no means improbable that they were an actual advantage, since by killing off all the weakly and maimed individuals of the various kinds of game they led to a survival of the fittest.

The Ferret is a pale-coloured and almost albino domesticated variety of the Polecat, which is, however, much improved by crossing with the dark-coloured wild race. Mr. Trevor-Battye says :—" A wild-caught Polecat, though always difficult to handle, can easily be worked like a Ferret for Rats; and in this work they are far superior to Ferrets, owing to their extreme agility. They do not delay in the hole, but, on the Rat bolting, follow it out and catch it in a couple of bounds."

III THE STOAT, OR ERMINE. MUSTELA ERMINEA.

Mustela erminea, Linn., Syst. Nat. ed. 12 vol. i. p. 68 (1766); Bell, British Quadrupeds 2nd ed. p. 191 (1874).

Fœtorius erminea, Keyserling and Blasius, Wirbelthiere Europ. p. 69 (1840).

Putorius ermineus, Owen, Brit. Foss. Mamm. p. 116 (1846).

(Plates XII. and XIII.)

PLATE XIII.

STOAT IN WINTER DRESS.

Characters.—Size considerably smaller than the last; fur short; tail shorter than the body; colour reddish-brown above, with the chin and under-parts, as well as the inner surfaces of the limbs and the feet, yellowish-white; tip of tail black. In winter, in high latitudes and altitudes, the colour is yellowish-white, with a black tip to the tail. Length of head and body of male about 10¾ inches; of tail, 6½ inches; female considerably smaller.

Although by non-zoological persons the Stoat or Ermine is often confounded with the Polecat, it is, in addition to its smaller size, such a very different-looking animal that there ought not to be the slightest difficulty in distinguishing between the two. Macgillivray, in the original edition of the " Naturalist's Library," describes it as having the body " much elongated, and of nearly equal thickness in its whole length ; its neck rather long and nearly as thick as the body; its head oblong, flattened above, with a rather obtuse muzzle ; the tail of moderate length, and the fur short. On the fore-foot the first toe is very small, the second longer than the fifth, the third longest, the fourth a little shorter; under the last joint of each is a bare tubercle. On the hind-feet are also five bare tubercles, and the toes have nearly the same proportions as those of the fore-feet; the soles covered with hair. The ears are rather large, broad, and rounded, with a slit in the posterior margin, forming a lobe there. The pile is shortish and soft ; the hairs acuminate, a little flattened, and slightly curved or undulated ; the under-fur very soft and woolly ; the moustache-bristles long ; the coarse hairs on the terminal half of the tail very long."

The most remarkable peculiarity about the Stoat, and one whereby it differs widely from all its congeners, is the assumption, in the colder portions of its habitat, of the yellowish-white winter-dress. Universal in the higher regions of Scotland, this change takes place comparatively seldom in the south of England, while in the northern counties, although frequent, it is by no means general. Somewhat curiously, the change from the brown to the white dress does not appear by any means always coincident with the advent of winter, or even the approach of cold weather, Stoats having been often killed, even in the south of England, which had undergone a partial change of colour during the early autumn. Mr. Harting states, indeed, that he knew an instance of a pure white Stoat being killed in Monmouthshire in the beginning of August. It is possible, however, that this may have been a case where the white coat was retained throughout the year; since, according to Messrs. Harvie-Brown and Buckley, the Stoats on the summit of Ben Nevis are to be seen at all seasons in their white winter-dress. Much discussion has arisen how the change from brown to white in the fur takes place, Bell observing that "this is effected not by the loss of the summer coat and the substitution of a new one for the winter, but by the actual change of colour in the existing fur." This theory has, however, been called in question; and it is now generally admitted that Macgillivray was right when he attributed the change to growth of new hairs differing in colour from those of the old coat. With regard to the spring change, he writes that "so early as the end of March, and the beginning of April, if the weather be mild, the colour of the upper-parts changes to a dull brownish-red, but the lower remain white, and the black hairs of the extremity of the tail are the same at all seasons. This change is not effected by an alteration in the colour of the same hairs, but by the gradual substitution of brown for white hairs. . . . On the whole, it appears to me that in spring, and the beginning of summer, when the animal had assumed its white colour in winter all the red hairs that appear are new. Towards December, earlier if the weather be very cold, later if less so, the hairs of the upper-parts become white. In an individual obtained in December, 1834, the colour was a mixture of white and brownish-red. The hairs of the latter colour were not in the least degree faded, and those of the former were much shorter, and evidently just shooting; so that the change from brown to white would seem to take place by the substitution of new white hairs for those of the summer-dress. But in mild winters the hairs retain their red colour, and if new hairs come in, they are also red; if the weather become colder, the new hairs that appear are white, although the old hairs do not vary; and, if there are alterna-tions of severe cold and temperate weather, the animal becomes mottled." Owing to the mild climate in Ireland, the Stoat, which is there very common, does not, according to Thompson, undergo a seasonal colour-change.*

Distribution.—Unlike the two preceding representatives of the genus, the Stoat is a circum-polar animal, ranging through Northern Europe, Asia, and America. Commonly distributed throughout the British Islands, it appears in England to be less abundant than the Weasel, although the reverse of this obtains in Scotland. In the latter country this animal is an inhabitant of the Hebrides and other islands, but, according to Mr. de Winton, it is absent in Lewis. In common with those of the Polecat and Weasel, fossilised remains of the Stoat have been found in several of the English caverns.

Habits.—As regards its mode of life, Macgillivray writes that

* I have received the following note from Mr. W. E. de Winton :— "The changes of fur are the same in all the *Mustelidæ*. The Stoat is, normally, yellow in winter and brown in summer. The female turns white in winter more often than the male, and is generally flecked with white, even in summer, in old animals. White males are hardly known in England. The male has a yellow stain through the whole pelage, and is paler than the female."

" the Stoat frequents stony places and thickets, among which
it finds a secure retreat, as its agility enables it to outstrip even
a Dog in a short race, and the slimness of its body allows it to
enter a very small aperture. Patches of furze, in particular,
afford it perfect security, and it sometimes takes possession of
a Rabbit's burrow. It preys on game and other birds, from the
Grouse and Ptarmigan downwards, sometimes attacks poultry
or sucks their eggs, and is a determined enemy to Rats and
Voles. Young Rabbits and Hares frequently become victims to
its rapacity, and even full-grown individuals are sometimes
destroyed by it. Although, in general, it does not appear to
hunt by scent, yet it has been seen to trace its prey like a Dog,
following its track with certainty. Its motions are elegant,
and its appearance extremely animated. It moves by leaping
or bounding, and is capable of running with great speed, although it seldom trusts itself beyond the immediate vicinity of
cover. Under the excitement of pursuit, however, its courage
is surprising, for it will attack, seize by the throat, and cling to
a Grouse, Hare, or other animal strong enough to carry it off,
and it does not hesitate on occasion to betake itself to the
water." The young, usually from five to eight in number, are
born in April or May, and are blind for nine days after birth.
They remain with the mother till the autumn, and are full-
grown by the following spring. It may be added that the
Stoat is an expert climber, having been known to ascend trees
for the purpose of attacking birds on their nests and eating
their eggs or young. Mr. de Winton writes :—" Old Stoats
whose teeth are worn are inveterate egg-eaters. I took forty-
two Pheasant's eggs from one hole in May, 1894, and have
got the skin of the old ' Hob ' who amassed this larder."

In the autumn large parties of Stoats have, on several occasions, been encountered on the march, as though they were un-
dertaking a kind of migration, and at such times they are stated

WEASEL.

to be actually dangerous to man, as the whole body will, with but slight provocation, proceed to attack anyone who attempts to bar their progress. They have also been observed to combine in hunting Rabbits and Hares, which they follow by scent like a pack of hounds in full cry. The curious kind of paralysis which seizes a Hare or Rabbit when a Stoat, or even the dimunitive Weasel, is on its track, is too well known to need more than passing mention. At such times the hunted Rodent, after running a short distance, stops, incapable of further movement, until its relentless foe comes up and speedily puts a term to its existence. If taken in such a paralysed condition, a Rabbit will be found to have its eyes closed, its heart palpitating violently, and its limbs almost useless; and it is not till left alone for several minutes that it will revive.

Although, owing to the shortness of its fur, the British Stoat in its winter-dress is of no great commercial value, the longer furred skins from Northern Europe and America, constituting the "ermine" of the fur-trade, have a very high value indeed, and are imported in enormous numbers. The Russian skins are sold in bundles of forty, constituting a "timber," of which the present market price varies from twenty to thirty shillings, although as much as nine pounds has been realised. According to Mr. Poland, to whose work on "Fur-bearing Animals," we are indebted for the foregoing details, over 5,000 Ermine skins were sold in London in 1891 by the Hudson Bay Company alone; while in 1836 the enormous number of 264,606 were imported.

Of late years Stoats have been introduced into New Zealand for the purpose of checking the spread of Rabbits; no less than 3,000 Stoats and Weasels having been sent out from Lincolnshire in 1885.

An albino Ermine with a white coat in summer, and lacking the usual black tip to the tail, is on record.

IV. THE WEASEL. MUSTELA VULGARIS.

Mustela vulgaris, Erxleben, Syst. Rég. Animale p. 471 (1777); Bell, British Quadrupeds 2nd ed. p. 182 (1874).

Fœtorius vulgaris, Keyserling and Blasius, Wirbelthiere Europ. p. 69 (1840).

Putorius vulgaris, Richardson, Fauna Bor.-Amer. vol. i. p. 145 (1829).

(*Plate XIV.*)

Characters.—Smaller than the last species, from which it is readily distinguished by the absence of a black tip to the relatively shorter tail; no seasonal change of colour.* Average length of head and body of male about $8\frac{1}{4}$ inches; of tail, $2\frac{1}{2}$ inches; the corresponding dimensions in the female being about 7 and 2 inches.

To describe in detail the form and general coloration of the Weasel would be but to repeat the statements given under the heading of the Stoat, although the Weasel is a redder animal than the latter.

Distribution.—Having, like the Stoat, a circum-polar distribution, the Weasel, although common throughout England, Wales, and Scotland, appears to be unknown in Ireland, where, however, the first-mentioned animal has usurped its name. It is true that in the *Zoologist* for 1877 the occurrence of the Weasel in county Mayo is reported; but even if the animal seen were rightly identified, it is possible that it may have been introduced. In the north of Scotland, Messrs. Harvie-Brown and Buckley state that Weasels are common on the mainland; "and there is not much reason to believe that their numbers have sensibly decreased, though kept, no doubt,

* Mr. de Winton writes to me:—"The Weasel is paler in colour in winter. I believe that none of the *Mustelidæ* shed their hair in autumn. The white dress is assumed by a change of pigment, as well as by an accession of white hairs."

in wholesome check by the efforts of keepers and trappers." The species is, however, quite unknown in the Hebrides and other Scottish islands.

Habits.—Nearly akin to the Stoat in its mode of life, the Weasel, from its inferior dimensions, has the advantage over the latter of being able to pursue in their tortuous underground runs both the Field-Vole and the Mole ; and from its relentless pursuit both of the former and the common Rat, this little Carnivore ought to receive all encouragement at the hands of the farmer, more especially in districts subject to seasonal "Vole-plagues." We by no means intend to imply that the Weasel, like other benefactors of the human race, has not its faults—quite the contrary ; but, taking all in all, we have little hesitation in saying that the benefits it confers far outweigh the injuries it inflicts. That it has a partiality for small birds, and that it may make an occasional onslaught on the smaller denizens of the poultry-house, may be freely admitted ; but the former depredations are necessarily limited to a few weeks in the year, while the latter are few and far between.

In addition to hunting Voles and Rats in their subterranean retreats, the Weasel will likewise pursue them if they attempt to escape by ascending trees or shrubs, as, among his other accomplishments, he is an excellent climber. Whether the Weasel is of sufficient size to carry off hens' eggs in the same manner as the Stoat, that is, by taking one between the chin and chest, and holding it there safely by bending down the head, we are unaware.

Writing in the original edition of the "Naturalist's Library," of the habits of this species, Macgillivray states that it will pursue Rats and Mice "into barns, granaries, and corn-stacks, despatching them generally by a single bite which perforates the brain. In the fields and pastures it has been seen following its prey by scent, turning and doubling on the track, and pursuing it even into the water. Among grass or herbage it frequently raises itself on its hind-legs to look around, and in a place of security will sometimes allow a person to make a near approach to it. . . . When its nest is plundered, it defends itself against all assailants, springs upon the Dogs, and even attempts to vent its fury upon their masters. It produces five or six young ones, and is said to litter two or three times in the year." The extreme playfulness and activity of a litter of young Weasels is well described by Bell.

"To the extreme boldness of the Weasel on occasion," writes Mr. Trevor-Battye, "the following fact bears witness. In September, 1892, at about one o'clock in the afternoon, when walking along a high road in Kent, a Weasel ran across the road in front, and disappeared in a hole. In a moment it reappeared, and began quartering the ground with that undulating rapidity characteristic of this creature. It was quite regardless of my presence, and presently disappeared again. I moved down the bank, and noticing a movement at the mouth of a little hole, put my hand quickly down and caught a large Field-Vole. As I picked it up, the Weasel followed my hand, and would I am sure have jumped at it for the Vole : but, without thinking, I stupidly threw down the Vole, which the creature seized instantaneously, and carried off into the hedge."

That the Weasel will take to the water when in pursuit of its prey is mentioned in Macgillivray's account, but it does not appear that it will voluntarily swim for any long distance. An instance is, however, recorded by the Rev. H. A. Macpherson, of one of these little animals being taken while swimming across Ulleswater, at a point where the lake is three-quarters of a mile in width.

Occasionally, though very rarely, the Weasel is stated to turn white in winter, the tail then retaining its reddish hue, although becoming paler than ordinary.

The Weasel is subject to considerable variation in size, which once gave rise to the idea that there might possibly be two species. Thus Gilbert White wrote that " some intelligent country people have a notion that we have, in these parts, a species of the genus *Mustelinum*, besides the Weasel, Stoat, Ferret, and Polecat ; a little reddish beast, not much bigger than a Field-Mouse, but much longer, which they call a *Cane*." It is, however, now ascertained that the so-called Cane, or Kine, is nothing more than an unusually small female Weasel. Such very small, although fully adult, females have been recorded not only from Hampshire, but likewise from Kent and Sussex.

As an example of the pugnacious habits of the Weasel, we may mention that (as we are informed by Mr. Harvie-Brown) there is in the Banff Museum an extraordinary mummified group of these animals, found in a hole of an old tree-stump, all the members of which evidently perished while fighting together.

THE BADGERS. GENUS MELES.

Meles, Storr, Prodromus Méthod. Mamm. p. 34 (1780).

The Badgers and their allies, which are assigned to several distinct genera, represent the second sub-family of the *Mustelidæ*, and are characterised as follows. The feet are elongated, with straight toes, and the claws non-retractile, slightly curved, rounded, and blunt, those on the fore-feet being especially elongated. The upper molar tooth, although variable, is generally very large and elongated longitudinally. In habits the members of the sub-family are mostly terrestrial and burrowing animals, and the group has a wide geographical distribution, although unrepresented in South America. .

From their plantigrade feet, short ears and tail, and somewhat Bear-like general appearance and gait, the more typical Badgers were long classed with the Bears, and even in the second edition of Bell's "British Quadrupeds" the Common Badger will be found described as the sole existing British representative of the family *Ursidæ*. It is, however, now well ascertained that such resemblances as these animals present to the Bears are for the most part superficial, and that their true affinities are with the Weasel tribe.

As a genus, the true Badgers, or those included under the head of *Meles*, may be defined as follows :—Upper molar tooth very large and longer than broad, exceeding the flesh-tooth in length ; bony palate not greatly produced backwards ; head pointed, with the nose prominent, and the ears small and rounded ; body thick and heavy ; limbs short and stout ; feet plantigrade ; tail short. Number of teeth 38, of which four on each side of both the upper and lower jaws belong to the premolar series.

The members of the genus are confined to the northern half of the Old World, and do not range into India, although represented in Persia.

It may be mentioned as a peculiarity of the Badger group in general, although the feature is more developed in some genera than in others, that the lower jaw is so strongly articulated to the skull, by means of overhanging processes from the latter, that it is almost or quite impossible to disarticulate it without fracture. This is the secret of the terrible biting power of these animals.

THE COMMON BADGER. MELES TAXUS.

Ursus meles, Linn., Syst. Nat. ed. 12 vol. i. p. 70 (1766).
Meles taxus, Boddaert, Elenchus Animal. vol. i. p. 80 (1785);
　　　Bell, British Quadrupeds 2nd ed. p. 158 (1874).
Meles vulgaris, Desmarest, Mammalogie p. 173 (1820).

(*Plate XV.*)

PLATE V.

Characters.—General colour yellowish-grey, washed with black; under-parts and limbs black; face white, with a black longitudinal streak on each side passing through the eye and ear. Length of head and body about 27 inches; of tail, 7½ inches

With regard to the nature and coloration of the pelage, Macgillivray writes as follows:—"On the head and face the hairs are adpressed, and of ordinary texture; on the lower-parts coarse, but of the nature of fur or under-hair; on the upper-parts of two kinds, a coarse fur and still coarser and longer, stiffish, undulated, flattened, and pointed hairs. The head, chin, and hind-neck are white, with a broad brownish-black band on each side from before the eye over the ear, of which the tip is white, down the back of the neck. The throat, fore-neck, middle of the breast, fore-limbs, and hind-feet are brownish-black; the upper-parts and sides light grey, variegated with black, a large portion of each hair near the end being of the latter colour; the long hairs at the tip of the short tail whitish." It may be added that the long hairs of the body are three-coloured, namely reddish, white, and black, and it is the blending of these that produces the well-known " Badger-colour." The soles of the feet are completely covered with hair.

Distribution.—Ranging over the greater part of Northern Europe and Asia, the Badger was formerly an abundant animal in the British Isles, where it has left its remains in the Pleistocene deposits of Kent, as well as in many English caverns, and likewise in Shandon Cave, Ireland. Owing to its shy and retiring habits, and the secluded nature of the spots in which it takes up its subterranean haunts, the Badger, or, as it used to be called in many parts of England, the "Brock," is very generally supposed to be an exceedingly rare, if not a nearly exterminated, animal in our islands. This, however, is very far indeed from being the case, and Badgers occur sporadically in most English counties ; while in some districts, owing to the protection they receive at the hands of land-owners, they are actually on the increase. Within the last thirty years the presence of Badgers has been recorded in up-wards of twenty-nine English counties. Its former abundance in England is attested by the frequency with which its title enters into the names of places, and it is curious that in all these cases it is the ancient name of "Brock,"and not the more modern one of "Badger,"that is employed in the compound word. Thus we have, as pointed out by Mr. Harting, the names of Brockhurst, Brockenhurst, Brockenborough, Brockford, Brockhall, Brock-hampton (in four counties), Brockham Green, Brockholes (in two counties), Brock-le-Bank, Brocklesby, Brockley (in four counties), Brockmoor, and Brockworth. The name Brock, it may be observed, apparently refers to the striped face which forms such a characteristic feature in the animal under con-sideration. As an instance of the apparent increase in the number of Badgers in certain parts of England, we may mention that, in Leicestershire, according to Mr. Montagu-Browne, they now breed in several places and seem to be more abundant than formerly. On the other hand, in certain districts where, from the wild nature of the country, they might naturally have been expected to have survived, they have been more or less nearly, if not completely, exterminated. Thus in the Lake district, according to the Rev. H. A. Macpherson, Badgers appear to have been completely extirpated since the end of the first third of the present century, when a few individuals still survived on the fells of Windermere and Cartmell. It is true that a few solitary Badgers are now and then recorded from the districts in question, but these are all stated to be individuals that have escaped from confinement. We may mention, however, that Badgers have been re-introduced on one or two estates in Westmoreland, so that there is some hope that, under due protection, the county may be partly re-populated with these interesting animals.

In Scotland Mr. Harvie-Brown states that the Badger occurs pretty generally throughout the mainland, but that it is not a native of any of the islands, although it has been introduced into Jura and upon Ailsa Craig. In all districts it appears, however, to be much less common than formerly. In Thompson's time (*circiter* 1855), the Badger was stated to maintain its ground throughout Ireland, probably in every county, examples existing some ten years previous to that date within a few miles of the city of Belfast.

Habits.—A nocturnal animal, living generally in pairs, though several have not unfrequently been observed in company, the Badger passes its days securely concealed in its burrow, which is generally excavated in some unfrequented part of a wood or thicket, in the side of a hill densely covered with bushes, or in a deserted quarry, whence it issues forth to feed in the evening or during the night. Although having but a single entrance, the " earth " is described as consisting of several tortuous passages, opening out at their extremities into larger chambers. Its food consists mainly of roots of various kinds, fruits and nuts, birds' eggs, together with the smaller mammals, reptiles, frogs, and insects. It is also particularly fond of the grubs of wasps, which are dug out from the nests and extracted from the combs without any fear of the stings of the adult insects, against which the thick fur of the Badger appears to afford an effectual protection. Except that it may destroy a certain number of the eggs of game-birds, the Badger is harmless alike to the game-preserver and the farmer; and the persecution to which in this country it has always been subject at the hand of man, is due rather to the innate desire of killing and hunting, than on account of any actual damage inflicted. It is true, indeed, that these animals are frequently charged with

killing and otherwise interfering with young Foxes ; on which
account a war to the death is too often waged against them
by over-zealous huntsmen.   This charge has, however, been
effectually disproved, several writers recording instances where
the cubs of Badgers and Foxes have been inhabitants of
the same "earth," where they have lived together in perfect
good-fellowship and harmony.   Mr. Trevor-Battye says that
the only harm the Badger does in the above direction is by
re-opening Foxes' "earths" that have been stopped.   Mr.
de Winton writes :—"Badgers sometimes frighten sheep at
night, when they are feeding on turnips in pens, and I have
had some harm done by them, as the sheep are very fat and
heavy-coated, and hurt themselves over the feeding troughs.
This is the only damage which Badgers have done to me, and I
have lived side by side with them all my life, and have had
many as pets."

Having formed a bed of soft grass at the bottom of the burrow, the female Badger brings forth in the spring from three
to four young ones, which do not make their appearance
abroad until they have attained a considerable size.   Writing of
the breeding habits of some Badgers on his estate near Lough-
borough, the late Mr. A. Ellis, who had especial opportunities
of making observations, states that "the Badger breeds later than
the Fox, and it was the middle of March this year [1877] before
the preparations for the coming family were made.   These
consisted in cleaning out the winter-bed and replacing it by a
quantity of dry fern and grass, so great that it would seem impossible the earth could receive it.   In June the first young
Badger appeared at the mouth of the earth, and was soon
followed by three others, and then by their mother.   After
this, they continued to show every evening, and soon learnt to
take the food prepared for them.   The young are now [Octo-
ber] almost full-grown, and, forgetting their natural timidity.

will feed so near that I have placed my hand on the back of one of them. The old ones are more wary, but often feed with their family, although at a more cautious distance. Their hearing and sense are most acute, and it is curious to see them watch, with lifted head and ears erect, then, if all is quiet, search the ground for a raisin or a date. But the least strange sight or sound alarms them, and they rush headlong to earth with amazing speed." As is so generally the case among the Carnivora, the young of the Badger are born blind, and remain so for several days after birth. It is generally stated, in the case of the Badger, that the young open their eyes on the ninth day; but Dr. A. Nehring records an instance where a litter, born in the Zoological Gardens at Berlin, did not do so until the eighteenth day after birth.

A remarkable peculiarity in regard to the Badger is the length and variability of the period of gestation. The minimum duration of pregnancy does not appear to be fully ascertained, although Dr. Nehring is of opinion that it cannot be less than six months. Instances are on record where female Badgers that have been kept in solitary confinement have brought forth young after periods of ten and twelve months; and one very important one is recorded by Captain F. H. Salvin, in which a Badger gave birth to one litter on February 27th, and to another on the sixteenth of the same month in the following year, showing that in this case the period of gestation was about seventeen days short of a twelvemonth. In other instances, however, the period is much longer, reaching in two of these to at least fifteen months. The probable explanation of these discrepancies is that in certain cases, as in the Roe-deer, the impregnated ovum undergoes a period of quiescence before development; such retardation of development being not improbably induced by captivity, which nearly always interferes more or less with the reproductive process of animals.

On the gestation of the Badger Mr. Trevor-Battye sends me the following note:—" As a rule, no doubt, the Badger pairs in October and the young are born in March or April. I lived for many years close to a stronghold of Badgers and had unusual opportunities for watching them. It has been said and written that Badgers do not breed till two years old. This is wrong. Some years ago I had a pair which were probably about six weeks old. They were called Gripper and Nancy. They would rest on my lap while feeding, and used to sit up and beg like Dogs. Their hearing and power of scent were remarkable. They were in a closed square yard, but if any of the dogs came near, even following a path which ran at a distance of about six or seven yards, they would instantly jump off my lap and disappear into a corner. These animals could walk and trot backwards with the greatest ease. I have never seen this mentioned; yet it is worth noticing because the movement is characteristic of the *Mustelidæ*, not being shared to my knowledge by any other Mammal—not, for instance, by the Bears. As I was leaving home I was obliged to send off my Badgers. They went to a friend in the New Forest. Here they escaped from confinement and took up their quarters under some faggots in an outhouse. They paired that October and made their nest (the contents of which would have filled a big wheelbarrow and more) in the beginning of April. But poor Gripper came back one night with a trap on his foot. The chain of the trap got wound round somehow in the burrow and held him prisoner. So he died; and Nancy forsook the earth and went to breed elsewhere. In those days I did not understand maceration. But, as I wanted Gripper's skeleton, I boiled him in the copper outside, after he had been dead a month. Out of this Badger soup I collected even the smallest vertebra. 'To stink like a Badger' is a lying libel on the living animal; it was not overstated in the case of Gripper dead—and boiling!"

With reference to the carnivorous propensities of the Badger, Thompson writes that "one gentleman, who kept a young Badger in confinement, reports that it was very fond of Rats, Mice, and birds, and that it devoured a pet Blackbird which he highly prized. At Tollymore Park (County Down) and Glenarm (County Antrim), where Badgers are numerous, they are sometimes taken in traps baited with Rabbits ; and I was informed by a gamekeeper, at the latter place, that they are destructive to young Rabbits in the nest, and, in such cases, do not make use of the Rabbits' entrance, but delve out a

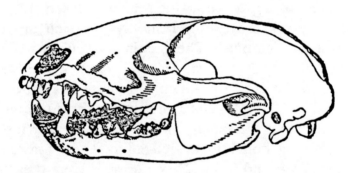

Skull of Badger.

circular hole immediately above the nest. From the peculiar footprint of the Badgers, always to be seen about these holes, he knows that they were the depredators." While admitting the truth of this latter statement, and also that a Badger may occasionally get hold of a sitting Pheasant, Mr. Harting considers that the harm done by Badgers to game-preserves is almost infinitesimal, Pheasants, except during the breeding-season, being at roost in the trees, and the Rabbits feeding in the open outside the coverts, at the time when these animals leave their lairs for the nocturnal prowl.

No account of this animal would be complete without some mention of the sport of Badger-baiting, which, although now illegal, was formerly a favourite with our ancestors. The creature was placed in a tub lying on its side, and attacked by Terriers or other Dogs, whose object was to draw the Badger from its place of security. As Bell remarks, it would be diffi- cult to say whether in this so-called sport, the cruelty were greater to the persecuted Badger or to his canine tormentors. Since, through the intervention of a London paper, the title of which need not be mentioned, a regular trade is even now carried on in live Badgers, the suspicion arises whether Badger-baiting is really as extinct as is commonly supposed.

To procure Badgers for the above-mentioned sport or other purposes, the usual plan was to place a sack within the margins of the "earth," with its mouth upwards and secured by a running string, at such time as the owner was ascertained to be absent from his dwelling. The surrounding coverts were then drawn with a few couple of hounds, which generally suc- ceeded in finding the Badger and hunting him to his hole, on attempting to enter which he was of course securely bagged beyond the possibility of escape.

THE OTTERS. GENUS LUTRA.

Lutra, Erxleben, Syst. Régne Animale, p. 445 (1777).

The Otters, all of which, with the single exception of the Sea-Otter, are included in the present genus, form the sole representatives of the last sub-family of the *Mustelidæ*, the characters of which are as follows :—The feet are short and rounded, with the toes webbed, and the claws small, curved, and blunt. The head is remarkably broad and flattened ; and the upper molar tooth is large and nearly square. In habits, all the species are thoroughly aquatic.

The genus *Lutra* is chiefly distinguished from the Sea-Otter by the cheek-teeth being furnished with a number of sharp

COMMON OTTER.

cusps, instead of being smoothed and mammillated, as well as by the moderate development of the toes of the hind-feet. Retaining the elongated bodily form and short limbs characterising the more typical *Mustelidæ*, the true Otters generally have the feet completely webbed, and either clawed or clawless. The soles of the feet are for the most part naked, although in the hinder pair the naked portion does not extend backwards to the heel. The flattened head is elongated and furnished with very small ears; and the fur is close, compact, and short, with a woolly under-fur; the tail being of medium length. There are generally four pairs of pre-molar teeth in the upper, and three in the lower jaw; the first of the upper ones is, however, always very small, and situated on the inner side of the canine, and in some species may be wanting.

All Otters have such a strong family resemblance, that the distinction between the various species is in many cases a matter of considerable difficulty; but, fortunately, there is but one, and that the typical, representative of the genus within the limits of our area. With the exception of Australasia and the extreme north, the genus is practically cosmopolitan; and its representatives are mainly fluviatile and lacustrine in their habits.

THE COMMON OTTER. LUTRA VULGARIS.

Mustela lutra, Linn., Syst. Nat. ed. 12, vol. i. p. 66 (1766).

Lutra vulgaris, Erxleben, Syst. Regn. Animal. p. 448 (1777); Bell, British Quadrupeds, 2nd ed. p. 167 (1874); Blanford, Mammals of British India, p. 182 (1888).

Lutra nair, F. Cuvier, Dict. Sci. Nat. vol. xxvii. p. 247 (1823).

Lutra indica, Gray, Mag. Nat. Hist. vol. i. p. 580 (1837).

(*Plate XVI.*)

Characters.—Size large; claws well-developed on all the toes; upper edge of naked portion of muzzle projecting backwards in the middle, and concave on either side, where it runs up to the hinder edge of the nostril; tail more than half the length of the body   General colour deep brown, with a more or less rufous tinge; woolly under-fur white at the base, then brown, and usually paler at the tips, especially in Indian examples; under-parts whitish; fur of chin and throat white throughout, elsewhere white at the base and tip, and brown in the middle. Length of head and body, from 25 to 29 inches; of tail, from 15 to 16 inches.

Distribution.—This species has a wide distribution in the Old World, ranging over the whole of Europe and Asia north of the Himalaya, while it is represented in India and some of the countries on the east of the Bay of Bengal by a form which is now generally regarded as a mere variety.   In the British Islands its fossilised remains are found in the Norwich Crag, belonging to the upper part of the Pliocene period, in the overlying forest-bed of the east coast, the brick-earths of the Thames valley, as well as in several of the English caves.   At the present day it is still pretty generally distributed over the country, although becoming scarce in the more cultivated districts where the rivers are small.   While, for instance, it is stated to be rare in Leicestershire and Rutland, as also in Hertfordshire, in the wild and rocky districts of Somerset, Devon, and Monmouthshire it is still abundant, as it is in the streams and lakes of Westmoreland and Cumberland.   It would be difficult indeed, as observed by the Rev. H. A. Macpherson, to find any part of Britain more exactly suited to the needs and habits of this animal than is the Lake district of the two counties last mentioned.   In the north of Scotland, according to Messrs. Harvie-Brown and Buckley, the Otter, although scarce, from incessant persecution, in the east of

Sutherland, is still far from rare in Caithness, while it is abundant in Argyllshire and the Isles. Some idea of its former numbers may be gathered from the fact that between the years 1831 and 1834 rewards were paid for upwards of 263 Otters killed on the estates of the Duke of Sutherland alone. In Ireland, forty years ago, Thompson wrote that the Otter still survived in suitable localities throughout the country and along the coast, in spite of persecution.

Habits.—Feeding almost exclusively on fish, which it pursues not only in rivers and lakes, but also in the open sea, the Otter, writes Macgillivray, in the north of Scotland and the adjacent islands, "resides among the blocks, or in the caverns along the coasts, and subsists on marine fishes, seldom appearing in the streams or lakes except in winter, during very stormy weather. In the south of Scotland, and in many parts of England, it inhabits the fresh waters. On shore it runs with considerable speed, but does not bound like the Weasels, and, in fact, is rather plantigrade than digitigrade. In the water it exhibits an astonishing agility, swimming in a nearly horizontal position with the greatest ease, diving and darting along beneath the surface with a speed equal, if not superior, to that of many fishes. It is capable of remaining immersed for a considerable time, but on seizing a fish it cannot devour it in the water, but must bring it to shore for that purpose, not always, however, carrying it to its ordinary retreat, but generally to the nearest point that seems to afford temporary security. While eating, it holds its prey down with its fore-feet, or, if small, secures it between them, and commencing at the shoulders, devours the fish downwards, leaving the head and tail. While thus occupied it is sometimes visited by Gulls and Hooded Crows, which, however, do not venture to attack it, but wait until it has finished its meal, contenting themselves with the remnants. It is alleged that it destroys great quantities of

Salmon, which may be the case when it inhabits rivers and estuaries, but in the open sea it feeds on a variety of fishes. Along the coast it generally finds a safe retreat in caves, of which the upper part is filled with blocks of rock, or beneath large stones; but in rivers and lakes it seeks refuge among the roots of trees, or burrows a hole for itself in the banks. Although properly piscivorous, it has been known to attack young domestic animals, and I found the stomach of one killed in June filled with a curious collection of larvæ and earth-worms."

The foregoing description, it will be observed, applies chiefly to the habits of the Otter in the rivers and on the coasts of Scotland; those of our readers desirous of becoming acquainted with the haunts and habits of the animal in the rivers of the south of England should peruse a graphic chapter in a little work entitled " Forest Tithes," by an author who writes under the *nom-de-plume* of " A Son of the Marshes." On the Upper Indus I have known a pair of Otters take up their abode among the timbers of a wooden bridge. In sporting phraseology, an Otter's lair is spoken of as its "holt." When a burrow is excavated by the animals themselves it may vary considerably in size and depth, but one described by Mr. Buckley, discovered on one of the Scottish islands, seems to be the longest and most complex on record. This tunnel, which was bored in peaty soil, amongst the burrows of the Storm-Petrel, was upwards of fifteen feet in length, with a diameter of about a foot, except near the extremity, when it became about four inches narrower. " Here and there it was widened out into most evident circular or oval chambers, and the sides and roof were smooth and glossy, rubbed and polished by the passage to and fro of the animals' fur. The habitation had a cunning and gradual incline from upwards into the peat-bank from the entrance. The latter was simply an uneven, rough, grassy-edged, and semi-concealed doorway in the face of the peat slope."

In the month of March or April, the female gives birth in the lair—whether this be a burrow as above described, or merely a hollow beneath the roots of some large tree, or a fissure among rocks—to from three to five young ones, after a gestation of only nine weeks. The young remain with their parents for a considerable period; and, in India at least, family-parties of six or seven nearly full-grown individuals may be seen together, these sometimes contriving to drive a shoal of fish into shallow water, where they may be easily captured. Although in this country mainly nocturnal in its habits, in less frequented regions the Otter may often be seen abroad well on in the day-time. Everywhere these animals kill far more prey than they can possibly eat, which is one of the reasons why their presence in a river is so cordially detested by fishermen.

When taken young, the Otter may be easily tamed, and may be trained without much difficulty to exercise its fish-catching skill for its owner's benefit.

Otter-hunting, either with Otter-hounds or Fox-hounds, is a favourite sport in Devon and Somerset, in the Lake district, and also in Wales. The hounds should be laid on the trail, or "foil," of the Otter as soon as possible after daybreak, since on many soils the scent soon disappears under a strong sun. Formerly the Otter was struck at on every possible opportunity with a barbed spear termed an "Otter-grains," until finally despatched; but the use of this weapon has happily been discontinued in the Lake district, as we learn from the Rev. H. A. Macpherson, and elsewhere.

Although from its comparatively small numbers the Otter is not much hunted in this country for the sake of its beautiful pelage, on the Continent this forms an important trade. According to Mr. Poland, Scandinavian skins, from their large size, thick fur, and dark colour, are among the most esteemed ; and some idea of the numbers of these animals killed and the. importance of the trade may be gathered from the fact that upwards of about 10,000 skins are annually sold at the Easter fair at Leipsic, these varying in value from five to thirty shillings each, according to size, colour, and quality. The same authority tells us that during the winter of 1885–86 more than 4,000 of these animals were killed in Prussia alone.

THE BEARS. FAMILY URSIDÆ.

Although closely allied to the *Mustelidæ* in the structure of the hinder part of the base of the skull, the Bear family (in addition to the vastly superior bodily size of the great majority of its members) may be readily distinguished therefrom by the greater number of their molar teeth, of which there are two pairs in the upper, and three in the lower jaw, or the same as in the Dogs. In character these teeth are, however, very different from those of the latter, the two upper ones being oblong and much longer than broad, with the crown finely tuberculated, and adapted for a mixed, rather than a purely flesh diet. Moreover, the flesh-teeth (the last pre-molar in the upper, and the first molar in the lower jaw) are exceedingly unlike those of the Dogs, being small in proportion to the molars, and having the suctorial structure so characteristic of Carnivora in general but little developed. All Bears are large, heavily-built animals, with thoroughly plantigrade feet, armed with strong curved claws, well adapted for digging, short ears, and a mere apology for a tail.

Generally adepts in climbing, but, in spite of the fossorial characters of their feet, not excavating burrows for their own habitation, Bears are distributed over the greater part of the globe, with the exception of Africa south of the Atlas mountains, and Australia Save for one species from India and another from Tibet, they are all included in the typical genus, the distinctive characteristics of which it will be superfluous to indicate in the present work.

THE TRUE BEARS. GENUS URSUS.

Ursus, Linn., Syst. Nat. ed. 12, vol. i. p. 69 (1766).

THE BROWN BEAR. URSUS ARCTUS.

Ursus arctos, Linn., Syst. Nat. ed. 12, vol. i. p. 69 (1766).

The Brown Bear, being a species exterminated within the British Islands during the historical period, has the same claim as the Wolf to be regarded as a British Mammal. Being, however, thus extinct within our area, and at the same time such a thoroughly well-known animal, we think that we shall best serve the interests of our readers by omitting all description, and confining ourselves to a brief notice of the records of its extermination. For these, as in the case of the Wolf, we are indebted entirely to Mr. J. E. Harting, who has so thoroughly investigated what remains of the history of the exterminated Mammals of our islands.

We may premise that the Brown Bear (which is still far from uncommon in many parts of the Continent), under a variety of local races, has a wide distribution in the Old World, ranging over the greater part of Europe and Northern Asia, and extending as far south as the Western Himalaya and the valley of Kashmir. In North America it is represented by the closely allied Grisly Bear. Although there is some difficulty in distinguishing between the different species of Bears of this group by their skulls and teeth alone, it is now well ascertained that remains of the Brown Bear have been obtained from the brick-earths of the Thames valley, the fens of Cambridgeshire, various superficial deposits in Scotland and Ireland, and also from several of the English caves. It should be added that some Ursine remains, from English and Irish, have been assigned to the Grisly Bear (*Ursus horribilis*), but the writer is by no means assured that this reference is correct.

Documentary evidence proves the existence of the Bear in England during the eighth century; and it is likewise on record, that in the time of Edward the Confessor, the town of Norwich was compelled annually to furnish a Bear for royal sport, such Bears being in all probability native British animals. It is likewise probable that the performing Bears which were led about England during this period by itinerant minstrels were also captured in the British Islands. During both the Roman and Anglo-Saxon periods it would appear, however, that the great Caledonian forest of Scotland was the principal stronghold of these animals; Caledonian Bears being well-known in the Roman amphitheatre.   There are even traditions still extant in the Highlands, together with certain Gaelic place-names, apparently referring to the former existence of Bears in these districts.

At what precise period the Brown Bear became extinct in Britain, there is, unfortunately, no means of ascertaining. That it disappeared at an earlier date than the Wolf, is, however, certain; and it has been considered probable that it had ceased to exist before the tenth century.

With regard to Ireland, Thompson writes that " I am not aware of any written evidence tending to show that the Bear was ever indigenous to Ireland, but a tradition exists of its having been so.   It is associated with the Wolf as a native animal in the stories handed down through several generations to the present time."

THE TRUE SEALS. FAMILY PHOCIDÆ.

The whole of the Carnivora treated of above, together with their foreign allies, collectively constitute the typical group of the Order, and are known as the true Carnivores, or *Carnivora Vera;* of which the leading characteristic, as already mentioned, is the presence of a pair of specially modified flesh-teeth in each jaw, the fore-feet, and generally also the hinder pair, being of the normal type, although in the Sea-Otter the latter are flipper-like. On the other hand, in the Seals and Walruses, which now claim our attention, there are no flesh-teeth, and both pairs of limbs are modified into flippers. From the latter feature, this second great sub-ordinal group of the Order is known as *Carnivora Pinnipedia*, or Fin-footed Carnivores.

The massive and more or less conical form of the body in the Seals and their allies is too well known to demand more than casual mention. The limbs, which are relatively short, have their upper segments more or less completely enclosed in the skin of the body ; while they are provided with five toes each, connected together by webs. Unlike the land Carnivores, the first and fifth toes of each foot are stouter and generally longer than the three middle ones. The tail is always short.

In regard to their teeth, it may be mentioned that, whereas only in the Sea-Otter among the true Carnivores are there less than three pairs of incisors in the lower jaw, in the present group such a reduction is invariably the case ; while very frequently also there are only two pairs of these teeth in the upper jaw. In the cheek-teeth the pre-molars (generally four in number in each jaw) are nearly similar to the molars ; the latter being generally reduced to a single pair, although in some instances there are two pairs in the upper jaw. The milk-teeth are shed at an exceedingly early age—sometimes even before birth,—and are consequently of no functional importance whatever, while collar-bones are totally wanting.

In habits, the whole of these animals are thoroughly aquatic; and they are, as a rule, inhabitants of the sea, although some ascend rivers, and a few are found in land-locked lakes. Although their movements on land are awkward and ungainly in the extreme, the members of one family (the Eared Seals, of which there are no British representatives) pass the whole of the breeding season on shore, during which prolonged period they undergo a complete fast.

The true Seals, or *Phocidæ*, which are the most specialised representatives of the entire group, are characterised by the circumstance that the hind-flippers, when on land, are ex-.ended backwards parallel to the tail, and are thus incapable of taking any share in those movements which, by courtesy, may be termed walking; this mode of progression being effected mainly or entirely by a kind of jumping movement of the body. All these Seals are further characterised by the total absence of any externally projecting ear; the passages to the brain opening flat on the surface of the sides of the head. Although the number of incisor teeth is subject to some degree of variation, the pre-molars and molars collectively always form five pairs in each jaw; these teeth generally having three well-marked cusps arranged longitudinally, with sometimes a smaller fourth cusp posteriorly, but being occasionally simple.

The British Seals, although not numerous, include representatives of three distinct genera.

GENUS HALICHŒRUS.

Halichœrus, Nilsson, Faun. Skandinav. vol. i. p. 377 (1820).

Three pairs of upper, and two of lower incisor teeth; cheek-teeth (*i.e.*, molars and pre-molars) mostly with single roots, and simply conical without accessory cusps. First and fifth toes of the hinder flippers not much longer than the three middle ones; and the webs on their feet not projecting be· yond the extremities of the toes.

The genus is represented solely by the under-mentioned species.

THE GREY SEAL. HALICHŒRUS GRYPUS.

Phoca grypus, Fabricius, Skriv. af. Nat. Selksk. vol. i. pt. 2, p. 167 (1791).

Halichœrus griseus, Nilsson, Faun. Skandinav. vol. i. p. 377 (1820).

Phoca gryphus, Fischer, Synops. Mamm. p. 239 (1829).

Halichœrus gryphus, Bell, British Quadrupeds, p. 278 (1837), and 2nd ed. p. 262 (1874).

Halichœrus grypus, Gray, Cat. Seals and Whales Brit. Mus. p. 34 (1866).

Characters.—General colour yellowish-grey, becoming lighter on the under-parts, with dark grey spots and blotches; but, as in most Seals, there is considerable of variation in tint according to age. Total length of male, about 8 feet.

Distribution.—The range of this species is restricted to the shores of the North Atlantic Ocean, where it is far more common and more widely distributed on the European than on the American side. Its chief haunts appear to be the British and Scandinavian coasts; its northern limits being seemingly marked by the Baltic, the Gulf of Bothnia, and Iceland. This Seal was first recognised as an inhabitant of the British seas in the year 1836; and while rare on the southern coasts of England, it is exceedingly abundant on the western and southern shores of Ireland, as well as in the Hebrides and Shetlands. The specimens taken on our southern coasts must be regarded in the light of stragglers from more northern regions; one of these having been taken many years ago in the Severn, while a second was captured on the Isle of Wight in 1857. It has likewise been recorded from the Welsh coast. On the more southern coasts of Scotland this Seal is likewise rare, but it becomes more numerous as we proceed north. Thus, although now diminished in numbers, a few are still to be found in suitable localities on the coast of Caithness, where they have been said to breed in the rocky caverns. According to Messrs. Harvie-Brown and Buckley, they "also occur in some numbers on Eilean-nan-roan, off the Kyle of Tongue, where specimens have been seen over eight feet long. They are most numerous on the outer island. At Souliskeir, to the north of Cape Wrath, they were once abundant, and parties of fishermen used to go from Orkney and the north Sutherland coast

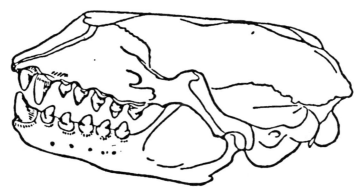

Skull of Grey Seal.

to kill them in "October." The same authors state that, although restricted and rare in the Inner Hebrides, it still frequents the more remote Outer Hebrides in some numbers, although, for obvious reasons, they refrain from mentioning its favourite haunts. They add that there are "few localities, even among the Isles, where they could be observed with any degree of regularity. We know of one single, very hoary, and very large individual, frequenting a portion of coast, and having done so unmolested for many years. What his age may be, it is vain to speculate upon, but he certainly has been known and recognised by natives for a very long series of years, frequenting always the same reach of shore. That great Grey Seals breed also even far in among the Inner Hebrides seems to be perfectly certain from notes in our possession, but it is quite open to doubt if such an occurrence as the birth of a Grey Seal has ever taken place anywhere upon the coast of the mainland " of Argyllshire.

On the southern and western coasts of Ireland these Seals appear to retain their hold more than elsewhere, and they likewise seem to congregate in larger parties than in most other places, at least a dozen having been seen together. Even here, however, their numbers appear to be diminishing steadily, although the persecuted creatures have, fortunately for themselves, now become so shy and wary as to make it very difficult to approach within range. A large specimen shot by A. G. More, on a rocky island off the coast of Connemara, in 1869, measured exactly eight feet in length, and weighed close upon four hundred pounds; but Scottish examples are stated to reach fully nine feet from the tip of the nose to the extremity of the hind-flippers.

Habits.—In habits the Grey Seal is essentially an insular and oceanic species, generally associating in pairs, although occasionally, as we have seen to be the case on the Irish coasts, consorting in small parties. In the Hebrides they take up their quarters in the most exposed situations ; and produce their young in September or October, or even as late as November. When first born, the young Seal is clothed with white hair, which is retained till such time as the creature is able to take to the water, when the adult dress is assumed. In Scandinavia, on the other hand, it is stated that the breeding season is not till February ; a difference which Bell suggests may be due to the difference in the climate of this region from Britain, although it does not appear to us that this explanation is adequate.

L 2

It may be mentioned that, like all the other British species, the Grey Seal has no under-fur, and therefore does not yield "seal-skin."

GENUS PHOCA.

Phoca, Linn., Syst. Nat. ed. 12, vol. i. p. 55 (1766).

Distinguished from the preceding genus by the relatively smaller and more pointed teeth, and by those of the cheek-series having accessory cusps, and mostly double roots. The head also is rounded, instead of flattened, and the muzzle naked and not truncated, while the brain-cavity of the skull is proportionately much larger.

The short front-flippers are furnished with five stout, somewhat compressed and curved, and rather sharp claws; while those of the hind-feet are narrower and less curved.

The genus includes several species from the northern hemisphere, among which are the majority of those frequenting the British coasts.

1. COMMON SEAL.   PHOCA VITULINA.

Phoca vitulina, Linn., Syst. Nat. ed. 12, vol. i. p. 56 (1766); Bell, British Quadrupeds, 2nd ed. p. 240 (1874).

Phoca variegata, Nilsson, Skandinav. Faun. vol. i. p. 359 (1820).

Callocephalus vitulinus, F. Cuvier, Dict. Sci. Nat. vol. xxix. p. 544 (1826); Gray, Cat. Seals and Whales Brit. Mus. p. 20 (1866).

(*Plate XVII.*)

Characters.—Considerably smaller than *Halichœrus grypus*, to which it closely approximates in general coloration, the upper-parts being yellowish-grey spotted with black and brown, while the under-parts are light silvery-grey. Cheek-teeth crowded together, and placed obliquely in the jaws. Total length, from 4 to 5 feet.

Distribution.—This Seal, the second of the two species which alone breed on the British coasts, has a wider and also a more northerly distribution than the Grey Seal, being found not only on both sides of the North Atlantic, but likewise in the North Pacific. Northwards its range includes Spitsbergen, Greenland, and Davis Straits; while southwards it is found commonly on the northern shores of France and Holland, but is stated to be rare in the Baltic. Formerly abundant, in such localities as are suited to its habits, throughout the British coasts, this Seal has now practically disappeared from those of the more southern and eastern counties of England, although even there an occasional straggler now and then

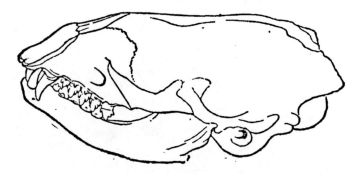

Skull of Common Seal.

makes its appearance, one such instance having occurred not many years ago at Brighton. On the more rocky shores of the western counties, as well as in Wales, it is, however, still far from uncommon; the same being the case in the northern English counties. On the coasts of the Lake district, where the shore is generally sandy and without islands, it is, however, decidedly rare, although, according to the Rev. H. A. Macpherson, a few old individuals occur now and again both in Morecambe Bay and in the main channel of the English Solway. On the coasts of the mainland of Scotland this species

may be still met with in considerable numbers, although
it is less abundant than formerly, even in the Hebrides and
other islands. On the coasts of Sutherland and Caithness,
Messrs. Harvie-Brown and Buckley write that it is not uncommon in some localities, especially in the Firths of the
north coast, and occurring all along the coasts in the west.
Another resort on the east coast is a sand-bank at the entrance
of the Dornoch Firth, visible from the town of Tain, where
Seals used to lie in large numbers, until persecuted by long-
range punt-guns. Although it has long been known that this
Seal will often ascend rivers for long distances in pursuit of its
favourite Salmon, it is not so much a matter of common knowledge that it will take up its residence for longer or shorter
periods in inland fresh-water lakes. The authors last mentioned
have, however, collected evidence of the occurrence of many
of these Seals both in Loch Awe, in Argyllshire, and also in
Loch Shiel. On the Irish coasts—and more especially on the
west and east—the common Seal was formerly abundant in
suitable localities, although even in Thompson's time they were
becoming scarce in Belfast Bay, where a portion of the coast,
where they were once common, bears the name of, "Craig-a-vad,"
or "Seal" rock.

Habits.—Unlike the Grey Seal, the present species is essentially gregarious, congregating in herds of as many as two or
three dozen individuals, which, when in repose, may be seen
lying on the shore as closely packed as possible, with their
heads all turned seawards. In spite, however, of its northern
range it is not an Ice-Seal, never frequenting the ice-fields or
ice-floes of the polar ocean, but generally resorting to sheltered
fjords and caves, where food is abundant, and the depth of
water not too great to render its capture a matter of difficulty.
Macgillivray writes that it "frequents estuaries, sea-lochs, bays,
and the channels between islands, where it may be seen

occasionally protruding its head above the surface, sometimes
following a boat or vessel at a distance, but generally keeping
beyond reach of shot. It feeds exclusively on fishes, in pursuit of which it can remain several minutes immersed. At
low water it often betakes itself to rocks or small islands, on
which it reposes until the return of the tide; and I have seen
droves of twenty or more individuals thus basking in the sun.
In estuaries they sometimes repose on the sands, where they
are liable to be surprised, if the water be distant, for their
movements on land are exceedingly awkward, and their hurry
in endeavouring to escape when approached forms an amusing
sight, as they seem to tumble about in a ludicrous manner, throwing themselves headlong into the water from the rocks. When
there are caverns on the coast, they find a more secure retreat
in them, since, if attacked, they can escape by diving."

While in the sea, the Common Seal lives largely upon Flounders; but it is also especially fond of Salmon and Sea-Trout, and
it is in pursuit of these latter that it so frequently ascends long
distances up rivers. The young—usually one, but occasionally
two in number—are born in June, or thereabouts, after a gestation of nine months. Although the new-born young are clothed
in a coat of white hairs, as in the case of the Grey Seal, yet it
appears that instead of being retained for two or three weeks,
as in the latter, this is replaced by the adult coat very shortly
after birth, the offspring at the same time taking to the water.

The fondness of Seals for musical sounds is well-known, and
the following account, communicated to Macgillivray by a
resident in the Hebrides, illustrates this very graphically. "In
walking along the shore in districts where Seals were abundant
in the calm of a summer afternoon," writes the narrator, "a
few notes of my flute would bring half-a-score of them within
thirty or forty yards of me; and there they would swim about,
with their heads above water, like so many black dogs,

evidently delighted with the sounds. For half-an-hour, or, indeed, for any length of time I chose, I could fix them to the spot, and when I moved along the water's edge they would follow me with eagerness, like the Dolphins, which, it is said, attended Arion, as if anxious to prolong the enjoyment. I have frequently witnessed the same effect when out on a boat-excursion. The sound of the flute, or of a common fife, blown by one of the boatmen, was no sooner heard than half-a-dozen would start up within a few yards, wheeling round us as long as the music played, and disappearing, one after another, when it ceased.

"Other occasions occurred during my residence in these islands of witnessing the habits of these creatures. While my pupils and I were bathing, which we often did in the bosom of a beautiful bay in the island, named, from the circumstance of its being the favourite haunt of the animal, Seal-Bay, numbers of them invariably made their appearance, especially if the weather was calm and sunny, and the sea smooth, crowding around us at the distance of a few yards, and looking as if they had some kind of notion that we were of the same species, or at least genus, with themselves. The gambols in the water of my playful companions, and their noise and merriment, seemed, to our imagination, to excite them, and to make them course round us with greater rapidity and animation. At the same time, the slightest attempt on our part to act on the offensive, by throwing at them a stone or a shell, was the signal for their instantaneous disappearance, each, as it vanished, leaving the surface of the water beautifully figured with a wavy succession of concentric circles.

"On hot days in summer I have seen great numbers of them stretched in groups on the rocks at the bottom of Seal-Bay, which had been left dry by the receding tide. There they would lie lazily along, basking in the warm sun, like so many large swine, and nearly of the same colour.

"The fishermen on the island used to assert that, like many other animals both of the land and the water, they never repose without stationing a sentinel on the watch. I cannot positively confirm this, but I have often observed that during the general slumber one of the number, but not always the same individual, would raise its head for a second or two, turning it half round, and again stretch itself in repose. Ever and anon, too, we would hear from some one of the group a melancholy moan coming slowly over the surface of the deep, wild and savage in the sound."

The proportionately much larger capacity of the brain in the Common, as compared with that of the Grey Seal, would naturally suggest that the former is a far more intelligent creature than the latter; and actual experience proves this to be the case. Thus, whereas the Grey Seal is a dull and phlegmatic animal, exhibiting no signs of pleasure in musical sounds and displaying no attachment to its owner when in captivity, the present species can be readily tamed, and exhibits not only a high degree of affection for its master, but likewise great general intelligence. A well-known story is related in Maxwell's "Wild Sports of the West" of a Seal which had been captured young in Clew Bay, on the west coast of Ireland, and tamed by the servants of a neighbouring landowner. There it remained for upwards of four years, and so great was its attachment to the house, that after being carried out to sea three times and there left, it returned home on each occasion. With unspeakable cruelty, on the last of these occasions, the poor animal had been deprived of its sight, but even then it returned after an interval of eight days. Another individual, which was tamed by an Irish gentleman in 1819, appeared, according to Thompson's account, " to possess all the sagacity of the dog, and lived in its master's house and ate from his hand. In his fishing excursions this gentleman generally took it with him, upon which occasions it afforded no small entertainment. When thrown into the water, it would follow for miles the track of the boat, and although thrust back by the oars, it never relinquished its purpose ; indeed, it struggled so hard to regain its seat that one would imagine its fondness for its master had entirely overcome the natural predilection for its native element."

From the value of its skin, and the amount of oil yielded by its fat, this Seal is much hunted by fishermen, which has resulted in the diminution of its numbers already alluded to. Although the flesh of the adult is dark-coloured and somewhat rank, that of the young is tender and by no means unpalatable. Unless killed outright by the first shot, when in the water, they are liable to be lost, as they dive immediately on being struck, and are seldom seen again. Moreover, even if killed, unless the boat is rowed up speedily and the body secured, it will likewise be lost, as a dead Seal, more especially if it be in poor condition, immediately sinks to the bottom.

II. RINGED SEAL. PHOCA HISPIDA.

Phoca hispida, Schreber, Säugethiere vol. iii. pl. 86 (? 1776);
    Bell, British Quadrupeds, 2nd ed. p. 247 (1874).

Phoca fœtida, Fabricius, in Müller's Zool. Dan. Prodr. p. 8
    (1766); without description, and the name subsequently
    withdrawn by its author.

Phoca annullata, Nilsson, Skandinav. Fauna, p. 362 (1820).

Callocephalus discolor, F. Cuvier, Dict. Sci. Nat. vol. xxxix., p.
    545 (1826).

Pagomys fœtidus, Gray, Cat. Seals and Whales Brit. Mus. p.
    23 (1866).

Characters.—Very similar in external appearance to the last, but of somewhat smaller size, and the colour of the upper parts blackish-grey, generally marked with more or less distinct oval whitish rings; under-parts whitish; hair soft, and nearly erect. Cheek-teeth not crowded together, and placed in a straight line. Total length, generally from 3 to 4 feet.

The skull may be distinguished by the pre-maxillary bones (those carrying the incisor teeth) running up some distance by the sides of the nasals, instead of not touching them at all, or only at the tips; while the hinder foramina on the palate open either on or behind the suture between the maxillæ and palatine bones, instead of in the maxillæ themselves.

Distribution.—But a very rare and casual visitor to the British coasts, the Ringed Seal is an essentially northern species, inhabiting the Arctic Ocean and the shores of the North Atlantic and North Pacific, being especially plentiful among the ice-floes of Davis Strait, but in Greenland mainly confined to the northern districts. An undoubted example of this Seal was taken on the Norfolk coast in 1846, and sold in a fresh con dition in the Norwich market; and there is some evidence that the species occasionally visits the Hebrides. It is also stated by Mr. J. Cordeaux that an example occurred on the Lincolnshire coast so recently as the year 1889. Sir William Turner records its remains from the glacial clays of various parts of Scotland.

Habits.—On this point it will suffice to say that this species is an Ice-Seal, dwelling in the neighbourhood of the coast-ice of the northern oceans, and seldom visiting the open sea. In such situations it preys on fish which are captured in a hole kept open, by some means not fully known, in the ice; passing such portions of its time as are not occupied in fishing, in sleep. The single offspring is born late in the winter or early in the spring on the solid ice, and is stated to take to the water before shedding its baby-coat of light-coloured hair, which is usually retained for about a month after birth. The skin, although used for clothing by the natives of Northern Greenland, is not so much valued as that of the Common Seal.

III. THE HARP-SEAL.   PHOCA GRŒNLANDICA.

Phoca grœnlandica, Fabricius, in Müller's Zool. Dan. Prodr. p.
 viii. (1766); Bell, British Quadrupeds, 2nd ed. p. 252
 (1874).
Callocephalus grœnlandicus, F. Cuvier, Dict. Sci. Nat. vol. xxxix.
 p. 545 (1826).
Pagophilus grœnlandicus, Gray, Cat. Seals and Whales Brit.
 Mus. p. 25 (1866).
 (*Plate XVIII.*)

Characters.—General colour tawny-grey or yellowish-white, sometimes spotted; males with a somewhat harp-shaped or crescentic blackish mark crossing the shoulders and extending down each flank, and the muzzle also dark-coloured. Cheek-teeth separated, and arranged in a straight line. Total length, from 4 to 5 feet.

The skull may be readily distinguished from that of either of the preceding species by the circumstance that the free hinder margin of the bony palate is almost entire, instead of being deeply and acutely notched; while the two branches of the lower jaw, in place of diverging at once, are nearly parallel in front.

According to Jukes, the young of the Harp-Seal are white until they are six or seven weeks old, during which period they are termed "White-coats" in Newfoundland; at the age of one year, small spots make their appearance, and in two years larger spots; while it is not till the third year that the males (then called "Saddle-backs") assume the characteristic dark harp-shaped markings.

HADD—1743.

Distribution.—As arctic in its distribution as the preceding species, the Harp, or, as it is often called, the Greenland Seal, is an equally rare and casual visitor to the British Islands, and, indeed, it is only recently that a skull has been definitely identified as pertaining to a British specimen. The general distribution of the species is the same as that of the Ringed Seal, since it occurs in the northern seas of both hemispheres. As regards its occurrence in Britain, two Seals killed in the Severn in 1836 were referred to this species by Bell, and although doubts were subsequently thrown on the correctness of this identification, the same gentleman maintained its

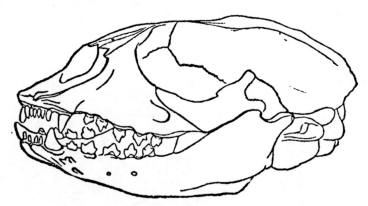

Skull of the Harp-Seal.

accuracy. Gray also identified with this species the skin of a young Seal taken in the Thames at Isleworth in 1858; and Macgillivray provisionally did the same with another from the Firth of Forth. More satisfactory is the evidence with regard to an immature Seal captured in Morecambe Bay in January, 1868, the skull of which is now preserved in the museum at Kendal; Sir William Turner (*Journ. Anatomy and Physiology*, vol. ix., p. 163) confidently assigning it to the species under consideration. Regarding its alleged occurrence in the Scottish Isles, Mr. H. D. Graham (*Proc. Nat. Hist. Soc. Glasgow*, vol. i.,

p. 53) gave an account of three Seals seen by himself in West
Loch Tarbet, off Jura, which he confidently identified with the
Harp-Seal; and three others have been reported from Loch
Scridain, in Mull.   Mr. Harvie-Brown records a Seal shot at
Kintradwell some time previous to 1870 as referable in all pro-
bability to this species; while he adds that one killed, although
lost, by himself in the Hebrides, was likewise a Harp-Seal.
Finally, a Seal shot in county Galway, about the year 1856,
is considered to indicate the right of this species to be included
in the list of Irish Mammals.

Habits.—Like the Ringed Seal, the Harp-Seal is found chiefly
on, or in the neighbourhood of, ice, frequenting both the solid
ice-fields and the detached floes.   It differs, however, from that
species in that it does not make a breathing-hole in the ice for
fishing.   Writing of its habits in Spitsbergen, Professor Alfred
Newton writes that the Harp-Seal "is of a sociable disposition,
and we saw it in herds of not less than fifty in number.   These
were very fond of swimming in line, their heads only above
water, engaged in a game of 'Follow-my-leader,' for, on the first
Seal making a roll over or a spring in the air, each Seal of the
whole procession on arriving at the same spot did the like, and
exactly in the same manner."   In addition to consuming large
quantities of Salmon and other fish, this Seal likewise feeds
upon molluscs and crustaceans.   During the month of March,
while on the field-ice, the female Seal gives birth to her offspring
which may be either one, two, or even, it is said, occasionally
three in number.   The white baby-coat is retained by the young
Seal for two or three weeks; and it is not till after losing this
that it takes to the water.

THE HOODED SEALS.   GENUS CYSTOPHORA.

Cystophora, Nilsson, Skandinav. Fauna vol. i. p. 382 (1820).

This genus differs from the two previously mentioned in that the incisor teeth are reduced to two pairs in the upper, and to a single pair in the lower jaw; the total number of teeth thus being only thirty. The cheek-teeth, with the usual exception of the last, are inserted in the jaws by a single root each; and the first and fifth toes of the hind-feet are much longer than the three middle ones, and are provided with small rudimental nails, while the webs connecting the toes project in the form of lobes considerably beyond the extremities of the latter. On the nose of the adult male is an inflatable sac lying beneath the skin, capable of being dilated so as to form a kind of hood extending backwards to cover the head.

HOODED SEAL. CYSTOPHORA CRISTATA.

Phoca cristata, Erxleben, Syst. Regne Animal. p. 590 (1777).
Cystophora cristata, Nilsson, Skandinav. Fauna, p. 327 (1820);
    Gray, Cat. Seals and Whales Brit. Mus. p. 41 (1866);
    Bell, British Quadrupeds, 2nd ed. p. 257 (1874).
Cystophora borealis, Nilsson, *op. cit.*, p. 383 (1820).
Stemmatopus cristatus, F. Cuvier, Dict. Sci. Nat. vol. xxxix.
    p. 551 (1826).

Characters.—In this, the only species of the genus, the general colour of the fur of the upper-parts is dark grey, marked with spots of a still deeper shade; the under-parts being lighter and uniform. Total length, from 7 to 10 feet.

Distribution.—This large and curious member of the Seal family is an inhabitant of the colder regions of the North Atlantic, although not extending to the extreme north, which probably accounts for its not being circum-polar. Migratory in its habits, occurring in South Greenland from April till June, and again making its appearance in August, some few individuals straggle as far south as Iceland and Northern Scandinavia, while still more rarely others make their appearance now and then on the coasts of Britain, or even of France. The first undoubted British example of this species was taken in the River Orwell during the summer of 1847 ; it was a very young animal, and its skin is preserved in the museum at Ipswich. A second young specimen was seen on a rock in the sea at St. Andrews in the summer of 1872, and was killed with stones. Other specimens are more or less vaguely reported to have been taken on the Scottish coasts ; while it is not improbable that a Seal seen many years ago near Westport, in Ireland, belonged to the present species.

Habits.—The Hooded, or, as it is often called, the Bladder-nosed Seal, is especially characterised by its migratory habits, to which allusion has already been made, and the extreme ferocity of its disposition. Not only do the males fight to-gether for the possession of females to add to their harem (this being one of the few species of true Seals which are polygamous), but when attacked on the ice they will boldly face their adversaries, instead of precipitately fleeing, after the general custom of their tribe. On such occasions the sac on the nose is inflated, as if with the purpose of terrifying the assailants. The chief food of this Seal is stated to consist of Cod and Flounders ; and the species spends the greater part of its time on the ice, upon which the young are born in the spring.

THE WALRUSES. FAMILY TRICHECHIDÆ.

The Walruses, of which there is but a single existing genus, differ structurally from the true Seals in that, when on land, the hind-flippers are bent forwards under the body, and aid in terrestrial progression ; this being a feature in which they resemble the Eared Seals (*Otariidæ*). In the absence of external ears they agree, however, with the true Seals. Their dentition, on the other hand, is quite unlike that of either of the other two Families of the sub-order, the upper canines forming enormous downwardly directed tusks, while all the other teeth are inserted by single roots, and have very simple crowns, which in those of the cheek-series are flattened.

TIIE WALRUSES. GENUS TRICHECIIUS.

Trichechus, Linn., Syst. Nat. ed. 12, vol. i. p. 49 (1766).

Size very large ; head rounded, with relatively small eyes, and the muzzle short and wide ; tail rudimental ; the five toes of the fore-feet of nearly equal length, and furnished with minute flattened nails ; in the hind-feet, the fifth toe slightly the largest, and, like the first, with a nail like those of the fore-feet, the nails of the three middle toes being long, narrow, and pointed ; the webs of the hind-feet projecting in advance of the toes in the form of lobes. In the adult only eighteen teeth, forming a pair of small incisors in the upper jaw, and another of enormous canines ; the lower canines being small, and very similar to the pre-molars, of which there are three pairs in each jaw.

THE WALRUS. TRICHECHUS ROSMARUS.

Trichechus rosmarus, Linn., Syst. Nat. ed. 12, vol. i. p. 49 (1766) ; Gray, Cat. Seals and Whales Brit. Mus. p. 36 (1866) ; Bell, British Quadrupeds, 2nd ed. vol. i. p. 269 (1874).

Rosmarus arcticus, Pallas, Zoogr. Rosso.-Asiat. vol. i. p. 269 (1811).

Odobœnus rosmarus, Allen (*ex* Malmgren), North American Pinnipeds, p. 23 (1880).

Characters·—Muzzle furnished on each side with a bunch of quill-like bristles ; hair short and closely pressed to the skin, of

5   M

a greyish-brown colour, but becoming lighter with age, and in very old individuals to a great extent disappearing, and leaving the body nearly naked. Total length, from 12 to 15 feet.

Distribution.—Essentially an inhabitant of the frozen regions of the north, the Walrus, or Morse, has but slight claim to be regarded as a British animal, so far at least as the historical period is concerned. Typically from the North Atlantic and Arctic Oceans, this species may probably be regarded as likewise an inhabitant of the North Pacific, since, in our

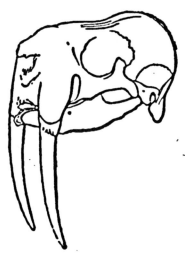

Skull of Walrus.

opinion, the view taken by the American naturalists that the Pacific Walrus is entitled to rank as a distinct species is untenable. Apart from certain early references to its reported occurrence on the coast of Scotland, the first definite record of the occurrence of the Walrus within our limits is one given by Macgillivray, who states that the example in question was shot while reposing on a rock at Caolas Stocnis, in the island of Harris, during the winter of 1817. This specimen, which was actually seen in the flesh by its describer, measured ten feet in length, and yielded two barrels of blubber. A second example was killed in the summer of 1825 on the island of Edday, in the Orkneys; while two years later a third is stated to have been seen in Hoy Sound. A fourth was killed in the spring of 1841 on the island of East Haskar, near Harris; while two others are reported to have been seen in the Orkneys—the one in 1857, and the other somewhere about the same date.

The discovery of a skull, now preserved in the Cambridge Museum, in the peat near Ely, would seem to indicate that in former times the Walrus not only visited the shores of the eastern coast, but that it ascended the larger rivers. Its former occurrence on the same coast is confirmed by a lower jaw dredged from the Dogger Bank (where teeth of the Mammoth are so commonly obtained), now in the British Museum.

At a still earlier epoch, when the climate was probably much colder than at the present day, Walruses (which have been referred to an extinct species) appear to have been by no means uncommon on our eastern coast, where they were doubtless resident. Fragments of the tusks of these animals have been disinterred not only from the so-called "forest-bed" of Cromer, in Norfolk, but likewise from the still older Red Crag of Suffolk and Essex, which belongs to the upper portion of the Pliocene epoch.

Habits.—In the case of animals like the Walrus, whose only claim to be regarded as British rests on the occurrence of some half-dozen stragglers which have wandered or been carried from their northern home, our notice of habits will be of the briefest. It may be mentioned, however, that Walruses are essentially gregarious animals, which in former days congregated on the ice or shores of the Arctic regions in herds often comprising hundreds of individuals. Their food consists mainly of molluscs and crustaceans, grubbed up from the mud by the aid of the tusks; and for crushing the hard shells of these the other teeth are most admirably adapted. Whether, as alleged, the tusks are also employed in aiding the creature to climb up on the ice, is a point in regard to which there is a difference of opinion among observers. The young, usually one, but occasionally two in number, are born on the ice from April to June, and are tended and defended by the female with remarkable solicitude and bravery.

THE RODENTS, OR GNAWING MAMMALS.
ORDER RODENTIA.

THE possession of a single pair of chisel-like incisor teeth in the lower jaw, which grow continuously throughout life, and are opposed by a similar pair of upper teeth, is of itself a sufficient character to distinguish the Rodents, or Gnawing Mammals, from all the other British representatives of the Class to which they belong. In the lower jaw only this single pair of incisors is developed, and the same is the case in the great majority of the members of the Order as regards the upper jaw, although in the Hares and Rabbits, as well as in their foreign cousins the Pikas, a small and functionless second pair of upper incisors is to be found behind the large ones. These chisel-like incisor teeth have, as an almost invariable rule, a coating of hard enamel only on their front surfaces, the result of which is that they have a cutting-edge formed and kept continually sharp by the action of gnawing food and other hard substances. Since these teeth form a segment of a circle and grow continuously throughout the life of their owner, if one by any chance happens to get broken it results that the opposing tooth, having nothing to wear against it, grows to a great length beyond the gums, curving round, and sometimes actually piercing the skull of its unfortunate owner. Although in many cases the enamel on the front of the incisor teeth of Rodents is of the ordinary white colour, in others it is stained some shade of yellow, brown, red, or even black.

Behind these incisors there occurs a long tooth-less gap, owing to the total want of canines. Then follow the cheek-teeth, which are generally only four in number on each side of both the upper and lower jaws, owing to the loss of the anterior pre-molars, there being never more than three pairs of the latter teeth, while in some cases they are totally wanting. The cheek-teeth have flattened crowns adapted for grinding ; and while in some cases these are surmounted by blunt tubercles, they are more generally inter-penetrated by in-folds of the enamel from the sides or summits, or both, by which in the worn state they are divided into laminæ, or have islands of enamel on the grinding surface.

The lower jaw is articulated to the skull by a knob, or condyle, elongated longitudinally, and thus permitting of the backwards-and-forwards "munching" movement so characteristic of these animals when eating.

The feet are either completely, or almost completely, plantigrade, and are usually furnished with five toes, generally armed with sharp claws, although in a few instances these terminal appendages partake more of the nature of hoofs. In nearly all cases collar-bones are present, although these may be incomplete, or even rudimentary. In no case is the socket for the eye in the skull surrounded by a ring of bone.

In number the Rodents exceed any other of the Mammalian Orders; and they have likewise a wider geographical distribution, being practically cosmopolitan and represented even in Australia. They are, however, by no means evenly spread over the globe, and attain their greatest development in South America. In accordance with this general numerical superiority, we find their British representatives exceeding in this respect the terrestrial members of any other Order belonging to our fauna.

With the exception of one South American species, existing Rodents are mostly animals of comparatively small size, many being very minute. Although some are aquatic, and others arboreal in their mode of life, the majority are terrestrial. By far the greater number are exclusively vegetable feeders, and there are scarcely any which do not eat vegetable food of some kind or other. Consequently they are, of all Mammals, the most harmful to the agriculturist.

Although the Order is divided into a very large number of Families, only four are now represented in the British Islands, two of which have but a single species each. Within the historic period a fourth Family—the Beavers—was, however, represented by its typical member within our area.

THE SQUIRRELS AND MARMOTS.
FAMILY SCIURIDÆ..

Confining our attention throughout our description to the British representatives of the Order, the Squirrels may be defined as Rodents with cylindrical hairy tails, having cheek-teeth furnished with roots and carrying tubercles on their crowns, and by the presence of two pairs of pre-molars in the upper, and one pair in the lower jaw, the first pair of upper pre-molars being, however, often minute, and not unfrequently shed at an early age.

With the exception of Australasia, this numerous Family is cosmopolitan in its distribution, and while its typical representatives—the Squirrels—are arboreal, the Marmots are terrestrial.

COMMON SQUIRREL.

THE TRUE SQUIRRELS. GENUS SCIURUS.

Sciurus, Linn., Syst. Nat. ed. 12, vol. i. p. 86 (1766).

Tail long and bushy ; ears generally well developed and often tufted ; feet adapted for climbing, the front pair with the first toe rudimentary. Teats four to six in number. First pair of upper pre-molar teeth minute, and frequently shed at an early state. Collar-bones complete.

THE COMMON SQUIRREL. SCIURUS VULGARIS.

Sciurus vulgaris, Linn., Syst. Nat. ed. 12, vol. i. p. 86 (1766) ;
Bell, British Quadrupeds, 2nd ed. p. 276 (1874).

(*Plate XIX.*)

Characters.—General colour brownish-red on the upper-parts, and white beneath; tail very bushy and coloured like the body ; ears tufted during a portion of the year; first upper pre-molar tooth frequently shed. Length of head and body, about 8⅓ inches ; of tail, exclusive of hair, 7 inches, with the hair, 8 inches.

The Squirrel is subject to certain variations of colour according to age and the time of the year, and there seems likewise to be some difference due to locality. After mentioning that the female is smaller, and generally of a lighter colour than the male, Macgillivray writes on this subject as follows :—In younger individuals the colour is redder than in adults, in which it is seldom destitute of a grey tinge ; "and I have seen some in which the grey predominated over the red. In April and May the hair of the upper-parts assumes a singularly faded appearance, losing its gloss and assuming a light yellowish tint. In the latter month the process of depilation commences, to be completed by the end of June, when the ears are destitute of tufts. It appears that the long hairs which fringe the ears are not proportionately longer than the rest until November, that they then gradually elongate, attain their extreme development in spring, and remain un-shed till June. In the northern regions of Europe the grey colour in winter is more decided, and the fur of denser and finer texture." Bell adds that towards the end of summer the tail not unfrequently becomes more or less decidedly cream-coloured. A variety inhabiting the Alps and Pyrenees is characterised by the back being dark brown, mottled with yellowish-white, while the under-parts are pure white.

Distribution.—The distribution of the common Squirrel is extensive, ranging from Ireland across Europe and Asia,

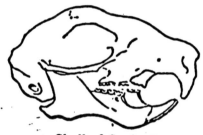

Skull of Squirrel.

north of the Himalaya as far as Japan, while in the opposite direction it embraces Northern Italy in the south and Lapland in the north. It will be obvious, however, that, from the nature of its habits, the animal is only found in more or less well-timbered districts. Throughout the whole of England the Squirrel appears to be pretty generally distributed in suitable localities. According to the Rev. H. A. Macpherson, there appears, however, to be some degree of probability that the existing breed has not inhabited the Lake district for much more than a century. Whether, however, the animal was originally indigenous to the district, and was destroyed by the felling of the forests, and afterwards again introduced, or whether it was originally unknown there, has not been decided.

Occurring throughout the lowlands, the Squirrel was formerly present in the north of Scotland, but, according to Mr. Harvie-Brown, appears to have become extinct towards the close of the last century—not improbably owing to the severe winter of 1795. In Sutherland it seems to have reappeared in 1859, but it was not till ten years later that, by the construction of a railway bridge, it was enabled to enter the east of that county. Since that date these animals have thriven and multiplied; although they are still unknown in Caithness, as they are in Argyllshire and the Hebrides. Apparently distributed over the whole or the greater part of Ireland, they seem to be in general less common there than in England; and it is not improbable that the species was introduced.

From the nature of its habits, remains of Squirrels are unlikely to be found in cavern-deposits, and it does not appear that any have hitherto been obtained therefrom. A limb-bone has, however, been disinterred from the "forest-bed" of the Norfolk coast, indicating the occurrence of the animal in our eastern forests at the comparatively remote epoch when that formation was deposited.

Habits.—Writing of its mode of life, Macgillivray observes :— "The agility of the Squirrel, its lively disposition, and beautiful form, render it a general favourite. It is amusing to watch it in its arboreal excursions, when you see it ascending the trunk and branches with surprising speed, running out even on slender twigs, always, when in motion, keeping its tail depressed, occasionally performing leaps from one branch to another, and when alarmed, scampering away at such a rate that you almost expect to see it miss its footing and fall down headlong. It feeds on nuts, beech-mast, acorns, buds, and the bark of young branches; generally, while eating, sitting on its haunches, with its tail elevated, holding the object between its paws, and

dexterously unshelling the kernel, from which it even removes
the outer pellicle before munching it. It does not reside
entirely on trees, but frequently resorts to the ground, where it
moves with nearly equal agility, leaping like a rabbit. The
female produces three or four young ones about Midsummer,
which are deposited in a nest, formed of moss, fibrous roots,
grass, and leaves, curiously interwoven, and placed in a hole,*
or in the fork between two large branches.

" In autumn it lays up a store of provisions for winter, but
usually in an irregular manner, depositing nuts in different
places in the ground, and in holes in trees. When the cold
weather commences, it becomes less active, and often dozes
for days in its retreat, but it does not become completely
torpid ; and I have seen it abroad in the midst of a most
severe snow-storm. If the weather be comparatively mild, it
exhibits its usual activity, feeding on ba.k and twigs."

The latter sentences of this account show conclusively that it
has long been a well-known fact that Squirrels do not hibernate
in the proper sense of the word, and, therefore, render superfluous a notice of a discussion which recently took place on
this subject in the pages of the *Zoologist.* One observer,
quoted by the Rev. H. A. Macpherson, states that even,
during the severe snow-storms in the spring of 1881, Squirrels
never failed to pay their accustomed daily visits to his house in
Cumberland ; while a second mentions that in the same county
he would feel sure of finding traces of these animals whenever
snow lies on the ground, adding that they dread damp and wet
far more than cold.

That the Squirrel is decidedly a harmful creature to the
owners of plantations, must, we think, be admitted ; since the

* With reference to this remark, Mr. Trevor-Battye writes :—" This, in
my experience, is not an unusual position for a nest, but a fir-tree bough is
much the commonest situation, though the nest is often found in a fork,
where the branches of a beech-tree separate off."

damage it does to the buds and bark of young trees, especially birch, sycamore, larch, and other conifers, is frequently very great. Mr. Harting states that " in plantations of Scotch fir, larch, and occasionally spruce, they attack the trees in spring, between April and June, when the sap is in full flow, biting off the outer bark and consuming the inner. This stops the flow of sap, which then becomes dry and resinous, and the first high wind blows the top off." Sometimes, indeed, the bark is peeled off in rings completely round the stems or branches of young trees, thus killing them at once.

In addition to the various kinds of vegetable food already mentioned, it has been ascertained that Squirrels will eat bilberries, truffles, and other fungi ; truffles being searched out by scent and dug out. Oak-galls seem to be rather a puzzle to Squirrels, which have been observed opening one after another of these growths, as if in search of a kernel, although it is just possible that grubs may have been the object. Less generally known is the fact, that these Rodents will devour both young birds and eggs ; such nests as are situated in holes of trees being, according to Mr. Harting, those most generally plundered. One instance is on record where a Squirrel was seen to kill and partially eat a fully-fledged Starling ; while in another case one out of a flock of Sparrows was the victim. This carnivorous habit, however, is only a depraved taste on the part of certain individuals, as when a Kestrel visits the Pheasant-coops.

As is well-known, if taken at a sufficiently early age, Squirrels can be readily tamed and domesticated, when they form interesting and amusing little pets.

Formerly, according to Mr. Poland, the fur of the common Squirrel was at one time largely employed in England for boas, no less than two-and-three-quarter millions of skins having been imported in the year 1839. Since that date, however, the trade has gradually declined, and is now mainly carried on in Germany. The backs are used for several purposes, the whitish under-parts are employed for the linings of cloaks, while the tails are used in the manufacture of boas, and also as trimmings. The so-called "Camels'-hair" paint-brushes are likewise made from Squirrel's hair.

THE BEAVERS. FAMILY CASTORIDÆ.

The members of this Family are aquatic Rodents, differing from the *Sciuridæ* in having but a single pair of pre-molars in each jaw, and in all the cheek-teeth being rootless and having re-entering foldings of enamel on their crowns, which become perfectly flat by wear; while, in the one existing genus, at least, the tail is broad, depressed, and naked, and the hind-feet are webbed. Moreover, the skull is devoid of projecting processes on its upper surface defining the hinder border of the socket of the eye.

GENUS CASTOR.

Castor, Linn., Syst. Nat. ed. 12, vol. i. p. 78 (1766).

Upper molar teeth sub-equal in size, with one fold of enamel on the inner, and three on the outer side. Form massive; fur soft and thick; tail as above; hind-feet with an additional rudimentary claw on the second toe.

THE EUROPEAN BEAVER. CASTOR FIBER.

Castor fiber, Linn., Syst. Nat. ed. 12, vol. i. p. 78 (1766).
Castor fossilis, Goldfuss, Nova Acta. Ac. Cæs. Leop.-Car. vol. xi. p. 488 (1823).
Castor europæus, Owen, Brit. Foss. Mamm. p. 190 (1846).

Characters.—Since the Beaver is no longer an inhabitant of the British Isles, it will be unnecessary to describe it, and it will suffice to point out that it differs from the North American Beaver (*C. canadensis*) by the greater length of the nasal bones of the skull, which extend upwards beyond the line of the anterior border of the sockets of the eyes.

Distribution.—The Beaver was formerly distributed over the greater part of Europe, and extending from the British Islands through France, Germany, Austria, Russia, Poland, and Livonia, to Lapland, and thence through the Scandinavian Peninsula, but, through incessant persecution, it has been exterminated from most of its ancient haunts, although solitary individuals, or small colonies, are still met with in certain parts of the Continent. It might have been supposed that, in the remote regions of the north, the animal would still flourish in numbers, although such appears not to be the case, the last known Lapland Beaver having been killed previously to 1830. There is, however, still a thriving colony in Norway. In Northern Russia the rivers Dwina and Petchora, respectively discharging into the White Sea and the Arctic Ocean, were the resort of Beavers as late as 1842, but there appear to be none left now. Formerly extending as far east as Amurland, in the basin of the Ob, in Western Siberia, they are exterminated in the valley of the Irtish, although they lingered in the tributary of the Ob, known as the Pelyin, up to 1876. From the Yenisei, in Eastern Siberia, they have completely disappeared ; but information is required with regard to the Lena.

In the British Isles the Beaver has long since been as completely exterminated as the Wolf and the Bear, although evidence of its former existence within the historic period is afforded either by the names of places or documentary records or tradition ; while the abundance of semi-fossilised remains attests its existence in still earlier epochs. For most of this evidence naturalists are indebted to the researches of Mr. J. E. Harting

Of its existence within the historic period in England, there appears to be neither documentary nor oral evidence; and we are therefore compelled to rely on the circumstantial evidence of place-names. Among these, may be mentioned Beverage in Worcestershire, Bevercater in Nottinghamshire, Beverley in Yorkshire, Beverstone in Gloucestershire, and Beversbrook in Wiltshire. Moreover, about a mile to the north of Worcester a small brook enters the Severn known as Barbourne, or Beaverbourne, while near by is an island known as Beaver Island, and higher up the river a second island called Beverege, or Beaverage, likewise giving the name to an adjoining hamlet, which is the one alluded to above.

Turning to Wales, we find Beavers' skins mentioned in the year 940 among the laws of Howel Dha; while Giraldus in 1188 makes reference to the fact that Beavers were then living in one of the rivers of Cardiganshire. It may be added that the name of Llyn-yr-Afange, which is said to be applied to more than one piece of water in the Principality, means the Beavers' lake.

With regard to Scotland, the historic evidence is unfortunately somewhat doubtful. Giraldus states, indeed, from hearsay, that Beavers were still occasionally seen in his time in Loch Ness, and Boethius made a similar statement in 1527; but Alston considered that by this date the Beaver had ceased to exist in Scotland. That it will flourish there, is demonstrated by the colony introduced by the Marquis of Bute into the island from which he takes his title.

If the foregoing evidence is scant and somewhat unsatisfactory, the semi-fossilised remains of the Beaver found in many parts of England, and also in the south of Scotland, afford conclusive testimony as to its former abundance. In various superficial deposits, such as the fens of Cambridgeshire and Lincolnshire, the turbaries of the Lea valley at Walthamstow in Essex, such remains are of more or less common occurrence, and are frequently found in a fine state of preservation. Some of these deposits, such as those of the Thames valley, undoubtedly belong to the Pleistocene period, but at least a portion of the fen-peat may be pretty safely assigned to the pre-historic epoch. The counties from which such remains have been obtained include Berkshire, Berwickshire, Cambridgeshire, Dumfriesshire, Essex, Hampshire, Lincolnshire, Norfolk, Perthshire, Roxburghshire, Wiltshire, and Yorkshire. Remains of the Beaver have likewise been obtained from Kent's Hole, near Torquay, in company with those of the Mammoth, Hairy Rhinoceros, and other extinct animals ; and likewise from the so-called " forest-bed " of the Norfolk coast.

In the case of Ireland, we have neither the evidence of history nor of fossil remains, and it is therefore quite likely that the range of the Beaver never included that island.

Following our general rule with regard to exterminated species, we shall not give any account of the habits of the Beaver. It may be mentioned, however, that the use of the additional claw on the second toe of the hind-foot is at present quite unknown, and that those who have an opportunity of observing the American Beaver in its native haunts will do good service by ascertaining what this may be.

. THE DORMICE. FAMILY MYOXIDÆ.

The Dormice are small arboreal Rodents, with long Squirrel-like tails, large ears and eyes, and short fore-limbs, and may be distinguished from all other British representatives of the Order by having a single pair of pre-molars in each jaw, and by all the cheek-teeth being rooted, and having their crowns interpenetrated by transverse enamel-folds, which in some cases assume a very complicated pattern. Internally these Rodents are distinguished from all other members of the Order by the circumstance that the intestine is devoid of a blind appendage or cæcum. The collar-bones are well-developed, and the first toe of the foot is rudimentary.

Dormice are found only in Africa, Europe, and Asia north of the Himalaya. Although not numerous in species, they have been divided into several genera; but on the whole, it seems preferable to retain only the under-mentioned one for the common Dormouse, and to refer the whole of the remaining members of the Family to the typical genus, *Myoxus*.

GENUS MUSCARDINUS.

Muscardinus, Kaup, Nat. Syst. Europ. Thierwelt, p. 136 (1829).

Tail cylindrical: cheek-teeth with flat crowns and complex infoldings of enamel; lower end of the œsophagus thickened and glandular.

COMMON DORMOUSE. MUSCARDINUS AVELLANARIUS.

Mus avellanarius, Linn., Syst. Nat. ed. 12, vol. i. p. 83 (1766).

Myoxus muscardinus, Schreber, Säugethiere, vol. iv. p. 835 (1792).

Myoxus avellanarius, Desmarest, Mammalogie, p. 295 (1820); Bell, British Quadrupeds, 2nd ed. p. 281 (1874).

Muscardinus avellanarius, Kaup, Nat. Syst. Europ. Thierwelt, p. 139 (1829); Flower, Cat. Osteol. Mus. R. Coll. Surgeons, pt. ii. p. 603 (1884).

(*Plate XX.*)

Characters.—General form rather stout; colour of upper-parts light tawny, beneath paler and yellowish; an elongated white patch on the throat and front of chest; tail rather shorter than head and body. Length of head and body, about 3 inches; of tail, 2½ inches.

DORMOUSE.

This beautiful little animal, with its prominent black eyes, has a rather large head, a pointed muzzle, and rounded ears, which are equal to about one-third of the head in length. Both fore- and hind-feet are adapted for grasping, and although in the former the first toe, as in the Squirrel, is rudimentary, in the hind-foot all five toes are well developed.

Distribution.—The Common Dormouse is distributed over the greater part of Europe, although not apparently ranging any distance into Northern Asia, even if it occurs there at all, and is the only British representative of the Family. In many continental countries the Fat Dormouse, or "Loire" (*Myoxus glis*), is, however, much more abundant than the present species, which is known in France as the "Loirot." Generally found in woods, plantations, or hedge-rows, but occasionally met with in open fields, the Dormouse appears to be spread over the southern and central districts of England, although much more abundant in some localities than others. In the writer's experience, one of the districts where it may be found in great numbers is the country on the borders of Hertfordshire and Buckinghamshire, between Hemel-Hempsted and Aylesbury, where one or more nests are almost sure to be met with, even in the open country, during a day's shooting. In the Lake district, according to the Rev. H. A. Macpherson, it occurs locally in the more thickly-planted portions of the country, but has not been detected in the eastern parts of Cumberland and Westmoreland. In Scotland, certainly so far as the north is concerned, it appears to be unknown, and it is also stated by Thompson to be wanting in Ireland.

Habits.—Deriving its specific name from its fondness for hazel-nuts, the Dormouse is especially partial to oak-woods with an undergrowth of hazels. In the stumps of the latter its winter-nest is very generally made, although, as already said,

5   N

this may be situated on the ground in an open field, while instances are on record where the deserted nest of a Thrush or Blackbird has been taken possession of and fitted up to suit the requirements of its new occupants. In addition to nuts, its food, according to Mr. Harting, comprises "acorns, seeds of the hornbeam and other forest-trees, grain, and fruit of different kinds, particularly grapes. In confinement, a bit of apple or pear is generally eaten with relish. The Dormouse will also suck the eggs of small birds, as a Squirrel will do, and it seems to be not generally known that it is insectivorous." In evidence of the latter habit the author quoted states that captive specimens have been known to eat aphides, nut-weevils, and caterpillars of various kinds.

Although so much resembling a diminutive Squirrel, both in form and habits, sitting up on its haunches and grasping its food with its fore-paws in true Squirrel-like fashion, the Dormouse is structurally much more nearly allied to the Mice, and its resemblance to the former animal is doubtless due to adaptation to a similar mode of life. Confirmation of this is afforded by the circumstance that certain arboreal Mice are exceedingly Dormouse-like in appearance.

The most remarkable peculiarity connected with the habits of the Dormouse is the length of time occupied by its hibernation, which sometimes extends uninterruptedly over a period of as much as six months. That this hibernation is, however, generally broken, is indicated by the circumstance that the Dormouse lays up a winter-store of provision; and, according to Bell, an unusually mild day is sufficient to waken the little creature from its slumbers, when it consumes a portion of its hoard, and once more curls itself to resume its sleep. Extremely fat at the commencement of its hibernation, by the time spring comes round the creature is much reduced in bulk. While adult Dormice commence their hibernation as early as the middle of October, the young ones are much later in retiring from active participation in the affairs of the world. A full account of the hibernation of the Dormouse will be found in the *Zoologist* for 1882, in which the variation in its temperature, its loss of fat, and the number of respirations during its sleep, as well as the length of the period of torpidity, are fully recorded.

The female Dormouse gives birth to her offspring in the spring, and the young, usually four in number, are born blind, but open their eyes in a few days, and are very speedily able to shift for themselves. Bell gives reasons for believing that in some cases a second litter may be produced in the autumn. In the first dress the young are of a mouse-grey colour, except on the head and flanks ; and it is only gradually that the reddish-brown hue of the adult is required.

If a sleeping Dormouse be found during the winter, and taken to a warm room, it soon awakens,* but after a short interval relapses into torpidity. Writing many years ago, Mr. Salmon observes that on one occasion he chanced to find "a little ball of grass curiously interwoven, lying on the ground. It was about eight inches in circumference, and on taking it up I soon ascertained, by the faint sound emitted from the interior on my handling it, that it contained a prisoner. I bore my prize homeward for examination, and on making a slight opening, immediately issued forth one of those beautiful little creatures, the Dormouse. The heat of my hand and the warmth of the room had completely revived it from its torpor. It appeared to enjoy its transition by nimbly scaling every part of the furniture in all directions. It experienced no difficulty in either ascending or descending the polished backs of the

---

* Mr. Trevor-Battye says that if warmed suddenly into waking, a Dormouse will die at the end of a minute or two, its heart beating with extreme rapidity, like a clock " running down."

chairs, and when I attempted to secure it, it leaped from chair to chair with astonishing agility for so small a creature. On taking it into my hand, it showed not the least disposition to resent the liberty; on the contrary, it was very docile. On being set at liberty, it sprang at least two yards on to a table. In the evening I placed my little stranger, with its original domicile, in a box, of which on the following morning I found it had taken possession, and again relapsed into a state of torpidity."

Even if fully adult when captured, Dormice are readily tamed; and in this state form, it is almost superfluous to add, favourite pets of children.

THE MICE AND VOLES. FAMILY MURIDÆ.

The members of this extensive and cosmopolitan Family differ from all the other British representatives of the Rodents, in having only three pairs of cheek-teeth in each jaw, owing to the absence of pre-molars. These molar teeth are very variable in structure, being sometimes furnished with roots and sur-mounted with tubercles, while in other cases they grow through-out life and thus never develop roots, while their tall crowns are divided into semi-detached prisms by angular infoldings of enamel. The first toe of the fore-foot is rudimentary; the tail is generally nearly naked and scaly; and complete collar-bones are present. The general bodily form of the more typical members of the family is so well known that the term "rat-like" forms a recognised standard of comparison in zoo-logical, if not in popular, language.

The British representatives of the Family are divided into two great sections or sub-families, readily distinguished by the character of their molar teeth; the first of these including the

Mice and Rats, and the second the Voles. In Britain each section is represented by a single genus only, although there are several other foreign genera in both.

In habits the majority of the British forms are mainly terrestrial, although one species is aquatic, and all are able to climb with more or less facility.

THE MICE AND RATS. GENUS MUS.

Mus, Linn., Syst. Nat. ed. 12, vol. i. p. 79 (1766).

Molar teeth furnished with roots and surmounted by tubercles ; the latter forming three longitudinal rows in the teeth of the upper jaw ; incisors narrow, and devoid of grooves on their front surfaces. Eyes and ears large ; extremity of muzzle naked ; first rudimentary toe of fore-foot with a short nail in place of a claw ; tail long, tapering, and nearly naked, with overlapping scales arranged in rings ; fur soft, and (in British species) without an intermixture of spines.

Light and active in their movements, and bright-eyed in appearance, the Mice and Rats, in addition to the distinctive character of their molar teeth, are specially distinguished from their British allies by their pointed muzzles, long scaly tails, and large ears. Purely terrestrial in their habits, they generally frequent houses, farm-buildings, stables, and corn-ricks, rather than the open fields, although the Harvest-Mouse is to a certain extent an exception to this rule.

The genus includes a larger number of species than any other in the whole Mammalian class, and, with the remarkable exception of Madagascar, is distributed over the whole of the Old World. Its head-quarters are, however, the Tropical Regions of that Hemisphere, whence there is a gradual diminution in the number of species, as we proceed north and south, till, in the Sub-Arctic region, they become very few.

I. THE HARVEST-MOUSE.   MUS MINUTUS.

Mus minutus, Pallas, Reise, vol. i. Append. p. 454 (1778);
    Bell, British Quadrupeds, 2nd ed. p. 286 (1874).
Mus messorius, Shaw, Gen. Zool. vol. ii. p. 62 (1801).

(*Plate XXI.*)

Characters.—Size very small; tail and ears relatively short,
the latter being about one-third the length of the head;
colour of upper-parts yellowish-red, that of under-parts white;
the line of demarcation between the two being sharply defined.
Length of head and body about 2½ inches; of tail nearly
the same.   The general form is rather more slender than in
most members of the genus, and the head is rather narrow,
with the eyes somewhat less prominent than is usually the
case.

Distribution.—Ranging over the greater part of Europe with
the exception of the extreme north, the Harvest-Mouse is an
inhabitant of most districts in England, although much more
abundant in some than in others.   In the Lake district, it appears
to have been only observed on two occasions, which leads the
Rev. H. A. Macpherson to suggest that in both cases it had been
accidentally introduced, and that it is not truly indigenous.
In Leicester and Rutland, it is stated by Mr. Montagu Browne
to be rare; and the writer has never observed it in the district of Hertfordshire where he resides.   On the other hand,
in Cambridgeshire, Devonshire, Gloucestershire, Hampshire
(where it was first recorded by Gilbert White as a member of
the British fauna), Warwickshire, and Wiltshire, it seems to
be fairly abundant.   In Scotland it has been recorded by
Macgillivray from Aberdeenshire, Fifeshire, and near Edinburgh, but is unknown in the more northern counties.   Although not definitely recorded by Thompson from Ireland,
it has been subsequently stated to exist there, but the writer

PLATE XXI.

is informed by Mr. A. G. More that its reputed occurrence is based on young specimens of the Wood-Mouse.

Habits.—Next to the Lesser Shrew, the smallest of British terrestrial Mammals, the Harvest-Mouse differs from the other British representatives of its genus in not frequenting gardens, or the neighbourhood of houses or other buildings, although it is often found in corn-ricks, to which it is carried in the sheaves of wheat. After mentioning his discovery of a nest in Fifeshire, Macgillivray states that this "was composed of dry blades of coarse grass, arranged in a globular form, and placed in the midst of a tuft of *Aira cæspitosa*, at the distance of about nine inches from the ground. It contained six or seven naked and blind young ones. The young are said to vary from five to nine ; and as it litters several times in the season, it is occasionally numerous in corn-fields, on hedge-banks, and in dry pastures. Its food consists of seeds, especially of corn and grass, insects, and worms. In wheat-stacks it is often found in great abundance, but in general it forms burrows in the ground, in which it deposits provisions for the winter. Bingley relates that he fed one with insects, which it always preferred to any other food ; and the individual represented in the plate, here reproduced, devoured an earth-worm, which at first, by twisting round its body, upset it. Like the other species, it may be kept in confinement, but is said not to become so familiar as the Wood-Mouse."

In connection with the latter point, it may be mentioned that Mr. Harting has been successful in getting these pretty little creatures to breed in captivity, and also to rear their young ones, which became so tame as to allow themselves to be handled without attempting to bite, and also to take food from their owner's hand.

As a general rule, the nest is built between three or four

corn-stalks, to which it is firmly attached, at some little distance from the ground; and so compact and firm in its structure, that, as Gilbert White tells us, when detached, it may be rolled, with its living freight, across a table without sustaining the slightest damage.   So light is the Harvest-Mouse—its weight being only about one-fifth of an ounce—that it can ascend a wheat-stalk and feast on the corn in the ear; its descent being facilitated by its partially prehensile tail.   In possessing an imperfect power of prehension in that appendage, the creature is unique among British Mammals.   The nest generally has a small aperture on one side, through which the female gains access to her young; this aperture being carefully closed during her absence.   Since, in a short time after birth, the young, when numerous, more or less completely fill the nest, it would appear impossible for the female to pass the periods of repose within it.

II.   THE WOOD-MOUSE.   MUS SYLVATICUS.

Mus sylvaticus, Linn., Syst. Nat. ed. 12, vol. i. p. 84 (1766); Bell, British Quadrupeds, 2nd ed. p. 293 (1874).

(*Plate XXII.*)

Characters.—Size small; ears more than half the length of the head; tail nearly as long as the head and body; colour of upper-parts bright reddish-grey; under-parts whitish, with a patch of light brownish on the breast.   Length of head and body about 4⅙ inches; of tail nearly the same.

Resembling the Common Mouse very closely, as regards form, but slightly exceeding it in size, the Wood-Mouse may be readily distinguished by its coloration and longer tail, as well as by its very long hind-feet, which are white.   It is very generally known as the Long-tailed Field-Mouse, but since the term "Field-Mouse," with or without a prefix, is applied indifferently to this

WOOD - MOUSE.

species and to the Voles, we prefer the use of the name Wood-Mouse.

Distribution.—The general distribution of this species is probably very similar to that of the Harvest-Mouse, although, perhaps, it may not range as far north as Siberia, where the latter is found. In the British Islands it is universally distributed, its range including the Inner and Outer Hebrides and the whole of Ireland. Many years ago the late Rev. Leonard Jenyns (Blomefield), called attention to a small dark variety from the mountains of Kerry, which it was thought might prove to be a distinct species.

Habits.—Although its name would imply that woods were the favourite resorts of this species, yet, as a matter of fact, it is more commonly found, during the summer, in thickets, hedges, corn-fields, and gardens; while in winter it resorts for shelter to barns or other out-buildings, as well as corn-stacks; and Thompson records an instance where a specimen was taken in an inhabited house in Belfast.

Feeding on corn of all kinds, as well as bulbs, nuts, acorns, and various smaller seeds, together with insects and grubs, the Wood-Mouse is an unmitigated nuisance to the farmer and gardener; the amount of good it does by the consumption of such animal food as it devours, going but a small way towards recompensing the damage it inflicts on newly-sown crops of all kinds. Moreover, although this Mouse makes a regular winter retreat, it does not become torpid,—or at all events does so only for very short periods—and consequently needs a large supply of food during the cold season, so that the unfortunate farmer or gardener has to support the creature from one year's end to another. As a rule, the retreat takes the form of a burrow in the ground; but instances are on record where deserted birds' nests have been occupied and fitted up, while regular nests are often made in hedge-banks, or even in

standing grass. At other times old Mole-runs are selected as
dwelling places. In such safe retreats, of whatever nature
they may be, the Wood-Mouse during the summer and autumn
accumulates enormous stores of provender for its winter consumption; acorns, beech-mast, nuts, peas, beans, and corn,
being gathered in by the pint. It is not only the loss of
these various seeds that the farmer has to deplore, for, in
districts and seasons when Wood-Mice are very abundant,
pigs learn to hunt for and root up these hidden stores, and
may then do much damage, both to pasture and arable land.

Breeding several times in a season, after a gestation of only
three weeks, and producing from five to seven young in a
litter, the Wood-Mouse is one of the most prolific of Rodents,
famous as are many of these animals for their rapidity of increase. Some idea of the rate at which they propagate may
be gathered from some interesting observations published by
Mr. R. M. Barrington in the *Zoologist* for 1881, by whom
several of these Mice were kept in captivity. It is probable,
however, that the number of young in a litter would not be so
large as in the wild state. One of these captive specimens,
when about five and a half months old, gave birth to a litter of
three on the 7th or 8th of March. Observation was kept on
this female (A), and a second one (B), with the following
result :—

					Interval since last litter.
March 7 or 8	...	A	...	3 young ...	—
,, 19	...	B	...	5 ,, ...	—
,, 31	...	A	...	3 ,, ...	24 days
April 18	...	B	...	5 ,, ...	29 ,,
,, 24	...	A	...	3 ,, ...	24 ,,
May 11	...	B	...	5 ,, ...	23. ,,
,, 17	...	A	...	4 ,, ...	23 ,,
June 12	...	A (?)	...	4 ,, ...	26 ,,
July 9	...	A (?)	...	4 ,, ...	27 ,,

Had not one of the adult females made its escape in the beginning of June this record of the number of young produced by a couple of Wood-Mice in less than five months would probably have been still larger. "During April," writes the narrator, "we had twelve to twenty Mice, young and old, in the nest; they all slept together, and it was certainly a curious sight to see fathers, mothers, and children of all ages and sizes in the nest, the young of different ages suckling the same mother at the same time, and the mothers appearing to suckle each other's young indiscriminately."

To counteract this extreme prolificness, it is fortunate that the Wood-Mouse has a large number of enemies. Foremost amongst these are Kestrels, Owls, Stoats, and Weasels; while many of these Mice are killed by Foxes, which seem especially fond of them and their cousins the Voles. Rooks and Crows are also stated to aid in the extermination of these pests by digging up the nests and young with their strong beaks; while several other of the larger birds probably occasionally assist in the destruction.

Mr. Trevor-Battye writes :—" In the dry summer of 1893 the Black-headed Gulls breeding on Scoulton Mere (as I was assured by the keeper), frequently brought 'Mice' to their nests, killing them by dropping them from a height. The Mice were probably of this species."

The Wood-Mouse is as readily tamed as the Dormouse, and will soon learn to permit itself to be handled without resentment, although it always displays considerable timidity. Specimens have been kept in confinement for upwards of two years.

It may be mentioned that some imperfect lower jaws obtained from the "forest-bed" of the Norfolk coast are apparently referable to the present species.

III. THE YELLOW-NECKED MOUSE. MUS FLAVICOLLIS.

Mus flavicollis, Melchior, Danske Pattedyr. 1834, p. 99.

Characters.—Differs from *M. sylvaticus* in having a broad
yellow band across the breast, and it is larger and handsomer
than that species, the colours of the upper and under surface
being separated by a sharp line; while the belly is of a purer
white. Length of head and body, 4½ inches; tail about the
same.

Distribution.—This Mouse, first recorded as a British species
by Mr. W. E. de Winton in the *Zoologist* for December,
1894 (p. 441), is exceedingly abundant in Herefordshire.

IV. THE COMMON MOUSE. MUS MUSCULUS.

Mus musculus, Linn., Syst. Nat. ed. 12, vol. i. p. 83 (1766);
Bell, British Quadrupeds, 2nd ed. p. 297 (1874).

Characters.—Size as in the Wood-Mouse; ears about half the
length of the head; tail rather shorter than the head and body;
general colour greyish-brown above, becoming lighter beneath.
Length of head and body, about 3½ inches; of tail, 3¼ inches.

Although greyish-brown is the usual colour of the fur of the
Common Mouse, there is considerable individual variation in
this respect, some specimens being much darker than others,
with the fur of the back almost black; while in others white
hairs are interspersed, and in some cases the whole colour
may be pale grey. Pied Mice, in which the colours are dark
brown and white, or a larger or smaller admixture of white
with the ordinary greyish-brown hair, are also known; and
there is likewise a pale buff variety. In addition to these,
there are the so-called White Mice, which are true albinos,
having pink eyes, and the fur of a yellowish-white colour.
These albinos, as well as some of the pied races, will breed

true for many generations, if not permanently. There is likewise some variation in size.

With a tapering head and rather pointed muzzle, the Common Mouse has smaller eyes and ears than the Wood-Mouse, the latter being rounded, and also shorter and narrower than in that species; the limbs, tail, and whiskers are likewise relatively shorter than in the allied form.

Distribution.—Although it has received a large number of synonyms, to which it is unnecessary to allude here, it appears that the Common Mouse has a practically cosmopolitan range, at least so far as regions inhabited by Man are concerned. At one time, indeed, it was thought that the Indian Mouse was a distinct species, but this has now been shown not to be the case. It is, however, somewhat curious that, according to Mr. Blanford, there are certain parts of India, namely, the Punjab, Sind, Rajputana, and portions of the North-West Provinces, where the Common Mouse is totally unknown.

That the species had not originally its present cosmopolitan distribution, and that it has spread *pari passu*, with the advance of Man, may be taken for granted. Which country constituted its original home, it seems, however, quite impossible to decide. It has been frequently urged that the Common Mouse is a comparatively late immigrant into the British Islands, but if palæontologists are right in assigning to it certain fossilised remains found in the Pleistocene deposits of the Thames Valley and some of the English caves, it is quite certain that this cannot be the case.

Habits.—In the case of such a familiar animal as the Common Mouse, it is unnecessary to say much in the way of its habits, and we therefore content ourselves with quoting Macgillivray's account, premising that, although generally found in human habitations, the creature also sometimes frequents gardens and fields in the neighbourhood of towns and villages. Macgillivray observes that, in spite of its sombre coloration, the activity of this little creature and its graceful movements render it not uninteresting to the observant naturalist. " It is pleasant to sit quietly at midnight watching one which has ventured from its retreat and stolen to the hearth in quest of crumbs. It glides along, now slowly, now by sudden starts, and on finding some fragment of food, sits on its haunches, lays hold of it in its fore-feet, and raising it up, nibbles it, or, if apprehensive of danger, runs off with it to its hole. Although extremely timid, Mice sometimes exhibit considerable boldness, and venture quite close to a person who does not molest them. Their agility is astonishing, and to escape when pursued they perform extraordinary feats. I have seen one leap from the top of a stair-case upon a table, a distance of twelve feet, apparently without receiving any injury. If seized in the hand they bite severely, but if caught by the tail and thus suspended, are unable to turn upon their persecutor. Although when in small numbers they are scarcely injurious to a house, yet, owing to their fecundity, they soon become very destructive, devouring meal, flour, bread, cheese, butter, tallow, in short, almost every article of food that comes in their way, and often gnawing clothes, leather, and furniture. Their great enemy, the Cat, is not always able to extirpate them, so that the additional aid of traps and poison is required. The ravages of this species are not confined to houses, for it often betakes itself to the fields, and nestles in the corn-stacks, which are found towards the base traversed by its tortuous runs. The ground beneath is also filled with them, and on removing a stack numbers almost incredible are often met with. Besides Man, and his allies, the Cat, the Dog, and the Ferret, the Mouse has many powerful enemies, all of which, however, are unable to extirpate it, for it litters many times in the year, producing from five to

BLACK RAT

seven at a birth, and thus in favourable localities soon increases to a great extent. Its nest is composed of straw, hay, woollen cloth, linen, and other substances, generally gnawed into small fragments; and the young are at first blind and naked, but grow so rapidly that in a fortnight they are able to shift for themselves."

To this it may be added that subsequent observations have shown that the number of young in a litter may vary from four to seven, and that the female commences to breed considerably before a year old.

When poisoned in houses, both Rats and Mice have an unpleasant habit of retiring behind skirting-boards, canvased walls, and similar situations, to die. To detect their exact position when this happens, the best plan is to close the door and windows, and to introduce into the room two or three bluebottle flies, which will soon settle on the spot behind which lies the defunct Rodent.

V. THE BLACK RAT. MUS RATTUS.

Mus rattus, Linn., Syst. Nat. ed. 12, vol. i. p. 83 (1766): Bell, British Quadrupeds, 2nd ed. p. 302 (1874); Blanford, Mamm. Brit. India, p. 406 (1891).

Mus alexandrinus, Geoffroy, Descr. de l'Egypte, vol. ii. p. 753 (1812).

Mus rufescens, Gray, Mag. Nat. Hist. vol. i. p. 585 (1837).

Mus nitidus, Gray, Ann. Mag. Nat. Hist. vol. xv. p. 267 (1845); &c., &c., &c.

(*Plate XXIII.*)

Characters.—Size large; build relatively light; head slender ears large; tail thin and exceeding the head and body in length. In the typical English variety the fur of the upperparts is greyish-black, and below ash-colour. Size very variable;

in the English variety, length of head and body about 7 inches; of tail, 7½ inches.

Having a wide geographical range, the Black Rat is an exceedingly variable species, and, as is usually the case in such instances, has received an almost bewildering number of aliases. In addition to the typical form alluded to above, the following more important varieties may be noticed.

The Alexandrine Rat (*Mus alexandrinus*), from Southern Europe, Egypt, Palestine, and Gilgit, is a southern variety characterised by its softer reddish or greyish fur, and by the under-parts being usually white.

A third variety is the Tree-Rat (*Mus rufescens*), from India, Ceylon, and Burma, which is very similar to the preceding, but of inferior dimensions.

Next we have the Hill-Rat (*Mus nitidus*), from Nipal and Sikhim, distinguished by its shorter tail.

More remarkable than all is the Andamanese Rat (*Mus andamanensis*), distinguished from the Tree-Rat by the intermixture of a number of spines with the fur. From the characters of the skull, which can alone be relied upon in distinguishing allied *Muridæ*, Mr. Thomas has, however, shown conclusively that this form cannot be specifically separated from the Black Rat.

Distribution.—The distribution of the typical variety of the Black Rat has been pretty fully worked out by Mr. J. E. Harting, who has devoted a chapter in a volume entitled "Essays on Sport and Natural History" to this species. It appears to be spread over the greater part of Europe, with the exception of the extreme north, being unknown in Lapland. In Sweden, where it was formerly plentiful, it seems to be now nearly exterminated; and the same is stated to be the case in most parts of Germany, although in certain districts it has been reported to be on the increase. In France and Spain we know little more than that it is uncommon; while in Southern Italy it has been driven away by the Alexandrine Rat. In Northern Africa and Egypt, on the other hand, it appears still to hold its own. Further eastward it becomes more rare, but it occurs in the Caucasus, Georgia, and the Caspian district; while it has been introduced by vessels into parts of India, the Philippines, and even New Zealand. It was introduced into the New World about 1554, and is now found in both continents, as it is in the West Indies.

That the Black Rat was introduced into Britain from the Continent, appears to be evident from the circumstance that it is not mentioned as occurring here previous to the fifteenth century, coupled with the fact that its remains are unknown in the English cavern-deposits. It would seem, however, that subsequently to its introduction it became pretty generally distributed in England and Wales until routed out by the Brown Rat, and was known even in the Orkneys. There, however, it is now completely exterminated, as it is in most districts of our area. In Argyllshire and Caithness it is unknown, but one specimen was taken in Sutherland in 1879; while a small colony was observed near Pitlochry in 1860, and specimens are occasionally taken in old houses in Edinburgh. Unknown in Northumberland, a colony existed in 1879 at Stockton-on-Tees, in Durham; and in 1883 it was stated still to linger among the farms of Westmoreland. It would be tedious to mention the isolated occurrences of specimens of this Rat which have been recorded from various English counties from time to time during the last few years, more especially as many of these—and notably such as have been taken in or near sea-port towns—have in all probability been imported by vessels. It may be mentioned, however, that it still survived in Norfolk up to about 1834, while occasional specimens were met with for

twenty years later. In Warwickshire, where it is now extinct,
it was not uncommon even so late as 1850.

In Ireland, remarks Mr. Harting, the Black Rat has been
met with in various counties, and in localities widely distant
from each other; but there is no evidence to show that it was
ever plentiful, and it must now be regarded as very rare.

Habits.—Although a weaker animal than its supplanter the
Brown Rat, the habits of the species appear in this country to
be similar to those of the latter. In the East, where both the
typical form (which has probably been introduced into India in
ships) and the above-mentioned varieties occur, it frequently
exhibits very different habits. Mr. Blanford, in his "Mammals
of British India," observes, for instance, that "this Rat is
found both on the ground, where it burrows, and in trees,
where it builds nests among the branches. In the Laccadive
Islands, and other places, it inhabits the crowns of cocoa-nut
palms, and is said never to descend to the ground, but to live
on the nuts, and to do great damage by biting them off when
unripe. It is common in houses everywhere, often living on
the roofs. It feeds chiefly on fruit, grain, and vegetables, but
is more or less omnivorous, though less carnivorous than the
M. decumanus."

In England, when abundant, it used apparently to frequent
the same situations as the last-named species, and was an equal
pest to the farmer and owner of granaries. It is not in any
way owing to its want of fecundity that it has been so nearly
exterminated in this country, since it breeds several times
during the year, producing from seven to nine blind offspring
in each litter.

"In feeding," writes Macgillivray, "this species holds the
object, if small, between its fore-feet, sits on its haunches with
the body bent forward, and the back arched, while its tail is
curved along the ground. It runs with great agility, and

exhibits much liveliness in all its actions; is remarkably cleanly, taking care to remove whatever may happen to adhere to its fur, feet, or head; and, although occasionally quarrelsome, it, for the most part, lives a peaceful life in its own community. In affectionate concern for its young, it is not surpassed by any other animal, and were it not an unwelcome guest in our dwellings and stores, but confined itself to the woods and pastures, we should place it among the most interesting of our native quadrupeds. Its voracity, however, and the ravages which it makes among our corn and provisions, and its prolificacy, render it injurious and therefore hateful; at least, such it was when it abounded in the country, but in Britain its existence is, to appearance, nearly ended."

VI. THE BROWN RAT. MUS DECUMANUS.

Mus decumanus, Pallas, Glires, p. 91 (1779); Bell, British Quadrupeds, 2nd ed. p. 308 (1874).

Mus hibernicus, Thompson, Proc. Zool. Soc. 1837, p. 52; Eagle Clarke and Barrett-Hamilton, Zoologist, ser. 3 vol. xv. p. 1 (1891).

Characters.—Somewhat larger than the last, from which it differs by the shorter head and more obtuse muzzle, smaller ears, and relatively shorter tail, of which the length is less than that of the head and body. General colour greyish-brown above, and whitish beneath. Length of head and body, about 9 inches; of tail, 7½ inches.

A Rat, of which the typical specimen measured 7½ inches from the muzzle to the root of the tail, was described in 1837 from Ireland by Thompson, under the name of *M. hibernicus*, and had black fur on the upper-parts, with a white patch on the chest. By its describer it was regarded as nearly allied to the Black Rat, of which Bell was disposed to regard it merely as a variety. Subsequently it was considered that it might be a hybrid between the present and the preceding species ; but, in the article referred to above, Messrs. Eagle Clarke and Barrett-Hamilton finally came to the conclusion that it must be regarded as a black, or melanistic race of the Brown Rat. This variety has been recorded from several counties in the east of Ireland, mostly from the neighbourhood of the coast.

In addition to this form, pied and white varieties are known ; the latter being true albinos, with red eyes.

Distribution.—Being carried by vessels to all parts of the world, and thus having become a complete cosmopolitan, the Brown Rat was a later immigrant into Britain than its darker relative. As to the exact date of its arrival in our islands, there is still some uncertainty, and it is probable that the question will never be decided with exactness. Waterton, who detested this inter-roper with a hatred only less cordial than that which he bestowed on the Hanoverian dynasty, maintained that the first specimens were brought over from the Continent by a vessel which reached our shores soon after the year 1688, even if they did not arrive in the very ship which carried the first of the line of Hanover. It is, however, probable that this date is considerably too early. From the testimony of Pallas, it may be taken as certain that large troops of the Brown Rat, migrating westwards from Central Asia, succeeded in crossing the Volga in the year 1727, whence they populated the whole of Russia, and subsequently the rest of Continental Europe. They are reported by Erxleben to have reached Paris in 1750, and to have been carried to England twenty years previously to that date. Professor Boyd-Dawkins is, however, of opinion that the Brown Rat had reached this country a little before 1730, and we may perhaps therefore put the date of its arrival as 1729, or 1728. Be this as it may, no sooner had the intruder obtained a foothold on British soil than it at once commenced an internecine war against the weaker Black Rat, with the calamitous results to the latter already described.

There is another question connected with the migrations of the Brown Rat which has likewise given rise to a considerable amount of controversy among naturalists, namely, as to the country which has the doubtful honour of being the original birthplace of this unmitigated pest. India was suggested by Pennant as being probably the parent-country, but Mr. Blanford states that the Brown Rat was certainly not indigenous there, and that Chinese Mongolia may with more likelihood be regarded as its centre of dispersion.

It may be added that the terms "Norway," and "Hanoverian" Rat, which used frequently to be applied to the present species, are pure misnomers.

Habits.—Not only is the Brown Rat a larger and more powerful animal than its black cousin, but it is even more prolific, breeding several times in the course of a season, and commonly producing from eight to ten young ones at a birth, while the number sometimes rises to a dozen or even more, and never seems to be less than four. It is likewise a more carnivorous creature, frequenting slaughter-houses and such-like places, where it frequently swarms, and consumes, not only such offal as it can procure, but picks clean all the bones of animals left accessible to its attacks.

Macgillivray observes that "in cities it frequently inhabits in great numbers the drains and sewers, whence it makes its way into the houses. In maritime towns it often takes up its abode in the quays, among piles of wood, in buildings along the shores, or wherever it finds a secure retreat. But it is not confined to cities and villages, but establishes colonies in farmsteadings, on the banks of canals and rivers, and even in islands at a considerable distance from the mainland, or upon larger islands, to which it has been introduced by shipping. Thus, on many of the islets of the Hebrides it is found in considerable numbers, feeding on grass, shell-fish, and crustaceans, and burrowing in the banks ; for although not essentially amphibious, like the Water-Rat, it does not hesitate on occasion to betake itself to the water, and troops have been seen swimming from one island to another.

"It is a very cleanly animal, for even when its residence is a ditch or sewer in the midst of all sorts of filth, it almost invariably preserves itself from pollution ; and in parts remote from towns its fur is often possessed of considerable beauty, although, on account of the injury it inflicts upon us, and the abhorrence with which in childhood we are taught to regard it, few persons will be apt to discover much beauty in a Rat. Its food consists of almost every kind of animal and vegetable substance eaten by other quadrupeds. In granaries and cornfields it is extremely destructive, committing its depredations in the former by night, and in the latter feasting at leisure in the heart of the stacks, where it produces its young, and whence it cannot be expelled until they are taken down, when the quantity of grain it has destroyed is sometimes found to be enormous. In houses it feeds on bread, potatoes, suet, tallow, flesh, fish, cheese, butter, and, in fact, almost everything that comes in its way, including leather and articles of apparel. It gnaws its way through planks, partitions and chests ; burrows with facility under the floors and walls ; nestles behind the plaster, or in the roofs ; and when numerous becomes a source of perpetual annoyance. In the poultry-yard it sometimes destroys the young chickens, and sucks the eggs ; and in game-preserves commits similar depredations. Instances of its mutilating infants, and even of it attacking grown persons, are known ; and when hard pushed it will sometimes turn on a Dog or Cat, and defend itself with great vigour. In the fields it devours great quantities of corn, beans, peas, and other kinds of agricultural produce ; and, as it is extremely prolific, it often inflicts serious injury. When provisions fall short, it migrates, sometimes in large bodies, to a more favourable station ; and when settled in a place where its supply of food is ample, rapidly increases to an astonishing extent."

On board ship Rats are, if possible, a greater nuisance than on shore, as all can testify who have had the misfortune to sail in a Rat-haunted vessel. Sometimes they will even enter the cabins and gnaw the toe-nails of the sleepers down to the quick, if their feet happen to be uncovered. Ivory would not at first sight appear a very tempting kind of food for Rats. Nevertheless, according to the testimony of Frank Buckland, these animals do much damage to the tusks stored in the docks. As they select for their attacks those which contain the largest amount of animal matter, and as such are the most suitable for the purposes of the manufacturer, a Rat-gnawn tusk is sure to be one of the finest quality.

It has been mentioned above that Rats will suck the eggs of poultry, and it is also well known that in many cases this is not done in the hen-house, but the eggs are bodily removed to safer quarters. How this removal is accomplished has not, however, at present been ascertained. Mr. Trevor-Battye writes to me :—" Rats move eggs along the ground by rolling them against their chests. How they move them unbroken from a height I have never been able to find out. The only Rat I ever had a chance of obtaining at this form of depredation dropped the egg and broke it." That these animals can display considerable ingenuity in overcoming mechanical difficulties is proved by an anecdote related by Mr. T. W. Kirk, of the Wellington Museum, New Zealand. In this instance two Rats combined their efforts in order to get a four-inch biscuit between the bars of a building which were only two inches

apart, which was effected by tilting the biscuit. What is equally
noteworthy in this case, is the circumstance that after one of
these Rats had in vain attempted the task single-handed, he left
it, and soon returned accompanied by a comrade, thus showing
that these animals have some rapid means of communicating
their ideas.

In addition to the various kinds of provender above
mentioned, the Brown Rat will also eat snails—both land and
fresh-water; the *débris* which it leaves of the latter being
generally considered as the work of the Water-Vole. An
instance is also on record of a Rat entering the water and
dragging forth with some difficulty a young Eel. That these
animals are likewise chargeable with cannibalism is probably
well known to most persons living in the country, as it is a
common occurrence for one caught in a trap to be set upon
and devoured by its companions. Mr. Trevor-Battye observes :—" When Frogs are spawning, the Rat is fond of
catching them, and eating the contents of their insides. A
heap of dead Frogs, all treated in this way, may often be found
at a Brown Rat's favourite resting-place by the side of a pond."

With regard to the damage caused by the Rat to game-
preservers, Mr. Harting, after many years' practical experience,
is of opinion that not only is this animal one of their worst
enemies, but is likewise very frequently the means of bringing
unoffending creatures to death. "He is a great devourer of
Pheasants' food (to say nothing of young Pheasants), and when
the latter are gathered under the foster-hen at sundown, the
Rat may be seen issuing stealthily into the grass-ride, where
the food has been scattered, helping himself to all he can
find. This is the opportunity for the Brown Owl to render
important service. Gliding off the low branch of a tree in the
direction of the Pheasant-coops, the bird swiftly and noise-
lessly approaches, and a Rat is carried off ere he has time to

realise the presence of an enemy." Too often, alas! the Owl is rewarded by a shot from the keeper's gun, under the mistaken idea that it is after the Pheasants.

As a final indictment against the Rat, it must be mentioned that, according to Jesse, it will sometimes inflict damage upon fruit-trees growing against walls by eating the buds and young leaves.

Says Mr. Trevor-Battye, "Rats are remarkably clever climbers. I have seen a Rat more than once running nimbly all about the small branches of an oak-tree, and collecting lichen; presumably for a nest-lining."

THE VOLES. GENUS MICROTUS.

Microtus, Schrank, Fauna Boica, vol. i. p. 72 (1798).

Head with a blunt, rounded muzzle, and short ears, which are almost buried in the fur; tail short and hairy; soles of the feet naked; molar teeth generally growing continuously, and thus not developing roots, and composed of two longitudinal rows of triangular prisms set alternately to one another.

The Voles are more clumsily-built animals than the Mice, and have less agile movements; while, in addition to the points noticed above, their limbs are relatively shorter and their eyes smaller. They comprise a considerable number of species distributed over Europe, North America, and Asia north of the Himalaya, a few just impinging on the north-west frontier of India. Instead of frequenting the neighbourhood of human habitations and other buildings, like the Mice, the Voles are inhabitants of the open country, burrowing and forming runs in meadows and fields, or dwelling by the sides of rivers and ponds. All of them appear to be strictly vegetable feeders.

As to their affinities, the Voles show but distant kinship with the true Mice, but are closely allied to the Hamsters (*Cricetus*), of which there are no existing British representatives. Although the Hamsters have rooted and tuberculated molars, their tubercles, instead of forming three longitudinal rows, as in the Mice, are arranged in two such rows. By the development of such tubercles into prisms the root-less molars of the Voles have originated; and it is interesting to notice that in some of the extinct species of the latter these teeth, although composed of the same prisms, are shorter and show more or less distinct roots. We may accordingly regard the Voles as forming a highly-specialised side-branch which has taken origin from the Hamsters.

Till within the last few years, the Voles have been almost universally known by the geneiic name of *Arvicola ;* but it has been discovered that the title under which they are here entered antedates the latter by one year, and, therefore, by the rules of zoological nomenclature, has to be employed. In this particular instance the substitution of a strange name for one which had become so well-known, is much to be deplored; but it will be obvious that if exceptions are once made in enforcing the rule of priority in nomenclature, it cannot be logically maintained elsewhere.

I. COMMON FIELD-VOLE.   MICROTUS AGRESTIS.

Mus agrestis, Linn., Fauna Suecica, p. 11 (1761).
Mus gregarius, Linn., Syst. Nat. ed. 12, vol. i. p. 84 (1766).
Arvicola agrestis, Fleming, British Animals, p. 23 (1828); Bell,
       British Quadrupeds, 2nd ed. p. 323 (1874).
Microtus agrestis, Lataste, Le Naturaliste, 1883, p. 349, id.
       Act. Soc. Linn., Bordeaux, vol. xxxviii. p. 36 (1884).

(*Plate XXIV.*)

Characters.—Size small ; tail one-third the length of the head and body ; soles of hind-feet with six naked pads ; colour of

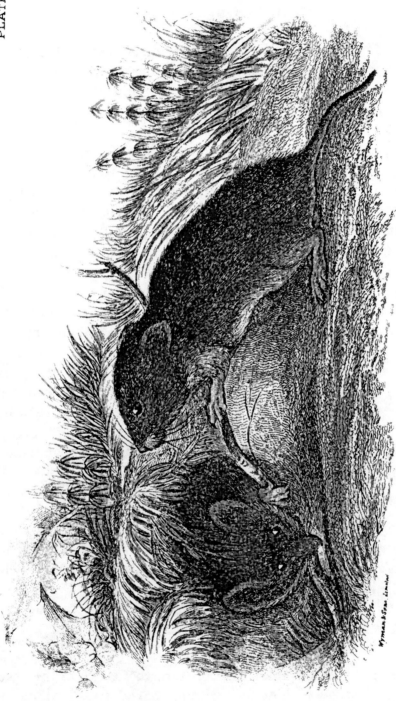

PLATE XXIV.

FIELD-VOLE.

upper parts dull greyish-brown; beneath greyish-white; feet dusky; first and second upper molar teeth with five prismatic spaces, and the third with six; in the lower jaw the first molar having nine such spaces, the second five, and the last three. Length of head and body about 3¾ to 4¾ inches; of the tail, 1¼ inch.

In the allied *Microtus arvalis* of the Continent, the second upper molar has only four prismatic spaces.

Distribution.—This species ranges over the greater part of Europe, from Finland in the north to Northern Italy in the south, and from England and Spain in the west to Russia in the east. In the British Islands it extends all over England and Scotland, inclusive of the Hebrides, but it is not found in Lewis, and is unknown in Ireland. While abundant in the more northern districts of the Continent, in the south it is exceeded in numbers by *M. arvalis*.

Habits.—The Field-Vole, or, as it may be generally termed, the Short-tailed Field-Mouse (in contradistinction to the Wood-Mouse, or Long-tailed Field-Mouse), is the most mischievous of all Rodents to the farmer, from the fact of its occasionally appearing in enormous numbers, as is likewise the case with its continental ally, *M. arvalis*. An exhaustive account of the habits of the latter has been given by Brehm, and since the two species appear to have somewhat similar modes of life, we cannot do better than quote therefrom. He observes that the food of the Voles "consists of every sort of vegetable substance. When they can obtain seeds, they feed only on these, but at other times they content themselves with fresh grass and herbs, roots and leaves, clover, fruits, and berries. Beech-mast and nuts, corn, turnips, and potatoes are badly attacked by them. When the corn begins to ripen, they assemble in hordes in the fields, bite the stalks through at the base till they fall over, then gnaw them through, above, and drag the ears into their burrows. During the harvest they follow the steps of the reapers from one crop to another, devour the corn that has dropped among the stubble, gather the ears up which have fallen in binding up the sheaves, and at last find their way to the stack-yard, where they find provision for the winter. In the woods they collect the fallen haws, juniper-berries, beech-mast, acorns, and nuts in their burrows. During the hardest weather they fall into uninterrupted hibernation, but when milder weather returns they rouse up, and feed on their stores. They are incredibly voracious, and require much to satisfy them ; but they cannot do without water.

"Field-Voles are very gregarious, and live socially together, at least in pairs, but more commonly in great hordes, and therefore they link one burrow to another. They multiply with extreme rapidity. Even in April we find from four to eight young in their warm nests, which lie from one to two feet below the surface of the ground, and are softly lined with fine frag· ments of grass or hay, and moss ; and in the course of the summer the female produces young from four to six times more. It is highly probable that the young of the first litter are themselves ready to breed in autumn, and the amazing increase in their numbers is thus easily explained.

"'Under favourable circumstances,' says Blasius, 'the Field-Vole multiplies in an incredible manner. Many instances are known in which a large part of the harvest has been destroyed over large tracts of country by their inordinate increase, and more than a thousand acres of young birch-trees have been destroyed by their gnawing the bark. Those who have never experienced such a Vole-year can hardly form a conception of the almost incredible swarms of Voles in the fields and plantations. They often appear in a particular neighbourhood without their gradual increase having been observed, as if they had suddenly come upon the earth by magic. It is possible that they sometimes migrate suddenly from place to place. But their rapid multiplication is generally foreshadowed for weeks beforehand by the increase of the Buzzards.'

" During the twenties, the Lower Rhine was repeatedly visited by such a plague. The fields were so undermined in places that you could scarcely set foot on the ground without touching a Vole-hole, and innumerable paths were deeply trodden between these openings. On fine days it swarmed with Voles, which ran about openly and fearlessly. If they were approached, from six to ten rushed to the same hole to creep in, and unwillingly impeded each other's progress by crowding together. It was not difficult in the crush to kill half-a-dozen with one blow from a stick. All seemed to be strong and healthy, but mostly rather small, and for the greater part were probably young ones. Three weeks after I revisited the place. The number of Voles had actually increased, but the animals were apparently in a sickly state. Many had mangy places or sores over the whole body, and even in those which appeared sound, the skin was so loose and delicate that it could not be roughly handled without destroying it. When I visited the place for the third time, four weeks later, every trace of them had disappeared ; but the empty burrows and passages awakened a much more dismal feeling than when they swarmed with life. People said that the whole race had suddenly disappeared from the earth as if by magic. Many may have perished from a devastating pestilence, and many have been devoured by their fellows, as happens in captivity ; but people also spoke of the innumerable hosts that had swum across the Rhine at several places in the open day. No extraordinary increase was noticed anywhere over a wide area ; but they seem to have disappeared everywhere at the same time, without reappearing elsewhere. Nature must have put a stop to their inordinate multiplication at the same period. It was fine warm autumn weather, apparently favourable to them to the last moment.

"In order to give some idea of the hordes of Voles which sometimes appear in certain districts, it may be mentioned that in 1822, in the district of Zabern, 1,570,000 Voles were caught in fourteen days; in the district of Nidda, 590,427; and in that of Putzbach, 271,941.

"In the autumn of 1856, says Lenz, there were so many Voles in one district of four leagues in circumference between Erfurt and Gotha, that about 12,000 acres of land had to be re-ploughed. The sowing of each acre at current wages 6s., and the ploughing-up was estimated at 1s. 6d.; so that the loss amounted to from £2,000 to £4,500, and probably much more. On a single large estate near Breslau 200,000 were caught in seven weeks, and delivered to the Breslau manure factory, which then paid a pfenning (half-a-farthing) per dozen for them. Some of the Vole-catchers were able to supply the factory with 1,400 or 1,500 per day. In the summer of 1861, 409,523 Voles and 4,707 Hamsters were caught and counted in the district of Alsheim in Rhenish Hesse. The local authorities paid 2,523 gulen (about £164) for them!

"In the years 1872 and 1873 it was just the same, and local complaints arose in all parts of the country about the Vole-plague. It might be compared to one of the plagues of Egypt. Even in the day, on the sandy plains of the Mark of Brandenburg, thousands of Voles were counted in particular fields, and in the rich corn-lands of Lower Saxony, Thuringia, and Hesse, they abounded to a fearful extent. Half the harvest was destroyed, hundreds of thousands of acres were left untilled, and thousands of pounds were spent on their destruction. Agricultural Societies and Governments were implored to seek ways and means of staying the plague."

In Britain "Vole-plagues," as they are called, have occurred several times, and we cull the following particulars from the Government Report on the most recent of these. The first on record took place in the year 1580, in the hundred of Danesey, in Essex, when it is stated that the roots of all the pasture-grass were destroyed by these pests. The second occurred during the years 1813 and 1814, and extended over the Forest of Dean, in Gloucestershire, and the New Forest, in Hampshire. An account of this plague has been furnished by Lord Glenbervie, from which it appears that about 98 per cent. of the Rodents composing the horde belonged to the present species, while the remaining 2 per cent. were Wood-Mice. Upwards of 30,000 Voles were destroyed by various means in the Forest of Dean, and 11,500 in the New Forest.* In 1874 and 1875 a similar plague made its appearance in Wensleydale, and lasted till about 1876, during which time the Field-Voles appeared in such numbers in the pasture-farms of the hill-districts of the borders of England and Scotland, and parts of Yorkshire and Wensleydale, as to destroy the grazing-ground. Reporting on this irruption, Sir Walter Elliot writes that "the district most seriously affected consists of a cluster of farms at the head of Borthwick Water, which falls into the Teviot, three miles above Hawick. The centre of the group is Howpasley, which, with Craikhope, Wolfcleughhead, and part of Craik, all in the parish of Roberton, belong to the Duke of Buccleuch ; adjoining them are Ramsay-cleughhead and Hislop, in the parish of Teviothead, and the estate of Tushielaw. Beyond them is Langshawburn ; which was too close to escape such dangerous neighbours, as were other farms in Eskdalemuir parish ; while

* Mr. W. E. de Winton writes to me :—"The Voles in the above-mentioned plagues have, I think, been proved to be the 'Bank' Voles. This animal is the only Vole which frequents woods, and its principal food, at all seasons, consists of seeds, bark, and shoots, and it is this species which does the damage in the woods. I have opened the bodies of many, and have invariably found the stomach filled with a yellow substance like peasepudding, while the stomach of the Field-Vole contains chewed grass."

several in Ettrick-head and Tema Water were attacked in a greater or less degree, but not to be compared with the first-mentioned six farms. In Nithsdale and Western Dumfries, the parishes of Tynron, Penpont, and Durisdeer were among those that suffered most.

"For two or three years previous to 1876, the Voles had been observed to be on the increase. In the spring of 1875 the ground, which had been covered with snow since December, was found to be riddled with holes under the wreath-drifts, and denuded of herbage, by the Voles that had found shelter there. Great numbers were seen throughout the summer, when cutting the bog hay. The shepherd at Craikhope described the children as 'amusing themselves by hunting them from morning to night, as long as they could find nothing better to do, so that each day,' he believes, 'they destroyed hundreds, and the dogs devoured them till they made themselves sick!' In the autumn of the same year they continued plentiful. The farmer of Howpasley, when cutting a four-acre field of corn, observed numbers to be driven inwards by the reaping-machine, so that when only a spot in the centre of about twenty feet by five remained, he made one of the men take a scythe and cut it slowly, a woman lifting behind. The others surrounded them, and killed the Mice as they came out; and somewhere between eighty and a hundred were thus destroyed, most of which were eaten by six dogs present. 'I used to kill scores of them,' he adds, 'with a stick while walking over the hills.'

"The same thing was observed, in a greater or less degree, wherever the conditions of the ground were favourable to them. A correspondent to a county paper relates that when 'removing a two-years' crop of hay in the autumn of 1875 from a meadow sloping down to the Bowmont, on the farm of Sourhope, near Yetholm, two to four nests were found under every rick, each with six to nine young ones, the nest lying in a cavity from which runs diverged in every direction. Great numbers were killed by the boys assisting. One little fellow got seventy-nine full-grown ones for his share, and his straw-hat was brimful of young ones.'

"Their numbers, already redundant, were augmented by the mild winter of 1875–6, and in the succeeding spring they made their presence felt in the doomed farms. During the three months from February to April they completely destroyed the pasturage of the bog-land in Borthwick water, and were then driven to the bents. Notwithstanding the means used for their destruction, which, however, were not very skilful, the swarms showed little diminution. The public journals suggested a trial of the plan which had been so efficacious in the New Forest, where holes were dug into which they fell, but the hint came too late. More efficient auxiliaries appeared in the shape of Hawks, Foxes, Weazels, &c., attracted by the abundant prey. Buzzards, which have long been strangers to the district, again made their appearance. A shepherd in Eskdale-muir saw seven of the rough-legged species (*Archibuteo lagopus*) on the wing at the same time, and the short and long-eared Owls were observed in still larger numbers. By the middle of April the herbage was so much impaired that the Voles themselves began to feel the want of food, and the occurrence of severe frost, with a sprinkling of snow, about the middle of the month, completed their discomfiture. Many died of starvation, and by the end of May they had mostly disappeared.

"When the Committee of the Farmers' Club made their inspection, they found that fully one-third of the pasture in the places visited had been destroyed. The true bog-grass especially, on which the sheep mainly depend in April and May, had been eaten down to the roots. The ground was strewed with dried stalks and blades, mixed with tufts of fur. limbs, and

other remains of the depredators. The sheep were in deplor-
able case; several had died; and the emaciated ewes, too weak
to make good nurses, suckled their lambs with difficulty.
Numbers of these had perished in consequence, and the survivors were poor and weakly."

In 1892 another alarming plague of Voles made its appearance in the south of Scotland, the districts chiefly affected
being the northern boundary of Dumfriesshire, east of Thorn-
hill, and the north-west of Roxburgh, where between 80,000
and 90,000 acres are reported to have been affected. The
border-districts in the south of Selkirk, Peebles, and Lanark,
as well as the parishes of Carpshain and Dairy, in the extreme
north of the stewardry of Kirkcudbright, suffered in a minor
degree. Reporting on the plague in Roxburgh, Mr. R. F.
Dudgeon writes as follows :—

"The districts of this county affected by the plague are the
west and south-west portions of Teviotdale adjoining the counties of Selkirk and Dumfries, and the south-west portion of
Liddesdale. The gross area of the farms seriously affected may
be stated as between 30,000 and 40,000 acres.

"The Voles, although more or less numerous than usual for
the previous two years, multiplied to an alarming extent during
the spring and summer of 1891. A correspondent in Teviotdale describes them as now swarming in millions. They
apparently first attack the deeper boggy and rough pasture-
lands, which are destroyed to the extent of nearly four-fifths
of their area ; one-half of the area of the hill-farms in the districts named may be said to be in bog or rough pasture, and I
think that I should not be far wrong in stating that some
12,000 to 15,000 acres have been rendered entirely useless by
reason of the plague. As the bog or rough pasture becomes
foul or exhausted, the Voles spread to the barer lea-land, and
even to the heather, which they bark, at the same time biting

off the young shoots. The grasses are first attacked close to the surface of the ground, and the stalk is consumed as far as it continues white or succulent; young shoots are also nipped off; and grass tufts are to be seen completely eaten through, what is left by the Voles being absolutely valueless. Sheep are suffering severely in the districts affected; large portions of many flocks have been removed to winterage, wherever that can be found, artificial food and purchased hay is being given to the stock on many hirsels; the lightness of last year's hay-crop and the present high price of purchased fodder, cakes, and corn adds very considerably to the difficulties of the far-mers. Plantations are in some instances attacked, buds being nipped off, and bark peeled. The arable land attached to some of the farms is not appreciably affected, although I am informed by one of my correspondents that during the leading of his corn last autumn Voles were discovered under nearly every stook, nests were also found, as well as eaten corn; fears are entertained that the seed-corn may be attacked, espe-cially in lea land, where the Voles can work their way up the furrows."

The reporter attributes the immediate cause of the outbreak to the unusual roughness of the pastures during the winter of 1890–91, and the mildness of the weather at that time, whereby the Voles gained an extraordinary advantage in the shape of shelter from their natural enemies, as also in facilities for breeding.

After various remedies had been tried, with more or less in-different success, the Voles seemed gradually to decrease in numbers, till by the beginning of 1894 affairs had resumed their normal conditions. In regard to the possibility of check-ing such epidemics, Brehm observes that, unfortunately, man is powerless; and although various remedies, such as inoculation with bacilli, have been tried, we are much inclined to agree with him. He writes that "all the means of destruction which have yet been devised seem insufficient to check the inordinate multiplication of these greedy hosts. Only Providence and the useful predacious animals, to which man is so hostile, can help him. 'Borers' have been used with good results, with which, where the soil permits it, holes are made in the ground 12–18 cm. in circumference and 60 cm. deep. When the Voles fall in, instead of burrowing their way out, they devour each other. When the fields were being ploughed, children followed with sticks, and destroyed as many as possible. Smoke has been driven into the burrows, poisoned grain thrown in, whole fields saturated with a decoction of strychnine or spurge. In short, every means has been adopted to get rid of this terrible pest; but in general all these methods have proved nearly useless, and some of them, especially poisoning, highly dangerous. The most efficacious poison not only destroys all the Voles in a field, but likewise their worst enemies, and consequently our friends, Foxes, Martens, Stoats, Weazels, Buzzards, Owls, and Rooks, besides Partridges, Hares, and domestic animals, from Pigeons to Horses and Oxen—a sufficient reason for abstaining altogether from the use of poison. It is painful to all naturalists and lovers of animals to see the enemies of the Voles, as in 1872, poisoned and destroyed instead of cared for and protected. Short-sighted people—farmers who cared more for hare-hunting than for making the best use of the land—were delighted when they found, besides dead Voles, hundreds of poisoned Rooks, Buzzards, Owls, Foxes, Weasels, and Stoats; but they did not consider what mischief they had entailed upon themselves in their senseless efforts to destroy the Voles. It was not the destruction of the useful but despised Vole-killers that concerned them, but when Hares, Partridges, and domestic animals were also poisoned, they were at last induced to give up the use of poison. Till then, the warnings of far-seeing

PLATE XXV

advisers were disregarded. The hints which they had given, both verbally and in print, that laying poison in the fields might perhaps benefit the infected land, but not agriculturists, were not appreciated till too late. Besides poison, smoking out the Voles was tried on suitable ground with satisfactory result. All the holes were stopped up, and poisonous coal and sulphur-smoke (bisulphide of carbon) was allowed to pour into the burrows which the Voles reopened : but this efficacious mode of destroying them could not be employed everywhere, and was very expensive. People knew not what to do, because they had neglected to destroy the Voles at the proper time." .

It may be mentioned, in conclusion, that fossil remains of the Common Field-Vole have been obtained from the Pleistocene brick-earths of the Thames Valley, and likewise from Kirkdale Cave in Yorkshire, and Kent's Hole Cavern near Torquay. A fact of still more interest is the occurrence of jaws of the continental *M. arvalis* in the "forest-bed" of the Norfolk coast, and also in a fissure near Frome, in Somerset-shire.

II. THE BANK-VOLE. MICROTUS GLAREOLUS.

Mus glareolus, Schreber, Säugethiere, vol. iii. p. 680 (1774).

Arvicola pratensis, Baillon, in F. Cuvier's Hist. Nat., Mamm., vol. iv. Tabl. gén. p. 4 (1834); Bell, British Quadrupeds, p. 230 (1837).

Arvicola riparia, Yarrell, Proc. Zool. Soc. 1832, p. 109; Jenyns, British Vertebr. p. 34 (1835).

Arvicola glareolus, Bell, British Quadrupeds, 2nd ed. p. 327 (1874).

Arvicola (Evotomys) glareola, Newton, Geol. Mag. decade 2, vol. viii. p. 258 (1881).

Microtus glareolus, Lataste, Act. Soc. Linn. Bordeaux, vol. xxxviii. p. 36 (1884).

(Plate XXV.)

Characters.—Size nearly as in the last; tail about one-half the length of the head and body, and thickly haired; colour of upper-parts rich reddish-chestnut, the flanks grey, and the under-parts nearly white; tail dark brown above and white beneath. Molars developing distinct roots in the adult; the first and third upper molars with five prismatic spaces, and the second with four; in the lower jaw, the first molar with seven, and the other two with three such spaces. Length of head and body about 3¾ to 4 inches; of tail, 1⅓ inches.

In the rooted molars of the adult, this species differs widely from the preceding; and, accordingly, while the latter is assigned to a separate sub-genus known as *Agricola*, the present form is sub-generically distinguished as *Evotomys*.

Distribution.—First recognised as a British species by Yarrell, the Bank-Vole ranges through England and Scotland as far north as Morayshire, beyond which it does not appear to have been met with; but, like both the other British members of the genus, it is unknown in Ireland. In England it is generally supposed to be a far less abundant species than the common Field-Vole; but among a large series of specimens of Voles recently collected for Mr. Oldfield Thomas, by far the greater majority proved to belong to the one under consideration. In Northumberland it occurs, but apparently not commonly; in Cumberland it has been recorded only from two localities; while in Durham it has not been noticed, although it must almost certainly occur. Mr. Montagu Browne also states that it is unknown in Leicestershire; while in Devonshire it is either extremely rare or very local. These instances will suffice to show that the distribution of the species over the country is far from uniform. In a fossil state, the Bank-Vole occurs in the "forest-bed" of Norfolk, as well as in several English caverns, such as Kent's Hole near Torquay, Wookey Hole in Glamorganshire, Brixham Cave, and another cave near Bristol.

Abroad, this species ranges across Europe from France to China, while in North America its place is taken by a closely-allied form known as *M. gapperi*. Recent investigations have, however, rendered it probable that both the European and American forms will eventually prove to be local southern races of the Arctic Vole (*M. rutilus*), of the circum-polar Regions, in which case the latter name will have to be employed for the species under consideration.

Habits.—In habits the Bank-Vole, or Red Vole, as it is frequently, and perhaps preferably, called, is generally very similar to those of the preceding species; but whereas the latter is essentially an inhabitant of the open fields, the former is more partial to sheltered situations, often frequenting gardens, where it does much damage by devouring the bulbs of crocuses and newly-sown peas and beans. Mr. Roper writes that its favourite haunts "are old rough ivy-covered hedge-banks, especially those from which the soil has been washed away in places, leaving the roots bare, and thus forming hollows behind them; banks adjoining woods and plantations seem particularly attractive to them. In spots like this, pleasingly varied by a sprinkling of mossy old stubs, brambles, and bushes, with the roots of overhanging trees backed by deep cavernous recesses, the Bank-Vole makes its burrow, and forms runs in all directions, partly above and partly below the surface; probably also making use of those of the Mole. I have caught them, too, among artificial rock-work, and in a plantation in which are banks thickly covered with the lesser periwinkle, among the roots and stems of which they had formed numerous runs."

Bell states that the Bank-Vole is more omnivorous in its habits than the common Field-Vole, and that it is less addicted to burrowing; while it is even more frequently seen abroad during the daytime. Its food comprises almost all kinds of vege-

table substances ; and it is probable that insects are also occasionally eaten.   In addition to the harm inflicted on roots and
bulbs, the Bank-Vole often does much damage to the bark of
fruit- and other trees, more especially in the spring and winter.
In parts of Scotland these animals have seriously damaged
young larch-plantations by their ravages on the bark and buds.
In Switzerland the charge has been brought against this Rodent
of robbing the nests of such small birds as build upon the
ground ; but further evidence on this point is desirable.   The
breeding-habits appear to be identical with those of the preceding species, from four to eight young being produced in a
litter.

In ridding gardens of Voles, the writer has found a common
4-trap made out of three pieces of lath and a couple of roofing-
tiles the most effective ; either a split bean or a piece of cheese
being used as a bait.

III. THE WATER-VOLE.   MICROTUS AMPHIBIUS.

Mus amphibius, Linn., Syst. Nat. ed. 12, vol. i. p. 82 (1766).
Microtus amphibius, Schrank, Fauna Boica, vol. i. p. 72
    (1798) ; Lataste, Act. Soc. Linn. Bordeaux, vol. xxxviii.
    p. 36 (1884).
Arvicola amphibius, Desmarest, Mammalogie, p. 280 (1820) ;
    Bell, British Quadrupeds, 2nd ed. p. 316 (1874).
Arvicola aquatica, Fleming, British Animals, p. 23 (1828).
Arvicola ater, Macgillivray, Mem. Wern. Soc. vol. vi. p.
    424 (1832).
Arvicola amphibia, Jenyns, British Vert. Anim. p. 33 (1835);
    Flower, Cat. Osteol. Mus Roy. Coll. Surgeons, pt. ii. p.
    610 (1884).
                        (*Plate XXVI.*)

Characters.—Size large ; tail about half the length of head and
body ; hind-feet long, with five naked pads on the soles ; fur

THE VAMPIRE.

long and thick, usually of a uniform greyish-brown, with a more or less distinct reddish tinge, but not unfrequently wholly black. First upper molar tooth with five, and the second and third with four, prismatic spaces ; in the lower jaw, the first molar has seven such spaces (of which the first three are generally imperfectly separated), the second five, and the third three. Length of head and body about 8¼ inches ; of tail 4½ inches.

The Water-Vole, or, as it is generally incorrectly termed, the Water-Rat, is a member of the sub-genus *Paludicola* (as defined by the number of prisms in the molar teeth), and may be compared to the Brown Rat in point of size. As in the case of the so-called Irish Rat, the black, or melanistic variety, which is as common in many parts of Scotland as it is in the Cambridge-shire fens and in Norfolk, was at first regarded as a distinct species, under the name of *Arvicola ater*.

The Water-Vole has the body full ; the neck very short ; the head short, broad, rounded, and convex above ; the limbs small ; and the tail rather long and slender. The short and rounded ears are entirely concealed among the thick fur, and are naked internally, and thinly covered with soft hairs exter-nally ; the aperture of the internal ear being capable of being closed by an operculum. On the fore-feet the claws are greatly compressed, but in the hind-limbs are longer ; while in neither are the toes webbed. The tail is cylindrical and slightly tapering, somewhat compressed towards the tip, and covered with short closely-adherent hairs. The fur is composed of two kinds of hairs, some being longer and a little thicker than the others. At the base all the hairs are bluish-black on the upper-parts, and bluish-grey below. The incisor teeth are brownish-yellow, the eyes black, the nose dusky, the soles of the feet pale flesh-colour, and the claws, according to Mr. de Winton, are "purple, as if dyed with black-currant juice."

Distribution.—The geographical range of this species is very extensive, including nearly the whole of Europe and a large portion of Asia north of the Himalaya, but it does not appear to be known further east than China. Unknown in Ireland, it is so universally distributed in England and Scotland that no special notice is necessary on this point, except that, while found in Sutherland and Caithness, it is unknown in Argyllshire and the Isles. Although locally abundant in some districts, the black variety appears much more common in Scotland than in England.

Not improbably occurring in the forest-bed of the Norfolk coast, in a fossil state, the Water-Vole is met with in the Pleistocene brick-earths of the Thames Valley, and likewise in a number of English caverns.

Habits.—Of the mode of life of the Water-Vole, Macgillivray, in the original edition of the " Naturalist's Library," writes that " its residence is in the banks of rivers, brooks, canals, mill-dams, and ponds, in which it forms long and tortuous burrows. It frequently betakes itself to the water, swims and dives with ease ; and generally has an entrance to its retreat beneath the surface, so that in cases of danger it may effect its escape without appearing on land. In fine weather, especially in the morning and evening, it may often be seen sitting at the mouth of its hole, nibbling the grass or roots there ; but in the middle of the day it usually remains underground. It feeds entirely on vegetable substances, chiefly roots, and has been known to deposit a store even of potatoes for winter use ; for it does not appear to become torpid in the cold season, although in time of snow it does not come abroad. Five or six young are produced early in summer, and deposited in a nest composed of dry grass and other vegetable matter."

Although generally found close to water, this Rodent occasionally wanders some distance away, and may make its burrow in a ploughed field; an instance of this habit being recorded by Gilbert White. In the Lake district, according to the Rev. H. A. Macpherson, these animals have taken to burrowing in the sandhills of Ravenglass. In summer the soft succulent inner portions of the stems of flags and horse-tails, form their favourite food; but when hard pressed in winter they will make raids on the farmer's store of root-crops, and will attack the bark of willows and osiers. The sins of the Brown Rat are often unjustly laid to the charge of the Water-Vole, in consequence of which it is often said to be carnivorous; but there is little doubt, as stated above, that it is a purely vegetable feeder. The only offences of which it can be justly convicted are of tapping the banks of mill-dams, rivers, and canals by means of its burrows, of damaging osier-plantations, and the aforesaid raids on root-crops.

When threatened with danger, the female Water-Vole has been observed to convey her young to a place of safety by taking them up in her mouth and carrying them, as a Cat does her kittens. One of the great enemies of this creature is the Weasel, which is able to enter its burrow and then attack it. In feeding, the Vole may often be observed sitting upon its haunches on the river-bank, and holding its food up to its mouth with its fore-paws after the manner of a Squirrel.

Mr. Trevor-Battye writes to me:—" It is worth noticing that when the Water-Vole is not hurried it will make use of its hind-legs alone in swimming, carrying its fore-paws at its sides, as the Seals do their flippers. I mentioned this fact in my book ' Pictures in Prose'; elsewhere I have not seen it referred to; yet it is one which anyone, given clear water, can attest for himself."

THE HARES AND RABBITS. FAMILY LEPORIDÆ.

The Hares and Rabbits, together with the Picas or Tailless Hares (*Lagomys*), of which there are no existing British representatives, form a group distinguished from all other Rodents by the presence of a second small pair of upper incisors placed immediately behind the large front pair. They are likewise peculiar in that the enamel on the large upper incisors, in place of being confined to their front surfaces, extends round to the back, although it is still thicker in front than elsewhere.

From the presence of the additional pair of upper incisors this group is spoken of as the *Duplicidentata*, whereas all the other members of the Order are collectively classed as *Simplicidentata*. In the young of the present group there are three pairs of incisor teeth in the upper jaw, but the hindmost of these are soon lost.

As a family, the Hares and Rabbits are distinguished from the Picas (*Lagomyidæ*) by the collar-bones, or clavicles, being imperfect, by the length of the hind-limbs being much in excess of that of the front pair, by the presence of a short, upwardly-curved tail, and the long ears. There are three pairs of upper, and two of lower, pre-molar teeth ; and the whole of the cheek-teeth are devoid of roots, and are divided into parallel plates by transverse infoldings of the enamel. The Family, which includes but a single genus, has, with the exception of Australasia (where Rabbits have been introduced with most disastrous results), a cosmopolitan distribution.

GENUS LEPUS.

Lepus, Linn., Syst. Nat. ed. 12, vol. i. p. 77 (1766).

Since this is the only genus of the Family, it will suffice to add to the above-mentioned characters that the fore-feet are furnished with five, and the hind with four toes, and that the soles of the feet are furred like the legs, while the inner surface of the cheeks are likewise covered with hair. With the exception of the Hispid Hare (*L. hispidus*), all the species are very similar to one another in external appearance, and all are

PLATE XXVII

COMMON HARE

terrestrial. Whereas, however, the majority are inhabitants of open fields, and produce furred and active young, the Rabbit and the Hispid Hare are peculiar in dwelling in burrows and giving birth to naked and helpless offspring. By far the great majority of the species are confined to the temperate regions of the Northern Hemisphere.

I. THE COMMON HARE. LEPUS EUROPŒUS.

Lepus europœus, Pallas, Nov. Spec. Glirium, p. 30 (1778).
Lepus timidus (nec Linn.), Bell, British Quadrupeds, 2nd ed. p.
   331 (1874).

(*Plate XXVII.*)

Characters.—Size large; hind-limbs and ears very long, the latter exceeding the head in length; tail nearly as long as the head; general colour of the upper-parts tawny-grey, more or less tinged with rufous; under-parts white; ears tipped with black; tail black above and white beneath. Length of head and body about 21⅔ inches; of tail, 3⅔ inches; of ear, 3⅚ inches.

Although the fur of the English Hare is usually of the colour mentioned above, there is considerable variation in this respect, depending upon the age of the animal, the season of the year, and locality, while there are also individual differences. As a rule, in Britain, the Hare becomes of a more pure grey in winter, while in more northern regions it tends to white at the same season. Leverets are more rufous than adult individuals; and in the south of Europe the prevailing colour tends to yellowish-red. Individuals occasionally assume a paler tint than usual, and sometimes resemble a Rabbit in colour; while very rarely black Hares have been met with.

As regards the general external form of the Hare, it may be added that the body is large, compressed, and deep; the neck very short; the head of moderate size, convex above, and broad and obtuse at the muzzle, with a depressed nose, and the upper lip tumid and divided by a vertical median cleft. The laterally-placed eyes are large and remarkably prominent; and the long ears are narrow, deeply concave, and rounded at the tips. The somewhat long claws are slightly curved, compressed, and rather sharp; although on the hind-feet they become blunted in old animals. The fur, as in the other members of the genus, consists of two kinds of hairs, of which the one is long and coarse, and the other short, fine, and somewhat woolly. In addition to the usual " whiskers," a few long bristly hairs are situated over each eye. A Hare generally weighs from seven to eight pounds when fully grown; but much heavier specimens occur, Bell recording one of eleven pounds, while in another just over thirteen pounds was scaled.

Distribution.—Before discussing the distribution of this species, it should be mentioned that by all the older writers on British Mammals, the Common Hare is alluded to under the name of *Lepus timidus.* Since, however, this species does not occur in Scandinavia, there can be little doubt but that the latter name was applied by Linnæus to the Mountain-Hare of that region, to which species the name in question must consequently be transferred.

With the exception of the Scandinavian peninsula, Northern Russia, and Ireland, the Common Hare ranges over the whole of Europe. That it extends to the Caucasus, and that it is unknown in Siberia, are ascertained facts, but we are not aware that the actual easterly limits of its range have been defined. Distributed over the whole of England and the Lowlands of Scotland, the Hare is less abundant in many of the northern districts of the latter country, on the higher tracts of which its place is taken by the next species. It occurs, however, commonly in Caithness, and is also found in the east of

Sutherland. In Argyllshire it is rare, and may have been introduced, as it has certainly been in Mull and some of the other islands.

Habits.—The following account of the habits of the Common Hare is taken from Macgillivray, who writes that, like the other species of the genus, it feeds entirely on vegetable substances, such as grass, clover, corn, turnips, and the bark of young trees, sometimes inflicting great injury on the latter, especially in winter. Towards evening it comes abroad in quest of food, and continues to search for it during the night, in conformity with which habits the pupil of its eye is large and of an oblong form. It advances by leaps, and as its hind-legs are much longer than the front ones, it runs with more ease up hill than down, especially on steep declivities. During the day it reposes in a crouching or half-sitting posture in its "form," which is a selected spot to which it usually resorts, among grass, ferns, or bushes. Its senses of hearing and seeing are extremely acute ; its eyes, being placed directly on the sides of the head, take in a wide range, while its long ears can be readily turned in any direction, forwards, outwards, or backwards, so as to catch the smallest sounds indicative of hostility. Being in a manner defenceless, and having no burrow or fastness to which it may retreat, the Hare trusts to vigilance and extraordinary speed to enable it to elude its numerous enemies.

It is chiefly to the lower and more cultivated districts that the Common Hare resorts, but it is also found in the upland valleys, and on the slopes of hills of considerable height. Timid and gentle as it is, yet it is by no means innocuous, for the injury it occasions to the young corn is often consider-able. In the winter it finds an abundant supply of food in the turnip-fields, and it sometimes visits gardens at night, more especially when pinched by hunger during continued frost. It has been observed to cross rivers by swimming, and even to enter the sea for the purpose of gaining an island or point of land, on which food was more abundant. We may add, that, as a rule, Hares do not take to water except when compelled to do so to escape from pursuit.

Mr. Trevor-Battye states, however, that as he was once waiting at evening for ducks by the side of the River Eden, in Kent, a Hare came quietly down the opposite bank through a copse, crossed about three feet of ice that fringed the stream, swam the open water, scrambled on to the ice on his side, and emerged close to him, shook itself, and, catching sight of him, ran off. This seemed quite a spontaneous act, as it was not being hunted.

The female goes with young thirty days, and more than once in the season produces from three to five young ones, which are born covered with hair, having their eyes open, and capable of running. The young squat in the fields, remaining motionless, like those of many birds, and are with difficulty perceived. Even the old Hares are not readily driven from their form, in which they will sometimes remain until a person is quite close to them, when they at length start off, exhibiting in their motions the haste and perturbation of extreme fear. The timidity of the Hare is, indeed, proverbial, as is its propensity to return when wounded, or even when hunted, to its usual place of repose.

In the foregoing account Hares are stated to skulk and lie close only when in their forms, but they will frequently do so —more especially in the early spring—on open fallows, or even on grass-land. From the similarity of their coloration to the surrounding clods of earth, they are then extremely difficult to detect, unless by a practised eye. When running away from a pursuer, the white under surface of the up-turned tail renders them, however, conspicuous in the extreme. The object of

PLATE XXVIII

MOUNTAIN-HARE.

this white on the tail is supposed to be (as in the case of the Rabbit) to aid the young in following their dam to a place of safety; but it is clearly a disadvantage to the animal when hunted by greyhounds, which follow only by sight, and in this have a conspicuous object to attract their eyes towards their quarry. The Hare, as Mr. Trevor-Battye has pointed out, does not, however, invariably carry its tail up, as the Rabbit does; and when cantering generally carries it down. When coursed, the Hare, as is well known, seeks to elude her pursuers by frequent doublings, being able to turn in a much smaller space than the dogs; and it is mainly for this reason that two greyhounds are invariably employed, as a single dog would have but a very poor chance.

Hare-skins are largely used in the manufacture of felt, the fur, before removal from the skin, being treated with acid, when it assumes a reddish colour, and felts more readily; this process being technically known as "carroting."

II. THE MOUNTAIN-HARE. LEPUS TIMIDUS.

Lepus timidus, Linn., Syst. Nat. ed. 12, vol. i. p. 77 (1766); Sclater, Cat. Mamm. Indian Mus. pt. ii. p. 118 (1891).

Lepus variabilis, Pallas, Nov. Spec. Glir. p. 1 (1778); Bell, British Quadrupeds, 2nd ed. p. 338 (1874).

Lepus arcticus, et *L. glacialis*, Leach in Ross' Voyage, pp. 151, 170 (1819).

Lepus albus, Jenyns, British Vert. Animals, p. 35 (1835).

Lepus hibernicus, Yarrell, Proc. Zool. Soc. 1833, p. 38; Bell, British Quadrupeds, p. 341 (1837).

Lepus borealis, et *L. canescens*, Nilsson, Skandinav. Fauna, pp. 19, 22 (1847).

(*Plate XXVIII.*)

Characters.—Size smaller than in the last; the head relatively smaller and more rounded; and the ears, hind-limbs, and tail

5 Q

shorter.   General colour fulvous grey, with black tips to the
ears, changing during the winter in the colder regions of the
animal's habitat to white, with the exception of the tips of
the ears, which are black at all times.   Length of head and
body about 21 inches ; of tail, 2½ inches ; of ear, 3¼ inches.

The reasons for applying the name of *Lepus timidus* to this
form, instead of to the Common Hare, have been already
given under the heading of the latter.

Distribution.—The geographical distribution of the Mountain,
Alpine, Blue, Irish, or Polar, Hare, as the animal is variously
called, is very extensive, embracing the circum-polar regions of
both Hemispheres, and including a considerable portion of
Europe and Asia north of the Himalaya.   This is the only Hare
found in Iceland and Scandinavia, and it ranges over Northern
Europe generally, while it extends eastwards as far as Japan,
and in Southern and Eastern Europe it is found in mountain-
ranges, like the Alps, the Pyrenees, and the Caucasus, which
have a climate and temperature suitable to its existence.   Although unknown in England, the Mountain-Hare is spread over
the whole of Ireland and the greater part of Scotland.   In the
latter country its range has of late years been steadily increasing, partly owing to artificial introduction, and partly to a westward immigration; it is, however, now unknown in the Orkneys,
where it is stated to have formerly existed.   According to Bell,
it was introduced into Peebleshire, Lanarkshire, and Ayrshire;
but in Argyllshire its increase of area is stated to be natural.
Thus it appears that, while it was unknown in Inverary about
1839, forty years later it was common there; and much the same
is reported of the Loch Lomond district.   In Mull it has
been introduced.   In Sutherland, from incessant shooting, the
number of these Hares has been greatly reduced; but of late
years they are once more increasing in numbers.

In Ireland, doubtless owing to the mild climate, the Mountain-Hare does not turn white in winter; and it is said that among those introduced into Ayrshire and the neighbouring counties, the change is much less complete and regular than in the north. Moreover, of those introduced into Mull, some become white in winter, while others do not; and it is, therefore, not improbable that those in which the change does not take place, were imported from Ireland. Elsewhere in Scotland the assumption of the white winter-dress is regular and complete.

Regarding this change, Macgillivray writes that " in September the colours begin to assume a paler tint, many of the dusky hairs having disappeared. In October the change is further advanced, and towards the end of the month, the muzzle, hind-neck, and feet are white, of which colour there are spots and patches dispersed here and there. In December the fur seems to be entirely white, but has an intermixture of long blackish hairs on the back; the anterior external part of the ear is brownish, and its tip black. The under-fur is light bluish-grey at the base, pale yellowish, or cream-colour towards the end. . . . . . From the examination of individuals at different periods of the year, I have inferred that in this species the hair is almost always changing; that in April and May there is a general but gradual shedding, after which the summer-colours are seen in perfection; that towards the middle of autumn many new white hairs have been substituted for coloured ones, and that by degrees all the hair and under-fur are shed and renewed before the end of December, when the fur is in the perfection of its winter condition, being closer, fuller, and longer than in summer." Bell, on the other hand, believed that the change was due to an alteration in the colour of the hairs themselves; but we have every reason for regarding the former as the true explanation.

Habits.—In its general habits this species resembles the Common Hare, producing active, furred young, and not burrow-

ing. Instead, however, of making a regular "form," it skulks
among stones, or in the clefts of rocks, or hides among heather or
fern. In summer keeping to the mountain-sides, although not
frequenting the summits, it descends in winter to the bottom
of the valleys, although even then generally avoiding the cultivated or low flats. In Northern Europe it not unfrequently
resorts to woods. When hard pressed by hunger in winter, it
will not disdain to eat lichens, and even the seeds of pines.
In point of speed, the Mountain-Hare cannot compare with the
English species. Only two litters appear to be produced by
the female in a season. The flesh is whiter and leaner, and
therefore, of inferior quality to that of the Common Hare.

Mr. Trevor-Battye writes :—"This animal has a habit that I
have never seen explained. When running, it goes crookedly
at more or less frequent intervals, twisting its hinder extremity
in a curious way. I used to think it was only changing its legs,
but the action is too marked for this."

In addition to an enormous number of carcases, with the
skins on, of the Mountain-Hare sent to this country for food,
from two to five million skins are annually collected, a large
proportion of which come from Siberia. According to Mr.
Poland, "a large quantity of these skins are used for fur-pur-
poses, both natural white, in imitation of White Fox, and dyed
Lynx-colour, brown, dark brown, black, and 'snow-flake.' The
peculiar dye called 'snow-flake' is effected by passing a solu-
tion of wax over the points of fur, and then dying the under-
fur a beautiful brown. The tips of the hairs thus retain their
natural white colour; the wax covering is removed, the skins
are cleaned, and the fur has then a beautiful appearance, somewhat like that of the Silver Fox."

It is noteworthy that fossil remains of this species have been
obtained from a cavern in the Mendip Hills, as well as from
two Irish caves.

III. THE RABBIT. LEPUS CUNICULUS.

Lepus cuniculus, Linn., Syst. Nat. ed. 12, vol. i. p. 77 (1766);
Bell, British Quadrupeds, 2nd ed. p. 343 (1874).

Characters.—Size small; ears and hind-limbs relatively shorter than in the two preceding species, and the former with a very small or no black terminal patch. General colour brownish-grey mingled with tawny, the under-parts white, and the tail blackish above and white beneath. Length of head and body about 16½ inches; of tail, 3⅔ inches; of ear, 3⅙ inches.

In form of body, the Rabbit is rounder and plumper than the Hare, and the flanks are less contracted, while the proportionately shorter ears and limbs give it a much more ordinary appearance. In this country pied, black, and fawn-coloured pure-bred wild Rabbits are not uncommon; and a wild albino specimen has been recently recorded from France. In weight, a wild Rabbit usually varies from between two-and-a-half and three pounds, but specimens which have turned the scale at five pounds are on record.

Distribution.—Originally, so far as can be determined, a native of the countries around the western portion of the Mediterranean, the Rabbit appears to have gradually spread thence, partly by human agency, and partly by migration, to the more northern countries of Europe; while the disastrous results of its introduction into Australia and New Zealand are only too well known. The date of its introduction into Britain does not appear to be ascertained, even approximately; but it was probably first imported into England, whence it was carried to Ireland, while its extension into Scotland was a gradual process, which is even now going on, this Rodent being now abundant in many districts where it was formerly unknown. As in the case of the northern isles, this widening of its distributional area in Scotland is largely due to human agency, although aided by the natural spread of the animal.

Habits.—Similar as is the Rabbit in appearance and structure to the Hare, it presents one remarkable difference, namely, that its young are born blind, naked, and helpless; while to protect them the creature lives in burrows excavated by itself in the earth.   Moreover, in place of being solitary animals, or consorting in pairs, Rabbits are social creatures, forming their burrows in continuity and connection with one another, and inhabiting such warrens in larger or smaller colonies.   So far as we are aware, the only other member of the genus which resembles the Rabbit in producing naked and helpless young and in dwelling in burrows, is the Asiatic Hispid Hare.

"The places most favourable to the Rabbit," observes Macgillivray, "are sandy heather or downs, overgrown with coarse grass and furze; the latter plant not only affording shelter, but also food.   There it congregates in vast numbers, digging burrows in the soil, in which it reposes, and to which it retreats from danger.   Although, on account of the comparative shortness of its legs, it is much inferior to the Hare in speed, it yet runs with great celerity; and a number of Rabbits scattered over a field afford a very pleasant sight, some scudding along in trepidation, others bounding over the shrubs or herbage, one disappearing here, another stopping a moment to look around before it plunges into its retreat, and perhaps a third peeping from the aperture.   Early in the morning, when old and young are abroad, they may be seen gambolling in fancied security.   If there are fields and pastures in the neighbourhood, they make excursions among the corn and grass, committing serious devastations when their numbers are great, so that the vicinity of a warren is a great nuisance to the farmer. Foxes, Polecats, Stoats, Weasels, and various Birds of Prey, destroy considerable numbers; but as their fecundity is great,

they rapidly increase in spite of natural enemies." The passing
of the Ground-Game Act has, of course, permitted the tenant-
farmer to reduce the number of Rabbits on his land to such
limits as he may think fit; and, in spite of their rapidity of
increase, we are never likely in this country to have swarms of
Rabbits like those which have devastated some portions of
Australia.

Favourable seasons have something to do with abnormal
increase, and Mr. Trevor-Battye observes:—"Last season
(1893), owing to the extraordinary weather, was remarkable as
a Rabbit-year. These animals almost amounted to a 'plague' in
some parts of England. Never can I remember in the palmiest
days, before the Ground-Game Act, more Rabbits in districts
with which I am familiar."

The remarkable paralysis, and loss of all kind of bodily and
mental power, which seizes a Rabbit or Hare when hunted by
a Stoat or Weasel, has been already alluded to when treating of
those Carnivores, and is one of the most curious physiological
peculiarities of the members of the group under consideration.
Although, when suddenly frightened, a Rabbit will plunge without hesitation into any water which may happen to be near, in
which it will swim strongly and boldly, it appears that these
animals take naturally to the water even less readily than the
Hare.

At the age of about six or eight months the doe Rabbit commences to breed; and as it produces several litters in a year, each
of which comprises from five to eight young ones, the rate of its
increase is very rapid. Although living in large colonies,
Rabbits are not polygamous animals, but associate in pairs, and
apparently remain thus attached for life. Before giving birth
to her offspring, the female forms a separate burrow for their
reception, at the termination of which is a soft nest lined with
fur plucked from her own body. Blind and naked as they are

at birth, the young Rabbits develop with amazing rapidity, and are soon able to feed and shift for themselves. It is by no means always, however, that they are allowed to see the light of day, for either the Polecat, Stoat, or Weasel may enter the burrow and destroy the whole litter (and not improbably the mother as well); or the Badger may dig straight down and ruthlessly root out the whole. Even after they venture abroad, many fall victims to prowling Cats, Foxes, and other Carnivores. When alarmed by impending danger, the old Rabbit strikes the ground forcibly with the hind-feet, thus making a sound which serves as a signal to her progeny, as well as to the rest of the colony, to follow her white tail back to the burrow with all the speed they can command.

It is scarcely necessary to say that the wild Rabbit is the ancestral stock from which have been derived the whole of the numerous domesticated races, some of which greatly exceed the wild form in size; while others are remarkable for their drooping ears, or the great length of their fur.

In addition to being largely used as an article of food, the Rabbit, both wild and tame, is an important animal in the fur-trade. According to Mr. Poland, the annual collection of French and Belgian skins is two millions, while the English collection reaches the enormous total of thirty millions. Of these skins, the majority "are dyed brown or black. They are sometimes clipped and dyed dark brown as imitation fur-seal, or clipped and dyed black, or they are dyed as imitation Beaver, and a few are dyed light brown; in fact, the fur of the Rabbit is used more extensively than any other fur, except that of the Musk-Rat and Squirrel. It exceeds these in size, is very cheap, and is of almost universal use, being employed on the Continent, in North America, and some also in Australia. The fur is, however, not otherwise desirable, as it soon wears out. Some white skins are clipped and dyed 'snow-flake.'"

THE HOOFED MAMMALS, OR UNGULATES. ORDER UNGULATA.

The whole of the terrestrial Mammals inhabiting the British Islands which remain for consideration are included in the great Order Ungulata ; a group comprising Oxen, Deer, Pigs, Horses, Tapirs, Rhinoceroses, Elephants, &c. The more typical members of this large assemblage, which alone need be considered in this work, are characterised by having the toes, which never exceed four in number on each foot, encased in horny hoofs, by the absence of collar-bones, and by the cheek-teeth having broad and flattened crowns adapted for masticating vegetable food. While in some forms, like the Pigs, these teeth have short crowns, surmounted by low and comparatively simple tubercles, in others, such as the Oxen and Horses, the crowns become very tall, and have deep infoldings of enamel on the summits, which are more or less completely filled with a softer substance termed "cement." By this means, especially when the tooth becomes worn, a very complicated pattern is produced, the plan of arrangement often taking the form of four more or less well-defined crescents.

The typical Ungulates are sub-divided into two main groups, readily distinguished by the structure of the foot. In the first of these, as represented by the Horses and Rhinoceroses, the middle or third toe (which may be the only one present), is larger than either of the others, and symmetrical in itself, and the members of the group are consequently termed the Odd-toed, or Perissodactyle, Ungulates. Of this group there have been no existing wild representatives during the historic period in Britain.

In the second group, on the other hand, which includes Oxen, Deer, and Pigs, the third and fourth toes (which are sometimes the only ones remaining) are larger than the second and fifth, and are symmetrical to a vertical line drawn between them, thus forming the so-called "cloven hoof." Consequently the forms included in this group are spoken of as the Even-toed, or Artiodactyle, Ungulates. The more specialised representatives of this section are very generally characterised by the presence of a pair of transversely placed bony appendages on the skull of the male sex at least, which may take the form of horns, properly so called, or of antlers.

THE OXEN, GOATS, ANTELOPES, &c.
FAMILY BOVIDÆ.

The members of this Family may be briefly characterised as being even-toed ruminating Ungulates, without incisor or canine teeth in the upper jaw, in which the appendages of the head, when present, take the form of a pair of hollow horny sheaths investing conical bony projections from the skull, such sheaths being never shed.

The function of rumination, which forms such an important portion of the foregoing definition, and is popularly termed "cud-chewing," is too well known to need much more than passing reference. It may be mentioned, however, that it consists of a regurgitation from the stomach of the hastily-swallowed grass or other vegetable food into the mouth, where it is subjected to a complete process of remastication, after which it is transferred into the true digestive portion of the stomach, it having been at first temporarily deposited in the paunch, or anterior chamber of the stomach. It will hence be evident that rumination is correlated with a complex form of stomach; while it may be added that it is likewise always associated with cheek-teeth of which the crowns have the complicated crescent-like pattern already alluded to. Moreover, there is always a long toothless gap between the cheek-teeth of the lower jaw and those in the front of the latter ; the lower canine tooth being placed alongside the three incisors, which it closely resembles in the broad, spatulate form of its crown. In the present family there is no canine tooth in the upper jaw of the adult.

Although the *Bovidæ* form a very extensive family, and one on which man chiefly depends for his food-supply, there is but a single representative entitled to be mentioned in the present work.

THE OXEN. GENUS BOS.

Bos, Linn., Syst. Nat. ed. 12, vol. i. p. 98 (1766).

Large, heavily-built "bovine" Ruminants, with horns generally present in both sexes ; broad naked muzzles ; long and cylindrical tails, usually terminating in a tuft ; tall-crowned and complex cheek-teeth ; and the males usually furnished with a large dewlap. The large horns are placed far apart from one another on or near the summit of the skull, and, although either rounded or angulated, are more or less smooth, and diverge to a greater or less extent outwards, with an upward curve at the tips.

Although the Bison and Buffaloes were separated as distinct genera, the whole of the Oxen are now included in the present genus.

PARK-CATTLE, OR AUROCHS. BOS TAURUS.

Bos taurus, Linn., Syst. Nat. ed. 12, vol. i. p. 98 (1766); Bell, British Quadrupeds, 2nd ed. p. 368 (1874).

Urus scoticus, H. Smith, in Griffith's Animal Kingdom, vol. iv. p. 411 (1827).

Bos primigenius, Bojanus, Nova Acta Ac. Cæs. Leop.-Car. vol. xiii. p. 422 (1827).

Bos scoticus, Swainson, Nat. Hist. Quadrupeds, p. 285 (1835).

Bos longifrons, Owen, Brit. Foss. Mamm. p. 508 (1846).

(Plate XXIX.)

Characters.—Horns cylindrical and placed at the very apex of the skull; no hump on the withers; tail long and descending below the hocks; colour frequently white, with black or reddish ears and muzzle.

History.—The numerous remains of gigantic Oxen specifically identical with the common domesticated Ox of Europe, found in the brick-earths of the Thames Valley, the fens of Cambridgeshire, and the peat of many parts of Scotland, prove incontestably that such animals were abundant in Britain during the pre-historic and Pleistocene periods. Although the written evidence as to the existence of such absolutely wild cattle in our islands during the historic period, is far from being so conclusive as we might wish, yet it appears to leave little doubt that such creatures were inhabitants of Britain. Thus, as we learn from Mr. Harting's researches, FitzStephen, writing about the year 1174, of the country round and about London, states that "close at hand lies an immense forest, woody ranges, hiding-places of wild beasts, of Stags, of Fallow Deer, of Boars, and of Forest Bulls." There are somewhat similar records for other parts of the country; and since it is quite evident (from the circumstance of their skulls having been transfixed by stone axes) that the absolutely wild cattle of the Cambridgeshire fens were in existence during the human period, it seems quite probable that these "Forest Bulls," their undoubted descendants, may have been equally wild. On the Continent there is decisive evidence that wild cattle existed in Cæsar's time in the Black Forest, and also, at a much later date, both there and in Switzerland; such cattle being known to the Romans by the name of Urus, and to the Germans as the Aurochs (the latter name being frequently incorrectly applied to the Bison).

Having said thus much in regard to the dearth of historical evidence relating to the existence of absolutely wild cattle in

PLATE XXIX.

CHILLINGHAM CATTLE.

Britain, we proceed to mention that from time immemorial there have existed in certain British parks peculiar races of half-wild cattle, which were long regarded as being directly descended from the original pre-historic Aurochs, without ever having undergone domestication. Although certain of these Park-Cattle (as they may be called), and more especially those of Chillingham Park, in Northumberland, are, in spite of their small size, evidently very nearly related to the gigantic wild Aurochs, there is now good reason for believing that they cannot trace back their ancestry directly to the latter without the intervention of a period of domestication. Hence they may probably be regarded as derived from a very ancient race nearly related to the wild Aurochs, which had undergone some degree of domestication.

Chillingham Cattle.—Although half-wild cattle were formerly kept in a considerable number of British parks, they remain now only in Cadzow Park, Lanarkshire, Chartley Park, Staffordshire, Chillingham Park, Northumberland, and Lyme Park, Cheshire. Since the wildest of these, and at the same time those which approach nearest to the wild Aurochs, are the Chillingham herd, our few remarks will be confined to these. These handsome animals have brown muzzles, and the insides and tips of the ears red, but are elsewhere milk-white; there is, however, evidence that originally the ears were, in most cases, black. Many of the cows are hornless. Writing many years ago, Mr. J. Hindmarsh observed that the Chillingham cattle "have pre-eminently all the characters of wild animals, with some peculiarities which are sometimes very curious and amusing. They hide their young, feed in the night, basking or sleeping during the day; they are fierce when pressed, but generally speaking very timorous, moving off on the appearance of anyone, even at a great distance." During the breeding season, the bulls are, however, very pugnacious, and it is then dangerous to approach the herd. To the effect of constant interbreeding may be attributed the small size of these cattle, and their slow rate of increase; and on more than one occasion, when attacked by murrain, they have been in danger of extermination.

THE DEER. FAMILY CERVIDÆ.

The Deer tribe may be defined as Ruminants differing from the *Bovidæ* in that the appendages of the head (which are almost invariably restricted to the males), when present, take the form of antlers, which are usually more or less branched, and are invariably shed every year; while, at least when such appendages are wanting, there are well-developed canine teeth in the upper jaw. The cheek-teeth may have either tall or short crowns. Like the *Bovidæ*, the originally separate metacarpal and metatarsal bones forming the lower part of the legs, and supporting the two middle toes, are each fused into a single cannon-bone; while the metacarpal and metatarsal bones supporting the small lateral toes are always incomplete; that is to say, they are represented only by their upper and lower extremities. This feature at once serves to distinguish the Deer from the Chevrotains, or so-called Mouse-Deer, in which the bones in question are always complete. In all Deer there is a large lachrymal gland, or "larmier," on the face; and the tail is generally short.

Although a few species, like the Asiatic Musk-Deer, are devoid of these appendages, the great peculiarity of the Deer is the annual reproduction of the antlers of the males. In spite of familiarity having produced the proverbial contempt, this process is really one of the most wonderful physiological effects to be met with in nature; and if it had been described as occurring in some previously unknown fossil animal, it would have required all the talent of a palæontologist to have rendered it credible. Not only is this enormous mass of bone annually shed and renewed, but immediately after its completion it becomes an absolutely dead structure, having no connection with the vascular system of its owner. Soon after the annual shedding of the antlers, there appear on the skull of a Stag a pair of velvety knobs, with a large number of blood-vessels traversing their tender and sensitive skin. These bony knobs grow very rapidly, and soon begin to branch into a larger or smaller number of tines according to the age and species of the Deer to which they belong. When the new antlers are fully formed, they develop at the base a rough ring of bone termed the "burr," which constricts and finally stops the supply of blood, thus causing the skin, or " velvet," covering the antler to dry up ; this dead velvet subsequently either peeling off by itself or being rubbed off by the animal against the stems or branches of trees. In young Stags the antlers are very simple, and in those species in which they are much branched in the adult, they gradually increase in complexity with advancing age, although this annual increasing complexity is not so regular as is often stated to be the case.

The Family is divided into a large number of genera, two of which are still represented in the British Isles, where there is evidence that a third also existed within the historic period. Although distributed over the greater part of the world, with the exception of Australasia, Deer are quite unknown in Africa south of the Sahara Desert.

THE TYPICAL DEER. GENUS CERVUS.

Cervus, Linn., Syst. Nat. ed. 12, vol. i. p. 92 (1766).

Antlers rising at an acute angle from the middle line of the forehead, large, and either rounded or flattened ; skull without prominent longitudinal ridges on the forehead, and with the canine teeth relatively small ; lateral metacarpal and metatarsal bones of the feet represented by their upper extremities only. Muzzle narrow and naked; and tail of medium shortness. In most cases the young are spotted.

This large and widely-spread genus may be divided into a number of groups, mainly distinguished by the characters of the antlers of the males ; such groups being regarded by some naturalists as entitled to rank as distinct genera.

I. THE RED DEER. CERVUS ELAPHUS.

Cervus elaphus, Linn., Syst. Nat. ed. 12, vol. i. p. 93 (1766); Bell, British Quadrupeds, 2nd ed. p. 348 (1874).

Cervus barbarus, Bennett, List An. Gard. Zool. Soc. 1837, p. 31.

Strongyloceros spelæus, Owen, Brit. Foss. Mamm. p. 469 (1846).

(Plate XXX.).

Characters.—Antlers rounded, and generally with a brow-, bez-, and trez-tine, above which are the cup-shaped sur-royals; tail short; general colour dark reddish-brown in summer, and greyish-brown in winter, with a large whitish patch on the rump including the tail. Height of adult male 48 inches, or more, at the withers.

As regards general form, the body is moderately full and rounded, the neck of moderate length, and the graceful head tapering to the obtuse muzzle ; the liquid eyes are large and full; the ears rather long and pointed ; and the limbs slender ; while the tail does not exceed half the length of the ear. The fur comprises both bristly and woolly hairs ; the former, which are much the more numerous, being moderately long and close, while the latter are short and fine. The fur is thinnest on the under-parts, longest on the rump and back, and more especially on the fore-part of the neck, while on the feet and face it is very short. The young are prettily spotted with white ; and

RED DEER.

very rarely, pure white adult individuals are met with in a wild state. From fifteen to twenty stone may be given as the average weight of an adult British Stag. The largest Deer in England are those of Warnham Court, in Sussex, where a Stag of fourty-four stone has been killed; while in the same park lived, in 1892, a stag with forty-eight points to its antlers.

The antlers of the male make their appearance at the age of about seven months, and for the second year are straight and simple ; in the third year they have a single "brow"-tine immediately above the burr, when the animal is termed a "Brockett." Subsequently the second, or "bez"-tine, and the third or "trez"-tine, frequently termed the royal, are developed ; and the complete antler terminates in a cup or crown of three or more points, collectively known as the sur-royals. The term "Royal Hart" is first applied to Stags after the development of the three anterior tines, namely the "brow," "bez," and "trez." The antlers of Red Deer found in the fens, turbaries, and caverns of the British Isles are vastly larger, heavier, and carry a greater number of points on the sur-royals, than do those of any existing Scottish Stag; this diminution in the size of the antlers being readily accounted for by the restricted area of deer-forests, in-and-in breeding, and the comparatively early age at which most Stags are killed. The finest antlers of a Scotch Stag on record were obtained by Lord Burton in the autumn of 1893, in the forest of Glen Quoich, each having ten points. Even these, however, are nothing to the antlers from the peat and caverns, or, indeed, to some of the recent ones preserved in certain German castles, which may have as many as twenty points each. In a full-grown Scotch Stag, the weight of the antlers seldom exceeds from twelve to fifteen pounds.

Distribution.—The Red Deer is a member of a group comprising several closely allied species or varieties, spread over Northern Europe, Asia, and America, and also represented in

5   R

Northern Africa. So closely, indeed, are these Deer allied to one another, that it is frequently difficult to say which should be regarded as species, and which as varieties ; and we ought, perhaps, to regard the whole number as local varieties or races of one widely-spread species. To point out how these various Deer differ from one another, would considerably exceed the limits of our space ; and we must, therefore, in the main, confine ourselves to the distribution of the species under consideration, although even this is a matter shrouded in some degree of uncertainty.

Originally distributed over the greater part of Europe, the Red Deer extends some distance into Western Asia, being found in many parts of Asia Minor, as well as in Trans-Caucasia, although it, at most, only just impinges on the confines of Persia. From the Caucasus, Deer of the present type extend eastwards right away through Northern and Central Asia to Amurland and the North of China. How far the typical Red Deer extends in this direction, or where it is replaced by the so-called *C. xanthopygus*, and also whether the latter is anything more than a variety, are matters on which our judgment must be suspended. Southwards the Red Deer extends into Algeria and other parts of Northern Africa, the African race being distinguished by the absence of the "bez"-tine of the antlers. Of the allied species, we may mention by name the North American Wapiti (*C. canadensis*), the nearly similar Thian Shan Stag (*C. eustephanus*), the Kashmir Stag (*C. cashmirianus*), represented by a variety in Yarkand, the Persian Maral (*C. maral*), the Shou (*C. affinis*) of the inner eastern Himalaya, and the Lhasa Stag (*C. thoroldi*) of the Tibetan plateau ; the last-named species agreeing with the North African variety of the Red Deer in the absence of the "bez"-tine.

As regards their distribution in the British Isles, Red Deer are still to be found in the wild state in three districts of England, but are elsewhere confined to the Scottish Highlands and some of the wilder parts of Ireland. In the west of England there are a considerable number in Devonshire and Somersetshire, the herd being estimated at about two hundred and fifty head in 1871. Martindale Fell, in Westmoreland, is likewise one of the last strongholds of the species, although the number of head now remaining is comparatively small ; and as these Deer are fed in winter they can hardly be considered as absolutely wild. According to the Hon. G. Lascelles, some fifteen or twenty head still remain in the New Forest. About a century ago there were wild Red Deer in Cornwall; and all readers of Gilbert White must be familiar with his description of the Deer in Wolmer Forest, in Hampshire, which, in the time of Queen Anne, numbered about five hundred head. Tame Red Deer are now kept in eighty-six English parks, out of which Batminton has the largest herd. In most of these parks Fallow Deer are also kept, but in Blenheim (Oxfordshire), Bolton Abbey (Yorkshire), Barmingham (Yorkshire), and Calcot (Berkshire), Red Deer alone are kept. In a few English parks, namely, Alnwick; Ashridge, Langley, Welbeck, Windsor, and Woburn, there is a white or cream-coloured variety of the Red Deer, in which the nose is flesh-coloured, while the eyes are either pale blue or straw-coloured. The origin of this breed is quite unknown. It may be remarked here that formerly there was a prejudice against keeping Red and Fallow Deer in the same park, as it was thought they would disagree ; but this is now ascertained to be a mistaken idea.

It will be unnecessary to refer to the distribution of the Red Deer in the Scottish Highlands, but it may be mentioned that even in comparatively recent times the range of the species extended to the south-west of Scotland. Deer are indigenous to the island of Mull, though there have been several importations of fresh blood in order to counteract the ill-effects of in-and-in breeding; and they likewise inhabit all the Hebrides, but are now unknown in Shetland and Orkney, although there is evidence of their former existence in the latter. Once abundant over the whole of Ireland, the Red Deer, even in Thompson's time, was confined to the wilder parts of Connaught, as Erris and Connemara, and to a few localities in the south, more especially the neighbourhood of the Lakes of Killarney.

Habits.—Essentially gregarious in their habits, Red Deer, in common with most of their kind, divide themselves according to sexes for the greater portion of the year, the old Stags only consorting with the herds of does and young males during the breeding-season. During the summer the old Stags, while apart from the hinds, are in the habit of feeding singly or in small herds on the higher parts of the hills, while the hinds and young, unless much disturbed, prefer the valleys and lower ground. In September the Stags commence their rambles in search of the hinds, the breeding-season lasting for about three weeks from the latter part of that month or the beginning of the next. During this season of excitement they make the mountains ring with their loud bellowings, which are uttered at night and early morning; and should two rival "monarchs of the glen" chance to meet, a deadly conflict at once ensues. During such conflict, the hinds, as so admirably depicted in some of Landseer's pictures, remain as silent spectators, awaiting the issue, and then betake themselves to the triumphant victor. After the excitement of this season, the old Stags become very poor, and seem dejected; their mutual hostility ceases, and they set to work to recruit their energies before the severity of winter. The fawns are born in May or June, after a gestation of eight months and a few days; the hind retiring to some sequestered situation, where she attends her offspring with the greatest care and solicitude. In the winter the hinds and fawns once more congregate in herds. It is but very seldom that more than a single fawn is dropped at a birth, and there are never triplets.

A certain amount of variation occurs in the time of shedding the antlers, according to the age of the animals and the nature of the season. In unusually mild seasons they may be dropped in the latter part of February or early in March, but April is a more usual time, while if the spring be very late they may be retained till May. An instance is recorded by Mr. J. Hargreaves where a "Royal Hart" shed his antlers in December; but this seems to be quite unique. The rarity with which shed antlers of Deer are met with has often been noticed; and it is now well ascertained that this is due to their being eaten by the Deer themselves; although it is a little difficult to understand how an animal devoid of upper front teeth can manage to gnaw so hard a substance. It should be added that young Stags retain their antlers longer than the old ones, and a two-year-old animal may frequently be seen with them in May or June. When in the velvet, the Stags keep to themselves in the most sequestered situations they can find.

Like other members of the Family, and, indeed, like Ruminants in general, Red Deer are very fond of salt, and will travel long distances in search of "licks." Their feeding-time is chiefly the morning and evening, the middle of the day being spent in repose and cud-chewing among the heather. Their food consists chiefly of grass, leaves, young shoots, beech-nuts, and acorns; and it is stated that they will also eat various fungi.

Both in sight and hearing, the Red Deer is one of the most acute of animals; nevertheless, Macgillivray states that he has succeeded in crawling within ten paces of one. "When you have fired from your concealment," he adds, "the herd immediately starts off, gathering into a close body as they proceed, and at

the distance of from two to four hundred paces, invariably turn
and stand for a few seconds, to discover whence the noise has
come." In thus giving a chance for a second shot before
their final stampede, Red Deer resemble nearly all other
Ruminants. That they swim well, and may be seen crossing
from island to island in the larger lakes, is a well-known fact.

As regards its flesh, the Red Deer is less highly esteemed
than the Fallow Deer.

II. THE FALLOW DEER. CERVUS DAMA.

Cervus dama, Linn., Syst. Nat. ed. 12, vol. i. p. 93 (1766);
  Bell, British Quadrupeds, 2nd ed. p. 358 (1874).
Dama vulgaris, Gray, List Mamm. Brit. Mus. p. 181 (1843).
                    (*Plate XXXI.*)

Characters.—Belonging to a totally different group of the
genus to that containing the Red Deer, the present species
is readily distinguished from the latter by the form of the
antlers, and may be characterised as follows. Antlers rounded
at the base and flattened or palmated in the region of the sur-
royals, with a " brow "- and "trez "-tine in front, and a third tine
behind, above which the posterior margin carries a number
of small points; no upper canine teeth (which are present
in the adult Red Deer); tail rather long, exceeding the ear in
length. General colour yellowish-brown, with rows of white
spots on the body, but sometimes uniform dark brown, and
in other cases milk-white. Height of adult buck at the withers,
about 35 or 36 inches.

Distribution.—As being apparently an introduced species, the
Fallow Deer, strictly speaking, has no right to be included
in the British Fauna, and on this account it is omitted
by Macgillivray. If, however, this rule be enforced, the two
species of Rats, as well as the Rabbit, would have to disappear
from our lists. When or whence this pretty Deer was in-

FALLOW DEER

troduced into Britain is not definitely known, although it is commonly reputed to have been brought by the Romans from the Mediterranean countries. The dark variety was long considered to have been imported from Norway by James the First, but Mr. Harting has shown that it existed here long before his time ; while equally erroneous is the theory that the ordinary spotted form (which used to be known by the name of *Menil*) was imported from Manilla. Kept in a more or less completely domesticated state in large numbers of British parks, Fallow Deer are found in an almost wild condition in the New Forest and Epping Forest ; those in the latter being characterised by the narrow palmation of their antlers. There is also a small remnant of a nearly wild herd in Rockingham Forest. Of the New Forest Fallow Deer, the Hon. G. Lascelles, in a letter to Mr. J. Whitaker, quoted in the work of the latter on English Deer-parks, observes that, at the date of writing (January, 1892), there may be from two to three hundred head. " They are all precisely alike in colour, viz., very dark brown, with dun legs and bellies in winter, and in summer all 'fallow,' *i.e.*, light red, with whitish spots on the sides. The brightness of the spots varies, but the colour never. They all change their coats simultaneously in May and October, just like Wild Roe, and in this respect of varying in colour are unlike any Park-Deer that I know.

"These Deer are the pure Old English (or Roman) stock. They have always run perfectly wild in the forest and adjoining woods, and the stock has never been quite extinct."

In a wild state Fallow Deer are met with in South-eastern Europe, while in Mesopotamian Persia the species is replaced by the closely-allied Mesopotamian Fallow Deer (*C. mesopotamicus*). It is noteworthy that fossilised remains of Fallow Deer very nearly related to the common species are met with in the "forest-bed" of the Norfolk coast.

Habits.—The general habits of nearly all Deer are so similar that it will be unnecessary to refer to those of the present species in any great detail.   The period of changing the coat varies in most parks according to the nature of the season, and it is somewhat remarkable that while the brown variety is darker in summer than in winter, the reverse is the case with the paler spotted race; some of these showing scarcely any trace in winter of the numerous spots with which they are adorned in the summer-dress.   The antlers of the old bucks are shed in May, and the new ones begin to sprout in about ten days afterwards.   The fawns are born early in June, and although occasionally there may be twins, Mr. Whitaker refuses to accept the alleged occurrences of triplets.   As a rare event, a fawn may be dropped in autumn.   As regards food, it is only necessary to mention that Fallow Deer show a special partiality for chestnuts.

Writing of the habits of Deer in parks, the author last mentioned observes that these vary according to the season. " From May till October they rest from about 9.30 a.m. until 2 p.m.; sometimes in the shade, sometimes on the top of a hill, where they catch what little breeze there may be.   During the period of rest they get up occasionally to stretch themselves, and after standing up, or scratching their sides and necks with hoof and horn, they lie down again, but always on the other side.   They pass their time in chewing the cud and sleeping, and if the day be hot and sunny, will lie with all four legs stretched out, exposing as much of their bodies to the sun as they can.   About 2 p.m. they feed, and wander about till 4, when they again lie down for about two hours, starting again about 6 p.m., and continuing until 9 p.m., when they rest until 5 the next morning, feeding from that hour until 9 or 9.30 a.m.   In the winter they feed most of the short days, but when well supplied with corn and hay, they rest during the middle of the day.

PLATE XXXII.

ROE DEER

"In parks which are heavily stocked, Deer have to work harder for their food, and rest for shorter periods. When rising from the ground, Deer get on their knees first, then raise their hind-quarters before getting on their fore-feet. In fact they get up as a Cow does, just reversing the actions of a Horse."

THE ROE-DEER. GENUS CAPREOLUS.

Capreolus, H. Smith, in Griffith's Animal Kingdom, vol. v. p. 313 (1827).

Antlers small, simple, and rounded, less than twice the length of the head, usually with only three tines each, of which the front one springs from the anterior surface of the upper half of the antler, and has an upward direction; tail very short; no upper canine teeth; lateral metacarpal and metatarsal bones of the feet indicated only by their lower extremities.

Roe-Deer are comparatively small animals, represented by two or three closely-allied species; the range of the genus being confined to Europe and Asia north of the Himalaya, one species extending as far eastwards as Mantchuria.

THE COMMON ROE-DEER. CAPREOLUS CAPREA.

Cervus capreolus, Linn., Syst. Nat. ed. 12, vol. i. p. 94 (1766).

Capreolus capræa, Gray, List Mamm. Brit. Mus. p. 176 (1843).

Capreolus caprea, Bell, British Quadrupeds, 2nd ed. p. 363 (1874).

(*Plate XXXII.*)

Characters.—Size small; ears moderately hairy; general colour reddish-brown in summer and yellowish-grey in winter, with a relatively large white disc on the rump. Height of male at the withers about 25 inches. Fawn yellowish-red in autumn, with several longitudinal rows of whitish spots.

In form the Roe has a moderately full body, long and slender limbs, the neck of moderate length and considerable thickness, the head tapering, with a rather narrow muzzle, the eyes large and full, the ears long and pointed, and the rudimentary tail concealed among the fur. The hair is close, stiff, of moderate length, and structurally very similar to that of the Red Deer ; there being a slight intermixture of woolly under-fur. For the greater part of their length the hairs are purplish-grey, then dusky, with the tips reddish-brown or yellowish-grey, according to the season. In addition to her considerably inferior stature, the doe is lighter coloured than the buck.

Although the antlers, as already said, normally have only three tines, they are very liable to "sport," and some remarkable specimens are contained in the collection of Viscount Powerscourt, at Powerscourt in Ireland, in which the antlers consist of a bushy mass of points.

Distribution.—The Common Roe is widely distributed in Europe and Western Asia ; but is replaced in Turkestan and the mountains between Russia and China by the Tartarian Roe (*C. pygargus*), distinguished by its larger size, more hairy ears, and the smaller size of the white disc on the rump.

That the Roe, although totally unknown in Ireland, was formerly distributed over the remainder of the British Islands, is attested by the occurrence of its remains in the Norfolk forest-bed, the brick-earths of the Thames Valley, the fens of Cambridgeshire and Lincolnshire, and also in a number of English caverns. Although at the present day mainly restricted to Scotland, Wild Roe are still found sparingly in Northumberland, Cumberland, and Durham, while at the commencement of the present century they were reintroduced _nto Dorsetshire, where they are now fairly common in the woods on the south side of the Blackmoor Vale. A few likewise exist in the woods about Virginia Water, as also in Petworth Park, Sussex, while in 1884 a number were turned down in Epping Forest, where the species had long ceased to exist. Regarding the Roes of Naworth, near Brampton, in Cumberland, the Rev. H. A. Macpherson writes that only a few now remain, "and a few more wander through the plantations of the Netherby property. On some rare occasions these animals have been known to cross the Eden, and even to wander up the valley of that river into the neighbourhood of Penrith." In Wales the Roe is stated to have lingered as late as the reign of Queen Elizabeth.

Although in Scotland the Roe is less widely distributed than it was in former times, the increase of plantations in the south has led to its re-occupying districts where it was once exterminated; and this steady enlargement of its distributional area is still going on. Into Mull it was introduced in the year 1865. In Argyllshire, Messrs. Harvie-Brown and Buckley state that these Deer are much more abundant in the recently-planted pine- and larch-woods than they are in the native copses of oak, hazel, or birch; a birch-clad glen of three or more miles in length seldom containing more than from two to four Roe at a time.

Habits.—Essentially a forest-loving species, the Roe is a non-gregarious Deer, usually consorting in parties of from two to four head, and the two sexes remaining together throughout the year. "Its agility," remarks Macgillivray, "is astonishing, for it will bound over a space of eight or ten yards with ease, and leap a wall five or six feet high with scarcely an appearance of effort. Its ordinary pace when not pursued is an easy canter, but when alarmed it bounds along with great spirit and grace. It feeds chiefly in the morning and evening, often also at night, when it sometimes commits depredations on the corn fields in the neighbourhood of its haunts, and reposes by day among the heath or fern, often, when not liable to be much disturbed, selecting a spot to which it resorts in continuance." The Roe displays great curiosity in its disposition, and has been known to walk up within a short distance of a party of gentlemen seated on the grass, remain there walking inquisitively round in half-circles for more than a quarter-of-an-hour, and not taking its departure till it got wind of them, when it wheeled round and rushed off with a snort.

Mr. Trevor-Battye writes:—"On two successive evenings when I was sitting sketching in a Perthshire glen, in September, 1891, a fine Roebuck came up and stood within twenty yards and challenged me, snorting and stamping like a Sheep, and sometimes beating the ground with both fore-feet at the same instant."

The most remarkable peculiarity connected with the Roe, relates to its breeding. The pairing-season is in July and August, and the young are born in the following May or June. The interval is, however, not entirely the true period of gestation, since the germ remains dormant till December, when it suddenly begins to develop, and passes through the usual stages. The doe usually produces two fawns at a birth, and in one case at least three have been observed. The fawns remain with their parent till the winter, and are most zealously protected by her from danger. The first antlers of the bucks are in the form of simple spikes, those of the second winter are forked ; while in the third season the three tines of the adult are developed. The flesh of the Roe is very dark coloured, and somewhat dry.

THE REINDEER. GENUS RANGIFER.

Rangifer, H. Smith, in Griffith's Animal Kingdom, vol. v. p 304 (1827).

Distinguished from all the other members of the Family by the normal presence of antlers in both sexes. The antlers are very large, and have a rounded beam, with both "brow"- and 'bez "-tines, both of which are either branched or palmated, while frequently one of the former is rudimentary, and the other greatly developed. At about the middle of its length the beam is suddenly bent forwards at an angle, a larger or smaller back-tine being frequently given off at this point, the main branch terminating in several snags. The main hoofs of each foot are very widely separated, to afford support by their divergence in walking on deep snow; and for the same object the lateral hoofs are likewise large.

THE REINDEER. RANGIFER TARANDUS.

Cervus tarandus, Linn., Syst. Nat. ed. 12, vol. i. p. 93 (1766).

Rangifer tarandus, H. Smith, in Griffith's Animal Kingdom, vol. v. p. 304 (1827).

The claim of the Reindeer to be enrolled in the British Fauna being the same as that of the Wolf and Brown Bear, we shall not describe the animal, nor enter into a description of its habits and geographical distribution, merely mentioning that at the present day it has a circum-polar range, and in the Eastern Hemisphere extends about as far south as latitude 52°.

That the Reindeer was an inhabitant of the British Islands during the Pleistocene and Prehistoric periods, is abundantly testified by the occurrence of its fossilised remains in the brick-earths, fens, turbaries, peat-bogs, and caverns of England, Scotland, and Ireland ; some of the antlers bearing distinct marks of stone or other implements. The evidence of their occurrence within our limits during the historical period is, however, much less satisfactory, and rests solely upon a passage in Torfæus's " History of Orkney," written at the close of the twelfth century. As commonly translated, this passage states that "the jarls of Orkney were in the habit of crossing over to Caithness almost every summer, and there hunting in the wilds the Red Deer and Reindeer." If we could depend on this translation of the passage, which refers to the middle of the twelfth century, there would be little doubt that Reindeer did exist in Caithness. Unfortunately, however, the experts who have examined the original are by no means agreed whether Reindeer are really the animals intended; and under these circumstances it must remain a matter of doubt whether the Reindeer was ever an inhabitant of Britain during the period taken into consideration in the present volume.

THE PIGS. FAMILY SUIDÆ.

From the two preceding Families and their allies, collectively constituting the true Ruminants, the Pigs are at once distinguished by the presence of incisor teeth in the upper jaw, by the lower canine teeth being unlike the incisors and in the form of tusks, by the simpler structure of the molar teeth, which have comparatively short crowns surmounted by blunt tubercles, and by the simple character of the stomach and the want of the power of chewing the cud. To these characteristics it may be added that the third and fourth metacarpal bones of the fore-feet and the corresponding metatarsals of the hind ones are separate, and do not unite to form cannon-bones; while the metacarpals and metatarsals of the lateral toes are complete. Since we have but a single species to deal with which does not exist at the present time in a wild state in Britain, we shall not give the characteristics or distribution of either the genus or species, but merely consider the claims of the latter to a place in the Fauna of the historical period of Britain.

THE TRUE PIGS. GENUS SUS.

Sus, Linn. Syst. Nat. ed. 12, vol. i. p. 102 (1766).

THE WILD BOAR. SUS SCROFA.

Sus scrofa, Linn., *loc. cit.;* Owen, Brit. Foss. Mamm. p. 426 (1846).

Sus scrofa ferus, Ball, Trans. Roy. Dublin Soc. ser. 2, vol. iii. p. 339 (1889).

Distributed at the present day over the greater part of Europe and Asia north of the Himalaya, but replaced in India by the closely allied *Sus cristatus*, the Wild Boar has long ceased to be a member of the British Fauna. The earliest formation in which its remains have hitherto been detected is the Norfolk forest-bed, belonging, as we have already had occasion to mention, either to the latter part of the Pliocene, or the early part of the Pleistocene period. Similar remains are likewise of common occurrence in the brick-earths of the Thames Valley and the contemporary formations of other parts of England; while they also occur in the fens and many English caves. They have likewise been obtained from peat-bogs, as well as from caves, in Ireland.

Of its existence in our islands to a comparatively late date of the historical period, we have abundant testimony, which, as in the case of the other Mammals exterminated during that epoch, has been carefully collected and arranged by Mr. J. E. Harting, in his work on "Extinct British Animals." We there learn that a painting in a manuscript of the ninth century represents a Saxon chief, attended by his huntsman and a couple of hounds, pursuing Wild Boars through a wood. Further, it is enacted in the Welsh laws of Howel Dha, promulgated towards the close of the tenth century, that the season for Wild Boar hunting should last from the ninth of November till the first of December; but it appears that later on, in the reign of Edward II., the season was fixed to embrace the period between Christmas Day and Candlemas Day. We learn, moreover, from the testimony of William of Malmesbury, that in the time of Edward the Confessor the forest of Bernwood, in Buckinghamshire, was infested by a notable Wild Boar, which was eventually killed by the King's huntsman, and its head presented to His Majesty. So delighted was the Sovereign with this exploit, that he presented a tract of land to his faithful henchman, who built upon it a mansion which he appropriately christened Bore-Stall.

At the Conquest, Inglewood Forest, in the Border Country, was stated to contain Red and Fallow Deer, Wild Boars, and other beasts; and the Rev. H. A. Macpherson quotes a passage from the pipe-rolls of Henry II., which seems to indicate that Wild Swine existed there as late as his reign. Again, the forest-laws of William the Conqueror refer to the Wild Boar as being as well known as the Red Deer and the Roe; and it is stated that Henry I. was especially fond of Boar-hunting, while Edward I. made several grants of land held by the serjeanty of providing Boar-hounds. Between the years 1153 and 1165 we find Robert de Avenel, when granting to the monks of Melrose Abbey the right of pasturage over the lands of Eskdale, especially reserving to himself the right of hunting Wild Boar and Deer; and there is actual evidence of a Boar-hunt taking place at this very time in the same district.

Among the animals inhabiting the great forest around London mentioned by FitzStephen in 1174, we find the Wild Boar occupying a prominent place; and from the fact that certain land in Oxfordshire was held on condition of furnishing the King with Boar-spears on the occasions of his visits, it may be inferred that Edward III. was in the habit of pursuing the Wild Boar in that county; this would be about the year 1340. Certain other documents refer to Wild Boars in the year 1573, and twenty years later

Erdeswick, in his description of Chartley Park, Staffordshire, speaks of the number of these animals contained therein. Again, Leland tells us that at Blakeley, in Lancashire, "wild bores, bulls, and falcons bredde in times paste," and that near by is a place called Boar's Green.

In Scotland Boethius speaks of a huge Wild Boar killed on land belonging to the See of St. Andrews; while at an earlier date a Latin MS., giving the history of the Gordon family, dated 1545, relates that in 1057 a Wild Boar had been slaughtered by a member of that family in Huntly Forest. In the Highlands there are many traditions referring to Wild Boars, whose former abundance is likewise attested by the names of many places; and much the same may be stated in regard to Ireland.

THE CETACEANS. ORDER CETACEA.

The Whales, Dolphins, and their allies, collectively designated Cetaceans, are distinguished from all other Mammals by their assumption of a remarkable fish-like form, the only other members of the order approaching them in this respect being the Sirenians, of which there are no British representatives, and which present marked structural peculiarities of their own.

Fish-like in external appearance, with a spindle-shaped body, into which the head passes without any indication of a neck, Cetaceans have the front-limbs modified into simple ovoid paddles, devoid of any trace of division into segments or toes, while externally hind-limbs are completely wanting. Towards the hinder extremity, the body gradually tapers, until it becomes of very small diameter at the tail, which terminates in a horizontally-placed, fibrous, fin-like expansion, termed the "flukes"; this is deeply notched in the middle of its hinder border, and has sharp lateral angles. Relatively large in size, the head has the nostrils, which may be either single or double, placed near the top of the crown, and thus far removed from the muzzle; this feature at once serving to distinguish Cetaceans from Sirenians. Both the eye and ear are small; the latter merely forming a minute aperture in the skin, placed some distance behind the former, and showing no trace of a conch. The majority of Cetaceans have a vertical fin in the middle of the back, very similar in appearance to the fin of some fishes, although lacking the bony internal skeleton found in the latter. With the exception of a few fine bristles in the neighbourhood of the mouth, which are frequently lost in the adult, the skin is entirely naked, and smooth and glistening in appearance; while beneath it lies a thick layer of oily fat—the blubber —to protect the body from the chilling effects of submersion in the water. In all existing members of the Order in which they are present, the teeth are of an exceedingly simple structure.

The foregoing characters being sufficient to distinguish the Cetaceans from all other Mammalian Orders, are all that need be mentioned here.

As regards their mode of life, it is almost superfluous to observe that all Cetaceans are purely aquatic Mammals, passing the whole of their time in the water, and becoming immediately utterly helpless when once stranded on the shore. Whereas the majority are denizens of the ocean—some keeping exclusively to the open sea, while others more generally frequent the vicinity of the coast—a few are inhabitants of certain large rivers of the warmer regions of the globe, many of them, which are normally marine, occasionally ascending tidal rivers. Carnivorous in their diet, Cetaceans vary greatly in the nature of their food, some of the largest species feeding on organisms of the most minute size. While many of the smaller kinds live on fish, the ferocious "Killer" Whale alone consumes other Mammals, such as Seals and its own kindred. Hunting their prey either near the surface of the water, or at a greater or lesser depth below, Whales are obliged to come up at stated intervals to breathe, when they renovate the air in their lungs by the well-known action of "spouting."

Roaming at will through the trackless ocean, most Cetaceans apparently conform but little to laws of geographical distribution; a large number of species being more or less cosmopolitan in their distribution. Certain species, such as the Greenland Whale, the White Whale, and the Narwhal, are however, more or less, exclusively confined to the Arctic and Sub-Arctic Seas; while others, like the Pigmy Whale (*Neobalæna*), are equally characteristic of the Southern Seas. In consequence of these widely roaming habits of so many members of the Order, it is somewhat difficult to say how many species have a right to be included in the British Fauna. We must, however, regard all such as habitually frequent our coasts as entitled to a place in our Fauna; while in the case of those occurring only now and again, we must rather look upon them as accidental visitors. Still, however, no "hard-and-fast line" can be drawn in this respect.

THE WHALE-BONE WHALES.
FAMILY BALÆNIDÆ.

This Family, which includes the whole of the larger Whales, with the exception of the Sperm-Whale, is at once distinguished from all the others by the total absence of teeth, and the presence of that peculiar substance in the palate known as whale-bone or baleen. The nostrils open by two slit-like apertures.

Since the structure, arrangement, and mode of action of whale-bone has been described in so many works, it will be quite unnecessary that this should be recapitulated here; and

we accordingly at once pass on to the consideration of such
members of the Family as habitually, or from time to time, visit
the neighbourhood of the British Islands.

THE RIGHT WHALES. GENUS BALÆNA.

Balæna, Linn., Syst. Nat. ed. 12, vol. i. p. 105 (1766).

Whale-bone Whales of large size, in which the skin of the
throat is smooth, the back-fin absent, the flippers broad and
short, the head of enormous size, the whale-bone very long,
narrow, highly elastic, and black in colour, and all the vertebræ of the neck immovably welded together. So far as
can be ascertained, the genus includes only two well-defined
species.

THE SOUTHERN RIGHT WHALE. BALÆNA AUSTRALIS.

Balæna australis, Desmoulins, Dict. Class. d'Hist. Nat. vol. ii.
p. 161 (1822).
Balæna biscayensis, Gray, Proc. Zool. Soc. 1864, p. 200; Bell,
British Quadrupeds, 2nd ed. p. 387 (1874); Southwell,
British Seals and Whales, p. 62 (1881).
Macleayius brittanicus, Gray, Ann. Mag. Nat. Hist. vol. vi. p.
198 (1870).

Characters.—Distinguished from the Greenland Right Whale
(*B. mystacetus*) by its relatively smaller head, shorter whale-
bone, the different contour of the margin of the lower lip, and
the greater number of ribs (15 instead of 12). The size is
also stated to be somewhat less; and there is a marked
difference in the form of the tympanic bone of the internal
ear. In colour, this Whale appears to be wholly black, instead
of having white on the lower lip, and at the roots of the flippers
and flukes.

Distribution.—Although they have received distinct specific

names, it appears that the Right Whales of the North Atlantic the North Pacific, the South Atlantic, and the South Pacific, cannot be satisfactorily distinguished from one another, and they are accordingly included provisionally under one name. Such specimens as have been observed in the British seas belong to the North Atlantic variety, *B. biscayensis.* Formerly common in the North Atlantic, this Whale has long since been practically exterminated in these seas, such stragglers as have reached the European coasts during the last century or so having probably travelled from the opposite side of the Atlantic.

Such few examples of Right Whales as are stated to have visited our coasts in the older works on British Mammals were believed to belong to the Greenland Whale; but it is now pretty certainly ascertained that that species never by any chance wanders so far south, and they must accordingly be referred, in all probability, to the Southern Right Whale.

The earliest record we have of the reported occurrence of Right Wales in British waters is one given by Sibbald, who states that in the year 1682 one visited Peterhead; and there is some evidence that a young specimen was stranded at Yarmouth, in the summer of 1846. At an earlier date than the latter, namely in the year 1806, a female Right Whale with her calf, was seen off the coast of Peterhead; the young one being killed by fishermen who started in pursuit. The only other instance is given on the evidence of Captain Gray, an experienced whaler, who, while walking at Peterhead in the autumn of 1872, saw what he believed to be a Right Whale within half a mile of the shore. It may be added that the united cervical vertebræ of a Right Whale dredged off Lyme Regis not later than the year 1853, belong to the present species.

Since this Whale has so little claim to be regarded as British, it will be unnecessary to say anything concerning its habits, except that it is reported to be a swifter and more active animal than the Greenland Right Whale, being much more violent in its movements when harpooned, and consequently much more difficult and dangerous to capture. It is also characterised by being infested by a species of barnacle, more especially in the region of the blow-hole, or nostrils.

THE HUMP-BACKED WHALES. GENUS MEGAPTERA.

Megaptera, Gray, Zool. Voy. of Erebus and Terror, p. 16 (1846).

Skin of the throat thrown into longitudinal grooves, or puckers; a low back-fin; flippers very long and narrow, and their skeleton with only four digits (in place of the five in *Balæna*); head of moderate size; whale-bone plates short, broad, and black; vertebræ of the neck free.

In conformity with the shorter and broader baleen, the upper jaw is much less arched and much broader than in the Right Whales; while the lower lip is not elevated into the curious arched form so characterisic of the latter. There is likewise a marked difference in the form of the tympanic bone of the internal ear, which is more rounded and shell-like. So far as can be determined, there appears to be but a single existing representative of the genus.

THE HUMP-BACKED WHALE.　MEGAPTERA BÖOPS.

?Balæna böops, Linn., Syst. Nat. ed. 12, vol. i. p. 106 (1766).

Balæna böops, Fabricius, Fauna Grœnlandica, p. 36 (1780).

Balæna longimana, Rudolphi, Mem. Ac. Berlin, 1829, p. 133.

Megaptera longimana, Gray, Zool. Voy. Erebus and Terror, p. 17 (1846); Bell, British Quadrupeds, 2nd ed. p. 392 (1874); Southwell, British Seals and Whales, p. 69 (1881).

Megaptera böops, Van Beneden and Gervais, Ostéographie des Cétacés, p. 120 (1869-1880); Flower, List Cetacea Brit. Mus. p. 4 (1885).

Characters.—Body deep and somewhat humped near the middle; the long flippers scalloped along their margins; in colour, nearly the whole of the head and body black, and the flippers, except near the root, white. Total length of adult from 45 to 50 feet; of flippers from 10 to 14 feet. Females exceeding the males in size.

Distribution.—If zoologists are right in regarding all Humpbacks as referable to a single species, this Whale is found in nearly all the large oceans, specimens having been obtained as far north as Greenland and as far south as New Zealand.

Although frequent in the higher latitudes of the North Atlantic, the Hump-back is but a rare visitor to most of the coasts of the British Islands. Of the recorded specimens, one was washed ashore in 1839; while a young one, of which the skeleton is now in the museum at Liverpool, was captured in the estuary of the Dee in 1863; a third was picked up dead at sea by a Banff boat in April, 1871, and was towed into Wick harbour; and a fourth full-grown individual entered the estuary of the Tay in the winter of 1883-4, where it was captured. According to verbal information communicated by Captain Gray to Mr. Southwell, it appears that in summer these Whales are by no means uncommon off the east coast of Scotland, and that several have been captured off Peterhead, no less than three having, it is stated, been killed in a single year.

Habits.—In place of feeding, like the Right Whales, on minute pelagic animals, the Hump-back subsists mainly on various molluscs, crustaceans, and fish. In disposition it is neither very timorous nor very fierce, and it is consequently easy to capture. Its yield of blubber is, however, small, and its whalebone of poor quality; and in times, when the Greenland Right Whale was less scarce than at present, this species, like the

Rorquals, was but seldom molested; although now, in common
with the latter, it is frequently hunted.   At times these Whales
are met with in enormous "schools," so numerous, indeed, that
ships have to be careful to avoid collisions.   At other times,
however, they may be seen singly or in pairs.   During calm
weather, Lilljeborg states that Hump-backs may often be seen
resting quietly on the surface of the water, sometimes turning
on one side and beating themselves with their long flippers, as
if trying to rub off something that annoyed them.   At times
they will come and swim fearlessly round any boats that may be
in their vicinity.

THE RORQUALS, OR FINNERS.   GENUS BALÆNOPTERA.

Balænoptera, Lacépède, Hist. Nat. des Cétacés, Table des
    Ordres, p. xxxvi. (1804).

Distinguished from *Megaptera* by the long and slender form
of the body, the relatively small, flat, and pointed head, and
the short, narrow, and pointed flippers, as well as by the more
numerous and more closely approximated groovings in the skin
of the throat.

Rorquals include the largest of all Whales, and are represented by four well-defined species, which appear to have an
almost world-wide distribution, although not ranging into the
polar oceans.   All are characterised by their great speed, and
as they are of much less commercial value than the Right
Whales, they were but little hunted, until the increasing
scarcity of the latter, coupled with the introduction of steam-
vessels and firearms into the whaling trade, rendered their
pursuit a profitable business.

I. SIBBALD'S RORQUAL.   BALÆNOPTERA SIBBALDI.

Physalus (*Rorqualus*) *sibbaldii*, Gray, Proc. Zool. Soc. 1847,
    p. 92.

Physalus latirostris, Flower, Proc. Zool. Soc. 1865, p. 28.

Cuvierius latirostris, Gray, Cat. Seals and Whales Brit. Mus. p. 165 (1866).

Cuvierius sibbaldii, Gray, *op. cit.*, p. 380.

Balænoptera sibbaldii, Bell, British Quadrupeds, 2nd ed. p. 402 (1874); Southwell, British Seals and Whales, p. 75 (1881); Flower, List Cetacea Brit. Mus. p. 6 (1885); Flower and Lydekker, Study of Mammals, p. 243 (1891).

Characters.—Size very large; flippers relatively long, measuring one-seventh of the total length; back-fin small, and placed far back; general colour dark bluish-grey, with a number of small whitish spots on the breast; whale-bone black. Total length of adult from 80 to 85 feet.

Distribution.—Sibbald's Rorqual, which is the largest of all Whales, has a very wide distribution, although it does not range so far south as some species. It has been split up into several nominal species, such as the " Sulphur-Bottom " of the American whalers.

Although uncommon, several examples of this magnificent Cetacean have been taken in British waters; the first specimen on record being probably one stranded near Abercorn in the year 1692, and described by Sibbald himself, although the specific determination is not absolutely free from doubt. A Whale found floating dead in the North Sea, in 1827, which was towed into Ostend, is likewise referred by Sir William Turner to the present species; and another example, of which the skeleton is preserved in the Museum at Edinburgh, was found dead near North Berwick in the autumn of 1831. More important than all is a young specimen taken in the River Humber in the year 1847, the skeleton of which is preserved in the Museum of the Literary and Philosophical Society of Hull, since it was on the evidence of this specimen that Gray gave the name by which the present species is known.   Hence the type-specimen of the largest of all living animals is of British origin.   Another large Rorqual belonging to this species was stranded in the autumn of 1869 on the shore of the Firth of Forth; while about the same date a female and calf were washed ashore in Shetland.   A Whale, doubtless belonging to this species, and said to measure 90 feet in length, was found dead off the north shore of Coll, in the Hebrides, in June, 1887.

Habits.—Since this Rorqual so seldom visits the British Seas, it will be unnecessary to say much about its habits. It appears that during the winter months it frequents the open northern seas between the North Cape and Spits-bergen, and that it is not till the latter part of April or beginning of May that it approaches the coasts of more southern districts, when it enters the Norwegian fjords to feed upon certain crustaceans which swarm in them at this season.   An onshore wind, or stormy weather is, however, sufficient to induce the Whales, like prudent mariners, to at once turn their heads seawards.   In spite of its enormous dimensions, it appears that this Whale feeds almost or quite entirely on crustaceans, and mainly on one particular species belonging to the genus *Thrysanopoda*.   These little crustaceans are generally found in shoals, and when in pursuit of them, the Rorqual passes backwards and forwards over the spots where they are most numerous, closing, at intervals, its enormous mouth upon those which have been captured in its passage. The young are born in the autumn, and are occasionally two in number.   In size, the female of Sibbald's Rorqual generally somewhat exceeds that of her partner.

II. THE COMMON RORQUAL.   BALÆNOPTERA MUSCULUS.

Balæna physalus, et *B. musculus*, Linn. Syst. Nat. ed. 12, vol. i. p. 106 (1766).

Balæna physalus, Fabricius Fauna Grœnlandica, p. 35 (1780).

Balænoptera rorqual, Lacépède, Cétacés, p. 126 (1804).

Balæna antiquorum, Fischer, Synops. Mamm. p. 525 (1829).

Balænoptera musculus, Companyo, Mém. de la Baleine échouée près de St. Cyprien, p. 20 (1830); Bell, British Quadrupeds, 2nd ed. p. 397 (1874); Southwell, British Seals and Whales, p. 70 (1881); Flower, List Cetacea Brit. Mus. p. 5 (1885).

Balænoptera physalus, Gray, Zool. Voy. Erebus and Terror, p. 18 (1846).

Physalus antiquorum, Gray, Proc. Zool. Soc. 1847, p. 90.

Characters.—Size smaller than in the preceding species, and the flippers relatively shorter; general colour slaty-grey above, and white beneath; whale-bone slate-colour, with yellow or brown markings. Length of adult from 65 to 70 feet.

Distribution.—Occurring in both the Atlantic and Pacific Oceans, this species has a more southerly range than the preceding, and is commonly found in the Mediterranean, where the former species is rare. Specimens are stranded on the British coasts, more especially those of the southern parts of England, almost every year, generally after stormy weather, and very frequently during the winter. It will accordingly be quite unnecessary to quote the instances of its occurrence on our coasts, and we may therefore content ourselves with mentioning a few specimens that have been recorded of late years. About the end of October, 1885, two dead Rorquals of this species were found floating in the Channel, and were towed into Plymouth, where they were exhibited. Another example was stranded at Skegness, in 1887; and it is probable that a Whale captured at Sea View, in the Isle of Wight, on the 21st of September, in the following year, likewise pertained to this species. Another specimen, which has been described by Mr. W. Crouch, was stranded in the River Crouch, Essex, on February 12th, 1891.

Habits.—There is nothing specially noteworthy in the habits of this species, except that it feeds largely on fish, herrings being an especially favourite food.

III. RUDOLPHI'S RORQUAL.   BALÆNOPTERA BOREALIS.

Balænoptera borealis, Lesson, Hist. Nat. Cétacés, p. 342 (1828); Flower, List Cetacea Brit. Mus. p. 6 (1885).

Balænoptera laticeps, Gray, Zool. Voy. Erebus and Terror, p. 20 (1846); Bell, British Quadrupeds, 2nd ed. p. 407 (1874); Southwell, British Seals and Whales, p. 77 (1881).

Characters.—Size medium; flippers very short, measuring only one-eleventh of the total length of the head and body; general colour of the upper-parts bluish-black, with oblong light-coloured spots; under-parts more or less white; tail, flippers, and whale-bone black, but the curling bristly extremities of the latter white. Total length about 50 feet, or rather less.

Distribution.—In the Atlantic, Rudolphi's Rorqual is a more northern species than either of the preceding, being very abundant in summer in the neighbourhood of the North Cape, where at that season it is a regular visitant, and apparently not known to range further south than the coast of Biarritz.

It will be found stated in the second edition of Bell's "British Quadrupeds" that a Whale stranded at Charmouth, Dorsetshire, in February 1840, not improbably pertained to this species; but Sir William Turner ("Journ. Anatomy and Physiology," 1892, p. 473) is of opinion that it was more probably an example of the Common Rorqual. A Rorqual stranded in the Isle of Islay in 1866, the skull and some other bones of which are perserved in the Zoological Museum at Cambridge, is likewise mentioned by Bell under the head of the present species; but, as noticed by Sir W. Turner on the page cited, this specimen really belongs to the Lesser Rorqual. The first authenticated British example of this Rorqual is, therefore, one described by Sir W. Turner, which was stranded in the autumn of 1872, near Bo'ness, on the Firth of Forth. This specimen measured about 38 ft. in length, and its skeleton is preserved in the museum of the University of Edinburgh. Another example was found by some fishermen struggling in shallow water near the mouth of the River Crouch, in Essex, on the morning of Nov. 1, 1883. This specimen, which was a male, was about 29 ft. in length, and is described by Sir Wm. Flower in the "Proceedings" of the Zoological Society for 1883, p. 513. When caught, the colour of the back was a rich glossy black, shading to a brilliant white below, the flippers being entirely black. In September of the following year (1884) a female specimen of this species was stranded in the Humber, the skeleton of which is now preserved in the British Museum. The entire length of this specimen was about 34 ft., and a brief reference to it will be found in the under-mentioned paper by Mr. Crouch. The fourth example was a male, captured in the Thames at Tilbury on Oct. 19, 1887. A brief notice of this Whale was given by Sir Wm. Flower in the "Proceedings" of the Zoological Society for 1887, p. 567, and a fuller account by Mr. W. Crouch in the "Essex Naturalist," for 1887, p. 41. The length of this specimen was 35 ft. 4 in. It was described by a correspondent in a local paper as "measuring 35 ft. 4 in. in length, its mouth 6 ft. wide, and 18 ft. 6 in. round the shoulders; while its tail (flukes) is 8 ft. across, and its weight 6 tons 5 cwt. This surprising visitor was found soon after daylight, lying with its snout nearly level with the top of the river wall, so that it must have come up the river at high water.   The dock was observed to be filled with a shoal of sprats, while the shrimps and eels were congregated in large numbers; and no doubt while in pursuit of these it ventured too far up the river."   Mr. Crouch adds that " it was subsequently towed off by a tug, and, with the aid of the Dock Company's derrick, was placed upon three trucks and taken to the engineer's yard, where it was exhibited for a few days, and whilst there was photographed (with its mouth open, showing the baleen or whale-bone) by Mr. Robert Hider of Gravesend."   Finally, a sixth specimen of Rudolphi's Rorqual was captured in the Medway on Aug. 30, 1888, of which an account is given by Mr. Crouch on page 361 of the " Rochester Naturalist" for that year.   Mr. Crouch states that this Whale, which was a female, was first seen swimming quietly along; soon, however, it got aground, but " managed to plunge into deeper water.   Meanwhile Thomas Jewess of Gillingham, who was fishing, approached as near as he dared to try and cut off the retreat, and the animal, approaching too near the shore, was driven into shallow water, and as the tide ebbed, was left floundering on the mud.   He then procured assistance, and several shots were fired into the blowholes and head, but the wounded creature only lashed up the mud more vigorously with his tail, and, according to the statement of one of the men, uttered sounds like the crying of a child.   It was at last killed by Mr. Thomas Cuckow with a large butcher's knife.   A rope was then inserted in the lower jaw, and as the tide rose in the afternoon it was towed to a small landing stage at the back of the White Horse Inn, where it was exhibited for several days, and attracted hundreds of visitors, such a catch having never before been recorded in the Medway."   This specimen was 32 ft. 2 in. in length.

Habits.—The diet of this species is very different from that of the last, since, according to observations made by Dr.

Collett in the Norwegian seas, it feeds almost exclusively on small crustaceans, and never touches fish.

IV. THE LESSER RORQUAL. BALÆNOPTERA ROSTRATA.

Balæna rostrata, Fabricius, Fauna Grœnlandica, p. 40 (1780).

Rorqualus minor, Knox, in Jardine's Naturalist's Library, vol. xxvi. p. 142 (1844).

Balænoptera rostrata, Gray, Zool. Voy. of Erebus and Terror, p. 50 (1846); Bell, British Quadrupeds, 2nd ed. p. 411 (1874); Southwell, British Seals and Whales, p. 78 (1881); Flower, List Cetacea Brit. Mus. p. 7 (1885).

Characters.—Size small; back-fin (as in the last species) relatively tall, and placed far forwards; colour of upper-parts greyish-black, with the exception of a broad white band across the flippers; under-parts, with the exception of the lower surface of the flukes, which is coloured like the back, but including the inferior aspect of the flippers, white; whale-bone yellowish-white. Total length of adult about 30 feet, or less.

Distribution.—Typically, the Lesser Rorqual, or, as it is often called, the Pike-Whale, is an inhabitant of the North Atlantic, ranging as far north as Davis' Straits, and often found on the Scandinavian coasts, but seldom entering the Mediterranean. Like the other species, it is represented by a closely-allied form in the Pacific, which in our own opinion is probably specifically the same.

To the British coasts this Rorqual is a comparatively common visitor, and there are several examples in our Museums which have been taken in our own seas. It will be unnecessary to allude to all the examples recorded from England; but we may mention that one was taken in Cornwall in

April, 1880, while another was caught off the Scilly Islands in May, 1887. The latter specimen was a young female measuring 12½ feet in length; and it will be found described by Mr. Balkwill in the "Report" of the Plymouth Institute for 1888.

As regards Scotland, Sir William Turner has published in the "Proceedings" of the Royal Society of Edinburgh a complete list of all recorded instances of this species; from which it appears that between the years 1808 and 1888 a total of eighteen specimens visited the Scottish coasts. Of these, one was taken in Orkney in November 1808; a second in the Firth of Forth in May, 1832, and a third in February, 1834. In September, 1857, a small male was captured off the Bell Rock; another specimen was taken in 1858 in the Firth of Forth, and the sixth in 1869 on the coast of Islay. July, 1869, saw the capture of a small example at Arbroath; while in 1870 one was taken at Aberdeen, another at Hilswick, in Shetland, and a third in the Firth of Forth. Dunbar was the scene of capture of a full-grown specimen in 1871; while in the following year examples were secured at Anstruther and Stornaway. No other specimen was observed till 1877, when a half-grown female was caught at Bervie. Two examples were taken in 1879, namely, one in the Firth of Forth during July, and a second four months later in Stromness, Orkney. The year 1888 was likewise one in which two of these Whales were taken, both in the Firth of Forth; and one of which formed the subject of a memoir by the celebrated anatomist whose name is mentioned above.

Habits.—The Lesser Rorqual is a species generally found solitary, more than two or three being seldom seen in company. A large number of females, which seek the neighbourhood of the coasts for the purpose of bringing forth their young, are annually captured by the Norwegian fishermen, who drive them into narrow fjords, the entrances of which they subsequently bar, and there spear them to death.

THE TOOTHED WHALES. FAMILY PHYSETERIDÆ.

The members of this and the remaining Families of the Order are distinguished from the *Balænidæ* by having no whale-bone in the upper, and by the presence of teeth in the lower jaw at least, although in some cases these may be reduced to a single pair. In consequence of this and other important structural differences, the *Balænidæ* are regarded as constituting one sub-order—the *Mystacoceti*—by themselves, while the whole of the other existing Cetaceans collectively form a second sub-ordinal group, termed the *Odontoceti*. In all the members of the latter group, the upper surface of the skull is more or less a-symmetrical; the nasal bones are in the form of mere nodules, and never roof over the hinder portion of the nasal cavity in the manner characterising the Whale-bone Whales; while the aperture of the nostrils is a single, more or less, crescent-like slit.

The members of the present Family are sufficiently characterised by the absence of functional teeth in the upper jaw ; and by the hinder region of the skull being elevated in the form of a high crest or ridge behind the aperture of the nostrils.

THE SPERM-WHALES. GENUS PHYSETER.

Physeter, Linn., Syst. Nat. ed. 12, vol. i. p. 107 (1766).

Head enormously large, and truncated in front, with the upper surface of the skull forming a hollow pit, surrounded on the sides and behind by a tall semi-circular wall of bone ; lower jaw long and narrow, with its two branches united in front for more than half their total length ; from twenty to

5 T

twenty-five pairs of stout, conical, recurved, and pointed lower teeth, which are of large size and have no enamel. Back-fin rudimentary.

The genus is represented only by the under-mentioned species, which has been greatly reduced in number owing to incessant pursuit on account of the spermaceti yielded by the cavity in the skull, and the high value of the oil obtained from the blubber.

THE SPERM-WHALE. PHYSETER MACROCEPHALUS.

Physeter macrocephalus, Linn., Syst. Nat. ed. 12, vol. i. p. 107 (1766); Bell, British Quadrupeds, 2nd ed. p. 415 (1874); Southwell, British Seals and Whales, p. 85 (1881); Flower, List Cetacea Brit. Mus. p. 8 (1885).

Catodon macrocephalus, Lacépède, Hist. Nat. des Cétacés, Tabl. des Ordres, p. x (1804); Gray, Cat. Seals and Whales Brit. Mus. p. 202 (1866).

Characters.—Size very large (far exceeding that of any other member of the sub-order); general colour black above, and grey on the under-parts, without any clear line of demarcation between the two. Total length of adult male from 55 to 60 feet. The female very much smaller.

Distribution.—Formerly abundant in almost all the warmer seas of the globe, and associating in large "schools," the Sperm-Whale, or Cachalot, is but an accidental visitor to our shores, such specimens as have been recorded from the British seas being either stragglers, or those which have died in the southern oceans and been carried northwards and eastwards by the Gulf-Stream. None have been recorded of late years, doubtless owing to the comparative rarity of the species at the present day.

Of the specimens recorded from the English coasts, we may notice the following. So far back as the year 1626, a Sperm

Whale was cast on the shore near Hunstanton, in Norfolk; while in 1646 a "school" comprising some eight or nine individuals appears to have entered the Wash, one of them coming ashore near Wells, and a second, towards the close of the same year, at Holme. Another individual was stranded near Yarmouth, Norfolk, during or previous to 1652; and an ancient seat, made out of a Sperm-Whale's skull, now preserved in the church of St. Nicholas in that town, which is known to have been in existence in 1606, indicates that another example was stranded in the same neighbourhood at a still earlier date. In the year 1788, upwards of nine dead Sperm-Whales were washed ashore after a strong gale, while a living one, which was, doubtless, a member of the same "school," entered the Thames. Better-known is the large male stranded at Holderness, in Yorkshire, in 1825, of which the skeleton is preserved at Burton-Constable; while, four years later, another male was washed ashore on the Kentish coast. According to the Rev. H. A. Macpherson, a large Sperm-Whale, measuring 58 feet in length, came ashore at Flimby, in Cumberland.

Turning to Scotland, we find from Alston's "History" of the Mammals of that country that from eight to ten specimens have been recorded, of which the earliest was in 1689, and the latest in 1871. Among these, one ran ashore in the Firth of Forth in 1769; and in May, 1829, another was stranded at Oban; while a third, of which the skeleton now ornaments the Central Hall in the British Museum (Nat. Hist. Branch), was washed on shore near Thurso, in Caithness, in July, 1863, being then in a much decomposed condition. The last Scottish specimen on record was one stranded in the Isle of Skye, during the summer of 1871, a description of which has been given by Sir William Turner in the "Proceedings" of the Royal Society of Edinburgh.

In Thompson's "Natural History of Ireland" we find the

following record of Sperm-Whales observed on the coasts of
that island.   The first record relates to three examples taken
during 1691 and the five preceding years on the western coast;
while some years before 1750 another was washed ashore near
Castlehaven.   A later writer, Young, states that about 1776,
examples of these Whales were not unfrequently seen in the
bays of the coast of Donegal; while a large specimen was
stranded near Dublin in 1766, from which a quantity of spermaceti was obtained.   Somewhere about 1773, another Sperm-
Whale appears to have been taken or stranded at Youghal;
and yet another about 1822 in Connemara.

In the case of such a casual visitor to our shores it will be
unnecessary to say anything about habits.

THE BOTTLE-NOSED WHALES.   GENUS HYPERÖODON.

Hyperödon, Lacépède, Hist. Nat. des Cétacés, Tabl. des
    Ordres, p. xliv (1804).

Teeth reduced to a single pair in the front of the lower jaw,
which are concealed by the gum during life; skull with a tall
curved crest, highest in the middle, overhanging the nasal
aperture, and with elevated longitudinal crests in the front of the
latter, which in old males are greatly developed, having flattened front surfaces, rising nearly at right angles to the beak,
and almost meeting in the middle line; beak short and rather
broad; a falcate back-fin, placed rather far back; aperture of
the nostrils (as in all the remaining members of the Order) in
the form of a distinct transverse crescent.

THE COMMON BOTTLE-NOSE.   HYPERÖODON ROSTRATUS.

Balæna rostrata, Müller, Zool. Dan. Prodr. p. 7 (1776).
Delphinus bidentatus, et *D. butskopf*, Bonnaterre, Cétologie, p.
    25 (1789).

Delphinus diodon, Lacépède, Hist. Nat. des Cétacés, p. 309 (1804).

Hyperoodon butzkopf, Lacépède, *op. cit.*, p. 349 ; Bell, British Quadrupeds, p. 492 (1837) ; Gray, Cat. Seals and Whales Brit. Mus. p. 330 (1866).

Hyperoodon latifrons, Gray, Zool. Voy. Erebus and Terror, p. 27 (1846); Bell, British Quadrupeds, 2nd ed. p. 425 (1874).

Hyperoodon rostratum, Gray, Cat. Cetac. Brit. Mus. p. 64 (1850).

Hyperoodon rostratus, Bell, British Quadrupeds, 2nd ed. p. 421 (1874); Southwell, British Seals and Whales p. 101 (1881); Flower, List Cetacea Brit. Mus. p. 9 (1885).

Characters.—In this, the only well-defined, species, the general colour of the upper-parts is nearly black, while the under surface is greyish-black. Length of adult males 30 feet, of females 24 feet, or less.

Great variation obtains in the form of the head and skull according to age and sex ; old males having the crests on the upper jaws greatly developed, and rising high above the beak ; while in the young of the same sex, as in females at all ages, they are much smaller. It was on the evidence of one of these aged males that the so called *H. latifrons* was named.

Distribution.—The Bottle-nosed Whale (which must not be confounded with the Bottle-nosed Dolphin) is a common species in the North Atlantic, ranging in summer as far north as Spitsbergen, while during the winter it seeks warmer quarters in more southern seas. In Britain this species is of very common occurrence, especially in the spring and autumn, being met with off the Shetlands in considerable numbers at the former season while on its northward migration. Being thus common on our coasts, where specimens are captured almost annually, and at times entering our larger rivers, it would be impossible, even if it were desirable, to give a list of its occurrences; but we may mention a few instances of specimens which have been observed during the last few years.

In 1886, Sir W. Turner, in the "Proceedings" of the Physical Society of Edinburgh (vol. ix., p. 25), notices specimens captured on the coasts of Scotland. In 1888, Mr. Baily, in the *Naturalist*, p. 114, mentions one captured on March 13 of that year at Flamborough. On Aug. 28, in the same year, several Whales were stranded near Hunstanton, in Norfolk, two of which were recognised by Mr. Southwell (*Zoologist*, 1888, p. 387) as an old and a young female of this species. Sir W. Turner, in vol. x. of the serial in which his earlier notice appeared (p. 19), records one captured in 1889 in the Shetland Islands. During September, 1871, a "school" of these Whales were observed in the Channel, some of which visited the coast of Normandy, while a pair entered the Thames, where they were killed, and their bodies were examined by Dr. Murie. In the summer of the following year the present writer had the good fortune to see a dead Bottle-nose, which was carried by the tide into Weymouth Bay.

Habits.—In addition to their migrating habits, these Whales are characterised by going in "schools," comprising from four to ten individuals in each, several of such "schools" frequently swimming within a short distance of one another. They feed almost exclusively on Cuttle-fish, which they procure at great depths. A specimen, of which the skeleton is now preserved in the British Museum, is said, when killed, to have had more than half a bushel of the indigestible heavy beaks of those molluscs in its stomach. Since the skull of the male Bottle-nose contains spermaceti, while the blubber yields a consider able amount of oil, these Whales are now hunted to a large extent. Although their ordinary colour is, as stated above, blackish, in very old males it frequently fades to a yellowish hue; those of intermediate age being light brown. Frequently the adult males separate themselves from the rest of the "school," to lead a more or less solitary existence.

THE BEAKED WHALES. GENUS MESOPLODON.

Mesoplodon, Gervais, Ann. Sci. Nat. ser. 3, vol. xiv. p. 16 (1850).

The Beaked Whales of this genus present the following characteristics. Head produced into a long beak, supported in the upper jaw by an elongated solid mass of ivory-like bone ; a single pointed and compressed tooth at each side of the lower jaw, generally situated at some distance behind the anterior extremity, and in one species attaining such an extraordinary development as to prevent the two jaws being opened to their full extent.

The genus is represented by a considerable number of species, which are mainly characteristic of the warmer, and especially the southern, seas, only one of them occasionally visiting our shores.

SOWERBY'S WHALE. MESOPLODON BIDENS.

Physeter bidens, Sowerby, Brit. Miscell. p. 1 (1804).

Delphinus (Heterodon) sowerbiensis, Blainville, Nouv. Dict. d'Hist. Nat. vol. ix. p. 177 (1817).

Delphinus sowerbyi, Desmarest, Mammalogie, p. 521 (1822).

Heterodon sowerbyi, Lesson, Man. Mamm. p. 419 (1827).

Diodon sowerbi, Hamilton, in Jardine's Naturalist's Library Mamm. vol. viii. p. 192 (1839).

Diodon sowerbæ, Bell, British Quadrupeds, p. 497 (1837).

Mesoplodon sowerbiensis, Gervais, Zool. et Pal. Franç. p. 291 (1849); Bell, British Quadrupeds, 2nd ed. p. 431 (1874); Southwell, British Seals and Whales, p. 105 (1881).

Ziphius sowerbiensis, Gray, Proc. Zool. Soc. 1864, p. 241 ; id. Cat. Seals and Whales Brit. Mus. p. 350 (1866).

Mesoploden bidens, Flower, Cat Osteol. Mus. Roy. Coll. Surgeons, pt. ii. p. 559 (1884), and List Cetacea Brit. Mus. p. 11 (1885).

Characters.—Teeth relatively short, wide, and pointed, placed nearly in the middle of the lower jaw ; general colour white above, and black beneath, with vermicular white streaks on the flanks. Length of adult from 15 to 18 feet.

Distribution.—Originally described from a specimen stranded in 1800 on the shores of Elginshire, this species, which enjoys such a multiplicity of names (by no means the whole of which are quoted above), probably has a wide distribution, although, until the distinctive characters of the other members of the genus are more accurately defined than is at present the case, the exact limits of its range cannot be indicated. This Whale is not only one of the rarest of British Cetaceans, but is likewise equally scarce on the coasts of other countries, only seventeen specimens, according to Sir William Turner, being known up to the year 1888, since which date another British example has been recorded, while a second, captured at Cape Breton, in August, 1838, brings up the total number to nineteen.

Of the British examples the first is the above-mentioned specimen stranded in 1800 at Brodie, Elginshire, the skeleton of which is now in the Museum at Oxford. The second was a male, taken in Brandon Bay, Ireland, in 1864, the bones of which are now in Dublin ; while the fourth, which was likewise a male, was captured at the same place in 1870, and is also preserved in Dublin. In 1872 a female, of which the remains are in the Museum at Edinburgh, was taken on some part of the coast of Scotland; and in April, 1881, an adult example, measuring 14 feet in length, was cast ashore near Burrafirth Voe, on the west coast of the main island of the Shetland group, this specimen being described by Sir W. Turner in the "Journal of Anatomy and Physiology," vol. xvi., p. 458; while a second male was obtained from Shetland in May, 1885. In September of the latter year another example was stranded in shallow water just inside the Spurn Head, at the mouth of the Humber, but subsequently managed to get away. This specimen, which measured 15 feet 9 inches in length, is the first which has ever been seen on the English coasts; it is noticed by Messrs. T. Southwell and Eagle Clarke in the *Annals and Magazine of Natural History* (series 5, vol. xvii., p. 53). Yet another specimen visited the Firth of Forth in 1888, of which mention is made by Sir W. Turner in the "Proceedings" of the Physical Society of Edinburgh (vol. x., p. 5); while in the *Field* for the second half of 1892 (p. 1003), Mr. Tegetmeier records the stranding of a fine specimen of this Whale on the coast of Norfolk in December of that year. The latter specimen, we believe, has been secured for Mr. Rothschild's Museum at Tring Park.

Habits.—Unfortunately, scarcely anything is known of the mode of life of the Beaked Whales of this and the allied genera, all of which are mainly or entirely known only from stranded specimens. From this rarity it may, however, be inferred that these animals are essentially inhabitants of the open sea, and probably only visit the coasts when driven thither by bad weather. That they were formerly abundant in the seas surrounding our islands, is attested by the frequency with which their fossilised beaks occur in the so-called crag deposits of the east coast, which belong to the Pliocene period.

GENUS ZIPIIIUS.

Ziphius, Cuvier, Ossemens Fossiles, 2nd ed. vol. v. p. 352
    (1823).

This genus of Beaked Whales, apparently represented only
by a single species, may be distinguished from *Mesoplodon* by
the characters of the skull, and the circumstance that the
single pair of lower teeth, which are directed upwards and forwards, are placed at the anterior extremity of the jaw.

CUVIER'S WHALE.   ZIPHIUS CAVIROSTRIS.

Ziphius cavirostris, Cuvier, Ossemens Fossiles, 2nd ed. vol. v.
    p. 352 (1823); Bell, British Quadrupeds, 2nd ed. p. 428
    (1874); Southwell, British Seals and Wales, p. 102
    (1881); Flower, List Cetacea Brit. Mus. p. 10 (1885).

This exceedingly rare Cetacean is so little known that
neither its characters nor distribution can be given with any
approach to exactness. From the circumstance that it has been
met with in regions so remote from one another as the Shetland
Islands and New Zealand, it is probable that it has a nearly
cosmopolitan distribution, although not ranging into the Polar
seas.

The single British example of Cuvier's Whale hitherto
recorded was taken off Hanno Voe, to the north-west of the
mainland of Shetland, and has been described by Sir William
Turner in the "Proceedings" of the Royal Society of Edinburgh for 1872.

THE DOLPHINS AND PORPOISES.
FAMILY DELPHINIDÆ.

The whole of the remaining British representatives of the
Cetacean Order are included in the Family *Delphinidæ*, most
of the members of which are distinguished from the
Physeteridæ by the presence of numerous teeth in both jaws,

although in two instances the teeth are greatly reduced in number. The skull lacks the elevated crests behind the nasal aperture which forms such a characteristic feature in the Family last named; while there are also differences in the arrangement of certain of the cranial bones, as there are in the conformation of the bones of the internal ear. In all cases the aperture of the nostrils assumes a perfectly crescentic form. with the horns of the crescent directed towards the muzzle.

THE NARWHALS. GENUS MONODON.

Monodon, Linn., Syst. Nat. ed. 12, vol. i. p. 105 (1766).

Head rounded, without a distinct beak; functional dentition usually reduced to a single, spirally-twisted tusk of enormous length in the left side of the upper jaw of the male, the corresponding right tooth usually remaining undeveloped in its socket, while, in the female, both such teeth are rudimental. No back-fin; and all the vertebræ of the neck either completely or partially separate from one another.

The genus is represented solely by the under-mentioned species.

THE NARWHAL. MONODON MONOCEROS.

Monodon monoceros, Linn., Syst. Nat. ed. 12, vol. i. p. 105 (1766); Bell, British Quadrupeds, 2nd ed. p. 435 (1874); Southwell, British Seals and Whales, p. 106 (1881); Flower, List Cetacea Brit. Mus. p. 14 (1885).

Narwhalus vulgaris, Lacépède, Hist. Nat. des Cétacés, p. 142 (1804).

Characters.—Upper-parts dark grey, and under-parts white, both mottled with various shades of grey and greyish-black. Length of adult, exclusive of the tusk, from 14 to 15 feet; of the tusk 7 feet, or more.

Distribution.—Essentially a denizen of the icy Arctic seas, the Narwhal has but little claim to notice here; the only instances

of its occurrence on our shores being three in number. The
first of these stragglers entered the Firth of Forth so long
ago as the year 1648; the second was taken near Boston, in
Lincolnshire, during 1800; while the third was found eight
years later among the rocks in the Sound of Deesdale, in
Shetland.

THE WHITE WHALES. GENUS DELPHINAPTERUS.

Delphinapterus. Lacépède, Hist. Nat. des Cétacés, p. xli.
(1804).

General characters as in the preceding genus, but no long
tusk, and from eight to ten pairs of rather small teeth in each
jaw; these teeth being conical and pointed when un-worn, but
usually becoming obliquely truncated by use.

Like the last, this genus is represented by a single species.

THE WHITE WHALE, OR BELUGA. DELPHINAPTERUS LEUCAS.

Delphinus leucas, Pallas, Reise, Russ. Reichs. vol. iii. p. 85
(1776).

Balæna albicans, Müller, Zool. Dan. Prodr. p. 7 (1776).

Delphinapterus beluga, Lacépède, Hist. Nat. des Cétacés, p.
243 (1804).

Delphinapterus leucas, Bell, British Quadrupeds, 2nd ed., p. 440
(1874); Southwell, British Seals and Whales, p. 108 (1881);
Flower, List Cetacea Brit. Mus. p. 14 (1885).

Beluga leucas, Gray, Spicil. Zool. vol. i. p. 2 (1828); Bell,
British Quadrupeds, p. 488 (1837).

Beluga catodon, Gray, Zool. Voy. Erebus and Terror, p. 29 (1846);
id. Cat. Seals and Whales Brit. Mus. p. 307 (1866).

Characters.—Adult of a pure glistening white colour; the
young bluish-grey. Length of adult from 10 to 12 feet.

Distribution.—As Arctic an animal as the Narwhal, although
ranging somewhat further south than the latter on the eastern
coast of America, the White Whale has equally slight claims

to a place in the British Fauna, although a few individuals have been stranded on the Scottish coasts, and there is some evidence of one having been seen off Devonshire. The first record relates to two young specimens stated to have been washed ashore in the Pentland Firth in the summer of 1793. A second example was killed in the Firth of Forth, where it had been seen for three months, in June, 1815 ; and the third was found off dead on the Island of Auskerry, in the Orkneys, in the autumn of 1845. In June, 1878, a large white Cetacean, which could scarcely have been anything else than an example of this species, was seen in Loch Etive ; while a year later a fine example was found caught by the flukes between two posts to which a stake-net was attached, about three miles to the westward of Dunrobin, in Sutherlandshire, a description of which is given by Sir W. H. Flower in the "Proceedings" of the Zoological Society for 1879. According to Messrs. Harvie-Brown and Buckley, a White Whale was repeatedly seen in the Kyle of Tongue in August, 1880 ; and another was taken alive in the salmon-nets off Dunbeath in April, 1884, its skeleton being now preserved in the museum of Aberdeen University.

The only record of the occurrence of this species on the English coasts is on the authority of Gosse, who, when off Berry Head in the summer of 1832, reports having seen a White Cetacean which he regarded as a Beluga.

THE PORPOISES. GENUS PHOCÆNA.

Phocæna, Cuvier, Règne Animal, vol. i. p. 279 (1817).

Skull with the beak rather short, broad at the base and tapering towards the muzzle ; teeth small, with spade-like crowns marked off from the roots by a constriction, their number varying from sixteen to twenty-six pairs in each jaw, of which they occupy nearly the whole length ; neck short, and (as in all the following genera) at least some of its vertebræ united together; back-fin absent or present.

THE COMMON PORPOISE. PHOCÆNA COMMUNIS.

Delphinus phocæna, Linn., Syst. Nat. ed. 12, vol. i. p. 108 (1766).

Phocæna communis, Lesson, Man. Mamm. p. 413 (1827); Bell, British Quadrupeds, 2nd ed. p. 458 (1874); Southwell, British Seals and Whales, p. 120 (1881); Flower, List Cetacea Brit. Mus. p. 15 (1885).

Characters.—Back-fin triangular, situated nearly in the middle of the back, its height less than its basal length, and with a row of small tubercles on its front edge; colour of back nearly black, the flanks lighter, and the under-parts nearly white. Length of adult from 4 to 5 feet.

Distribution.—The range of the Common Porpoise includes the greater part of the North Atlantic, extending northwards to Baffin Bay and westwards to America; southwards, the Porpoise is found rarely in the Mediterranean. In the British seas the Porpoise is the commonest of all Cetaceans, and is found there at all seasons; while not unfrequently it ascends our larger rivers for some distance.

Habits.—The Porpoise is a gregarious Cetacean, associating in large "schools," which seldom wander far from shore, and whose sportive gambols as they roll along near the surface of the water, showing first the head, next the back, and finally the flukes, must be familiar to all. Exclusively or mainly a fish-eater, the Porpoise consumes vast numbers of pelagic fish, such as Herrings, Pilchards, and Mackerel, in its headlong pursuit of which it often becomes entangled in fishing-nets, where, from its size and power, it does much damage. It is likewise partial to Salmon, and it is probable that it is often when in pursuit of that fish that it enters some of our rivers. The female produces a single young one at a birth. Formerly the flesh of the Porpoise was eaten by Roman Catholics as a Lenten dish; but at the present day it is only valued for the oil yielded by its blubber.

THE KILLERS. GENUS ORCA.

Orca, Gray, Zool. Voy. Erebus and Terror, p. 33 (1846).

Beak of skull about equal in length to the remainder of the same, broad and flattened above, and rounded in front; about twelve pairs of large, stout, recurved, conical teeth in each jaw; flippers large, ovate, and nearly as broad as long; back-fin very tall, sharply pointed, and situated nearly in the middle of the back; whole conformation of body very stout, and the front of the head much depressed and flattened.

THE COMMON KILLER, OR GRAMPUS.   ORCA GLADIATOR.

Delphinus orca, Linn., Syst. Nat., ed. 12, p. 108 (1766).

Delphinus orca, et *D. gladiator*, Bonnaterre, Cétologie, pp. 22 and 23 (1789).

Phocæna orca, F. Cuvier, Hist. Nat. des Cétacés, p. 177 (1836); Bel', British Quadrupeds, p. 477 (1837).

Orca gladiator, Gray, Zool. Voy. Erebus and Terror, p. 33 (1846); Bell, British Quadrupeds, 2nd ed. p. 445 (1874); Southwell, British Seals and Whales, p. 113 (1881); Flower, List Cetacea Brit. Mus. p. 18 (1885).

Orca stenorhyncha, et *O. latirostris*, Gray, Proc. Zool. Soc. 1870, pp. 71, 76.

Characters.—Black above and white beneath, with a white spot above each eye. Length of adult 20 feet, or more.

Distribution.—Owing to the uncertainty as to whether there is more than one existing species, the distribution of the Common Killer cannot be accurately defined, but it is not improbable that it may prove to be almost world-wide. To the British coasts, and more especially to the northern parts of our islands, the Killer is by no means an unfrequent visitor, and at times ascends our larger rivers. For instance, in March, 1864, no less than ten of these Cetaceans entered the River Parret, in Somersetshire, all of which were captured within a few miles of Bridgewater. More recently, three Killers swam up the Thames in the spring of 1890. They must have passed through the Pool during the night, since in the morning they were observed swimming rapidly up the open reach between Chelsea and Battersea bridges, where their movem.nts were watched by a number of spectators. After remaining there for several hours, apparently in a state of indecision, they were at length observed to continue their course down the river; and, since there is no record of their capture, they probably succeeded in making their way to the sea.

Habits.—Easily recognised when swimming near the surface by its tall back-fin, the Killer may be regarded as the Tiger of the Cetacean order, in which it is the sole member that subsists on warm-blooded animals, killing and devouring not only Seals, but likewise such Porpoises and Dolphins as it can capture. The Killer is, however, by no means content with such comparatively small game, three or four of these animals combining together to harass and attack the larger Whales, from which they tear huge masses of blubber and flesh, till the unfortunate Whales eventually succumb from loss of blood. Such an attack by a party of Killers the present writer had recently the opportunity of witnessing in the South Atlantic. Killers will, however, also catch various kinds of fish. The amount of food that a Killer will consume is perfectly appalling; a specimen having been killed with remains of more than a couple of dozen of Seals and Porpoises in its stomach.

THE BLACK-FISH. GENUS GLOBICEPHALUS.

Globicephala, Lesson, N. Tabl. Règne Animal Mamm. p. 200 (1840).

General form of skull somewhat as in *Orca*, but the fore part of the head high and rounded, owing to the pre ence of a mass of blubber; teeth, small, conical, curved, and sharp, forming from eight to twelve pairs, which are confined to the anterior half of the jaws, in old age blunt, and sometimes wanting; flippers very long and narrow; back-fin short and triangular the height being much less than the basal length.

As in the case of *Orca*, it is very doubtful whether there is more than a single ex·sting representative of this genus.

THE PILOT-WHALE, OR BLACK-FISH. GLOBICEPHALUS MELAS.

Delphinus melas, Traill, Nicholson's Journal, vol. xxii. p. 81 (1809).

Delphinus globiceps, Cuvier, Ann. Mus. vol. xix. p. 14 (1812).

Phocæna melas, Bell, British Quadrupeds, p. 483 (1837).

Globicephala melas, Lesson, N. Tabl. Règne Animal Mamm. p. 200 (1840).

Globiocephalus swineval, Gray, Zool. Voy. Erebus and Terror, p. 32 (1846); Gray, Cat. Seals and Whales, Brit. Mus. p. 314 (1866).

Globicephalus melas, Bell, British Quadrupeds, 2nd ed. p. 453 (1874); Southwell, British Seals and Whales, p. 118 (1881); Flower, List Cetacea Brit. Mus. p. 19 (1885).

Characters.—General colour black, with a whitish stripe along the middle of the under-parts, expanding on the throat into a heart-shaped patch.   Length of adult from 16 to 20 feet.

Distribution.—Typically occurring in the North Atlantic, it is probable that the Pilot-Whale has a nearly world-wide distribution, specimens from Australia presenting no points of difference from British examples. To the Faeroe Islands, as well as to Orkney, and, more rarely, to the Hebrides, the Pilot-Whale is a frequent, although irregular, visitor during its seasonal migrations from the Arctic to the Atlantic Ocean. In the southern parts of our coasts it is, however, of rare occurrence, although it has been recorded as far south as the Channel and Cornwall.

Habits.—The essential feature of the Pilot-Whale, Ca'ing (that is, Driving) Whale, or Black-Fish, as it is vicariously called, is the large "schools" in which it associates, these frequently including hundreds of individuals. It is likewise remarkable for the persistence with which the other members of the school will follow the direction taken by their leader, even when this leads directly into danger. Advantage of this habit is taken by the hardy fishermen of the Faeroe Islands, who, immediately a school is sighted, take to their boats and endeavour to get to seaward of the animals. Should they successfully accomplish this, it is generally an easy matter to drive the school into shallow water, where its members can be slaughtered at leisure. If, however, the leading Whale manages to make his way to sea, all the labour is in vain, as the other Whales will be almost sure to make their way after him, despite the utmost efforts on the part of the boatmen. Some fifty years ago the numbers of these Whales taken during two seasons in the Faeroes and Shetlands were to be reckoned by hundreds, if not by thousands, although it is to be wished that the statements as to the exact numbers were somewhat better authenticated than they appear to be.

THE GRAMPUSES. GENUS GRAMPUS.

Grampus, Gray, Zool. Voy. Erebus and Terror, p. 30 (1846).

Distinguished from all the other genera of the Family by the total absence of teeth in the upper jaw, the dentition of the lower jaw being reduced to from three to seven pairs of teeth which are confined to its anterior extremity. In general conformation of the head and body the single well-defined representative of the genus comes very close to the Pilot-Whale, although the fore part of the head is less rounded, and the flippers are shorter.

RISSO'S GRAMPUS. GRAMPUS GRISEUS.

Delphinus griseus, Cuvier, Ann. Mus. vol. xix. p. 14 (1812).

Delphinus rissoanus, Desmarest, Mammalogie, p. 15 (1822).

Grampus griseus, Gray, Spicil. Zool. p. 2 (1828); Bell, British Quadrupeds, 2nd ed. p. 450 (1874); Southwell, British Seals and Whales, p. 115 (1881); Flower, List Cetacea Brit. Mus. p. 21 (1885).

Grampus cuvieri, Gray, Ann. Mag. Nat. Hist. vol. xvii. p. 85 (1846); id. Cat. Seals and Whales, Brit. Mus. p. 295 (1866).

Grampus rissoanus, Gray Zool. Voy. Erebus and Terror, p. 31 (1846); id. Cat. Seals and Whales, Brit. Mus. p. 298 (1866).

Characters.—Colour very variable, from black above and white beneath, to a pale grey, passing into black towards the tail, everywhere marked with light spots and irregular streaks and stripes. Length of adult about 13 feet.

Distribution.—Although rare in collections, Risso's Grampus appears to be a widely distributed species, since it has been taken not only in the British seas and the Mediterranean, but likewise in the Azores, the Cape of Good Hope, Japan, the North American coasts, and New Zealand (the specimen from the last-named country having been described as *G. richardsoni*).

To our own coasts, this Cetacean is a very rare visitor, as is indicated by the following list of recorded examples. The first known specimen was taken in the spring of 1843 at Puckaster, in the Isle of Wight, its skeleton being now in the British Museum. In February, 1870, a female was caught in a mackerel-net near the Eddystone Lighthouse; its skeleton is likewise in the National Collection. A third example, also a female, was exposed for sale in Billingsgate Market in March of the latter year, having probably been taken in the Channel; both its skin and skeleton have found a home alongside of the two preceding specimens. In July, 1875, a young male, which was kept alive for some hours in the Brighton Aquarium, was captured at Sidlesham, and in February, 1886, a female was caught in a mackerel-net about twenty miles south of the Eddystone Lighthouse, and was exhibited at Plymouth, in the Museum of which town its skeleton is preserved. The last recorded English example was captured in the Solway, on September 30th, 1892, as mentioned in *Land and Water* for that year (vol. liv., p. 405). Lastly, six specimens were caught in Hillswick, in Shetland, in September, 1889, one of which has been carefully described by Sir William Turner in the " Proceedings " of the Physical Society of Edinburgh, vol. xi., p. 1.

THE SHORT-BEAKED DOLPHINS. GENUS LAGENORHYNCHUS.

Lagenorhynchus, Gray, Zool. Voy. Erebus and Terror, p. 35 (1846).

Head with a short but not very distinct beak, or beakless; the beak scarcely exceeding the remainder of the skull in length, depressed, and gradually tapering from the broad base to the extremity; teeth very small, and forming from 23 to 33 pairs in each jaw; from 80 to 90 vertebræ in the back-bone. This genus forms a kind of connecting-link between the preceding and following genera.

I. THE WHITE-BEAKED DOLPHIN.   LAGENORHYNCHUS ALBIROSTRIS.

Delphinus albirostris, Gray, Ann. Mag. Nat. Hist. vol. xvii. p. 84 (1846); Bell, British Quadrupeds, 2nd ed. p. 472 (1874).

Lagenorhynchus albirostris, Gray, Zool. Voy. Erebus and Terror, p. 35 (1846); Southwell, British Seals and Whales, p. 125 (1881); Flower, List Cetacea Brit. Mus. p. 22 (1885).

Characters.—Colour of upper-parts deep purplish-black, cf the beak, lips, and under-parts pure creamy white; the two colours being sharply defined.   Length of adult from 7 to 9 feet.

Distribution.—This Dolphin is a rare species inhabiting the North Atlantic, and was first recorded as British in 1846 by Brightwell, who wrongly identified a specimen captured in that year off Yarmouth, in Norfolk, with *Tursiops tursio*.   It appears, however, that a Dolphin killed at Hartlepool in 1834, of which the skull is in the Zoological Museum at Cambridge, likewise belongs to the present species.   The next recorded occurrence is in 1866, in which year a specimen was shot near Cromer; while a fourth was taken at the mouth of the River Dee in December, 1862; and a fifth on the south coast in 1871.   A young female was captured off Grimsby in September, 1875; a male in March of the following year off Lowestoft; while both in 1879 and 1880 a young female was captured at Yarmouth.   In the *Zoologist* for 1881, p. 41, Mr. J. M. Campbell records a young male caught by a fisherman on September 11, 1880, near the Bell Rock, on the west coast of Scotland.   This specimen, which measured 5 ft. 8 in. in length, is the first recorded example from the Scottish

coasts.   On September 10, 1881, a very young example was
landed alive by some fishermen at Yarmouth, but soon died ;
an account of it is given by Mr. Southwell in the *Zoologist*
for the same year, p. 420.   In 1887 Mr. R. L. Patterson, in the
"Report" of the Belfast Natural History Club for that year (p.
114), mentions a specimen captured on the Irish coast, this
being apparently the first record of the occurrence of the
species in Ireland. The next example is one observed in the
Colne in 1889, of which an account is given by Mr. H.
Laver in the "Essex Naturalist" for that year (p. 169).   Sir
W. Turner, in the "Proccedings" of the Physical Society of
Edinburgh, vol. x., p. 14, gives a notice of other Scotch specimens, namely, one caught off Berwick in July, 1881, a female
captured at the same place in August, 1883, another female
taken at Sutherland in 1882, and an adult female and young
male taken together off Stonehaven, Kincardineshire, in July,
1888.   Of the habits of both this and the following species, as
also of Risso's Dolphin, nothing definite is known.

II. THE WHITE-SIDED DOLPHIN.   LAGENORHYNCHUS ACUTUS.

Delphinus acutus, Gray, Spicil. Zool. vol. i. p. 2 (1828) ; Bell,
     British Quadrupeds, 2nd ed. p. 470 (1874).
Delphinus eschrichtii, Schlegel, Abhandl. Geb. Zool. p. 23
     (1841).
Delphinus leucopleurus, Rasch, Nova Spec. Descript. (1843).
Lagenorhynchus acutus, Gray, Zool. Voy. Erebus and Terror,
     p. 35 (1846) ; Southwell, British Seals and Whales, p. 125
     (1881) ; Flower, List Cetacea Brit. Mus. p. 23 (1885).

Characters.—Colour of upper-parts black, and of under-parts
white, with a white stripe on the flanks continued anteriorly
and posteriorly as a yellow or brownish band.   Length of
adult from 6 to 8 feet.

Distribution.—This is a rare North Atlantic Dolphin, originally described from an Orkney skull, and does not appear to have been recorded from the English seas, although stated to be not uncommon in the Orkneys. In addition to the typical skull, an adult female was captured in Orkney in 1835; while in 1858 a school of some twenty head were secured in Scalpa Bay, near Kirkwall. In their work on the "Fauna of Argyll and the Hebrides," Messrs. Harvie-Brown and Buckley state that a Dolphin captured at Ardrishaig has been identified as of the present species.

THE TYPICAL DOLPHINS. GENUS DELPHINUS.

Delphinus, Linn., Syst. Nat. ed. 12, p. 108 (1766)

In common with the members of the next genus, the Typical Dolphins differ from all the foregoing representatives of the Family in having a distinct and more or less elongated beak to the head, generally separated from the fatty mass in front of the blow-hole by a V-shaped groove. In the skull the length of the beak exceeds that of the hinder portion; while in the skeleton of the neck only the two first vertebræ are welded together. All of them have a well-developed back-fin, and numerous teeth, and they prey chiefly or entirely on fish.

From their allies the Typical Dolphins are distinguished by the long beak of the skull being generally about twice the length of the hinder portion of the same, and carrying from 40 to 60 pairs of teeth in each jaw; these teeth being of small size, conical, pointed, placed close to one another, and occupying almost the whole length of the beak. The narrow and pointed flippers are of moderate length, and tend to assume a hook-like form; while the number of vertebræ in the back-bone varies from 73 to 75. The genus is represented by several closely-allied species.

THE COMMON DOLPHIN. DELPHINUS DELPHIS.

Delphinus delphis, Linn., Syst. Nat. ed. 12, vol. i. p. 470;
1766; Bell, British Quadrupeds, 2nd ed. p. 462 (1874);
Southwell, British Seals and Whales, p. 121 (1881).

Characters.—Coloration somewhat variable, but the upper-
parts black and the under surface pure white, with the flanks
shaded, mottled, and streaked with various tints of yellow and
grey; the markings on the two sides of the body frequently
displaying perfect symmetry. Length of adult from 5 to 8
feet.

Distribution.—Frequent in the Mediterranean, and likewise
occurring in the Atlantic, the Common Dolphin is represented
by a closely-allied form in the North Pacific, and by a third in
the South Seas. Although not uncommonly visiting our
southern shores, it appears very rarely to range as far north as
Scotland, but Sir William Turner, in the "Proceedings" of the
Physical Society of Edinburgh for 1887 (p. 364), has recorded the capture in that year of a specimen in the Firth of
Forth.

Habits.—Like its allies, the Common Dolphin is essentially
gregarious, and all who have made a voyage in the Mediterranean must be familiar with the sportive gambols of these beautiful Cetaceans as they frolic round a ship in large schools,
which sometimes include hundreds of individuals. Their
favourite prey seems to be Pilchards and Herrings, and they
are consequently frequently taken in the nets of the Cornish
fishermen. A single young one is produced at a birth, and
is tended with marked solicitude by its female parent. Like
that of the Porpoise, the flesh of the Dolphin formerly formed
an article of diet.

BOTTLE-NOSED DOLPHINS. GENUS TURSIOPS.

Tursiops, Gervais, Hist. Nat. Mamm. vol. ii. p. 323 (1855).

Distinguished from the preceding genus by the beak of the skull tapering moderately from the base to the extremity, the shorter bony union of the two branches of the lower jaw in front, the stouter teeth, of which there are from 21 to 25 pairs in each jaw, and by the total number of vertebræ being only 64.

THE BOTTLE-NOSED DOLPHIN.   TURSIOPS TURSIO.

? *Delphinus tursio,* Fabricius, Fauna Grœnlandica, p. 49 (1780).

Delphinus tursio, Bonnaterre, Cétologie, p. 21 (1789); Bell, British Quadrupeds, 2nd ed. p. 467 (1874); Southwell, British Seals and Whales, p. 124 (1881).

Delphinus truncatus, Montagu, Mem. Wern. Soc. vol. iii. p. 75 (1821).

Tursiops tursio, Gervais, Hist. Nat. Mamm. vol. ii. p. 323 (1855); Flower, List Cetacea Brit. Mus. p. 26 (1885).

Tursio truncatus, Gray, Cat. Seals and Whales, Brit. Mus. p. 258 (1866).

Characters.—General colour of upper-parts black, gradually shading into white beneath. Length of adult from 8 to 10 feet.

Distribution.—So far as can be determined from our present imperfect knowledge of the distribution of Dolphins in general, it would appear that the present one is a comparatively scarce species, ranging at least from the Mediterranean to the North Sea. To the British coasts it is but a rare visitor, although several instances of its occurrence are recorded in the second edition of Bell's "British Quadrupeds" frcm England, Scotland, and Ireland, the latest of these being a school which visited Holyhead Harbour in the autumn of 1868. Since that date, in the *Zoologist* for 1888, p. 346, Mr. W. Jeffery mentions that a specimen was stranded that year on the coast of Kirkcudbrightshire; while Mr. J. Cordeaux, in the *Naturalist* for 1889 (p. 6), records that two individuals had been seen to enter the Humber.

THE ANCIENT MAMMALS OF BRITAIN.*

I. The Cavern and Brick-Earth Period.

Owing to various circumstances, among which denudation not improbably occupies a place, the geological record in Britain during the Tertiary Period is far more imperfect than usual, owing to the total absence in our islands of all traces of strata corresponding to the typical Miocene deposits of the Continent. Nevertheless, in spite of this imperfection, and the consequent absence of the remains of the species which lived during the missing epoch, Britain is remarkably rich in fossil Mammals, our caves, brick-earths, and river-gravels having preserved the bones and teeth of the later in almost endless profusion; while the so-called "forest-bed" and crags of the eastern coast are rich in those of a somewhat earlier epoch; and the deposits of the Hampshire and London basins have yielded evidence of the Mammalian life of the lower portions of the Tertiary Period. In some respects it is, indeed, fortunate that we have not the hosts of Tertiary Mammals known from the Continent, as, if so, it would be absolutely impossible to give any adequate account of them within the limits at our disposal; but as things are, the list of species is of manageable proportions.

In giving a brief sketch of the ancient British Mammals, we shall practically omit mention of those found in the most superficial deposits, such as the fens and turbaries, since the majority of these belong to species which are either still living

* This section of the work originally appeared in *Knowledge*, and has been reproduced by the kind permission of the Editor of that journal.

in the country, or are existing in other parts of Europe. Our regular survey will, therefore, commence with the Mammals found in the caverns and the various more or less nearly contemporary brick-earths and gravels, which generally form high-level plateaux in our river valleys, and are for the most part of more recent date than the epoch of maximum extension of the ice of the Glacial Period. The whole of these deposits belong to the Pleistocene, or latest Geological Period ; and the next in point of age are the formations exposed on the east coast of England, in the counties of Norfolk, Suffolk, and Essex. The highest of those deposits to which we shall specially refer is the series usually denominated the "forest-bed," so called on account of the relics of an ancient forest which it contains *in situ.* Although clearly antedating the Glacial Epoch, there is some doubt as to the precise geological age of this deposit, some authorities referring it to the top of the Pliocene Period, while others consider that it forms the base of the Pleistocene. As the majority of the Mammalian remains yielded by this bed belong to existing species, the latter view is the one which we feel inclined to adopt. Below the forest-bed come the crags, of which the Norwich crag belongs to the upper portion of the Pliocene Period, while the Red and Coralline crags may be assigned to the lower division of the same. The Tertiaries of the Hampshire and London basins belong solely to the Oligocene and Eocene Epochs; and the mention of the ages of these different horizons may accordingly be reserved till we come to the consideration of their fauna.

With regard to the epoch of our caverns and brick-earths, it may be observed, in the first place, that by far the great majority of the species whose remains are entombed in the various deposits, are still existing, although most of the larger ones have disappeared from Britain, having been either

destroyed by human agency, or because the climate became
unsuitable to them.   Of such existing species we shall only
make mention when there is something of special interest
connected with them, and the reader will therefore under-
s'and that we have no intention of attempting anything like a
complete list of the Mammalian fauna of this epoch.   The most
remarkable feature connected with this fauna is the apparently
contradictory evidence which it affords as to the nature of the
climate then prevalent.   The Glutton, Reindeer, Arctic Fox,
and Musk-Ox are strongly indicative of a more or less Arctic
climate; many of the Voles (*Microtus*), Picas (*Lagomys*), and
Susliks (*Spermophilus*), together with the Saiga Antelope,
appear to point equally strongly to the prevalence of a steppe-
like condition; while the Hippopotamus and Spotted Hyæna
seem as much in favour of a sub-tropical state of things.
Many attempts have been made to reconcile these apparently
contradictory circumstances; one of the older views being
that while the tropical types of animals lived during a warm
interlude, they migrated southwards with the incoming of
colder conditions to the Arctic type of Fauna.   Since, however,
it has now been ascertained that the remains of both Tropical
and Arctic forms have been found lying side-by-side in the
same bed, it is perfectly certain that such an explanation will
not meet the exigencies of the case.   We have, however, yet
much to learn about the effects of climate on animals—our
experience being, unfortunately, confined to a single epoch;
and the fauna of the highlands of Tibet shows that many types
of animals formerly regarded as more or less essentially tropical
can withstand a winter climate of extreme severity.

Among the forms that at first sight seem to indicate that
Britain enjoyed a mild climate during the deposition of the
brick-earths of the Thames Valley is a Monkey, more or less
closely allied to the existing Macaques (*Macacus*), but, unfor-

tunately, only known to us by a small fragment of the upper jaw containing a single tooth, which was obtained many years ago from the brick-earth of Grays, in Essex. Although the majority of the Macaques, together with their allies the Langurs, are now inhabitants of warm regions, it must not be forgotten that a representative of each is found in Tibet, where the winter cold is intense. This species is the only evidence yet known of the occurrence of Monkeys in Britain.

Passing by the Bats and Insectivores, as pertaining exclusively to existing species, we proceed to the Carnivores. Among these, the rarest is a species of Sabre-toothed Tiger (*Machærodus latidens*), of which specimens of the enormous serrated upper tusks have been obtained from Kent's Hole, near Torquay. These Sabre-tooths were widely distributed during the Pleistocene and Pliocene Epochs, having been discovered in Europe, Persia, India, and North and South America; but they seem to have been a type less adapted for persistence than the ordinary and less specialised Cats. Side-by-side with this extinct species lived the Lion, whose remains have been found, not only in most of the English caves, but likewise in many of the brick-earths and river-gravels. Although we are accustomed to regard the Lion as essentially an inhabitant of the hot districts of India and Africa, it must be remembered that even in the historic period it was common in South-eastern Europe, while its near ally, the Tiger, ranges northwards into Siberia, where an unusually long and thick coat protects it from the winter-cold. The Lynx (*Felis lynx*) and the Leopard (*F. pardus*) were likewise British animals during the Cavern Period; the former being to a great extent an inhabitant of northern regions. Although the great Cave-Hyæna was formerly regarded as an extinct species only, it is now considered to be merely a large race of the Spotted African species (*Hyæna crocuta*), differing from the Striped Hyæna, not only in its superior size and coloration, but likewise in the structure of its teeth, the hindmost of which approximate to those of the Cats. Although the present habitat of the Striped Hyæna is tropical or sub-tropical, there does not appear any valid reason why the creature should not have been able to withstand a comparatively cold climate. The Dog tribe, as we might expect, is well represented during the Pleistocene, remains of both the Fox and the Wolf being common in all caverns; the latter species having, indeed, been exterminated only at a comparatively recent date in our islands. More remarkable is the occurrence of the Arctic Fox (*Canis lagopus*), the remains of which have been recently identified from a fissure near Ightham, in Kent. The nearest country to Britain where this species now lives is Iceland, and it is certainly very curious to find in the same deposits remains of animals so widely separated at the present day as are the Spotted Hyæna and the Arctic Fox. Another compatriot of the former species is the Cape Hunting-Dog (*Lycaon pictus*), distinguished from the Wolves by the characters of the teeth and the smaller number of toes on the fore feet; and it is certainly remarkable to find this genus represented by an extinct species from the Glamorganshire caverns. Passing on to the Bears, we naturally expect to find the common Brown Bear, which was only exterminated at a late epoch of the Historic Period, common in the Pleistocene; and in this we are not disappointed, its remains occurring not uncommonly in the English caverns as well as in those of Ireland. A large proportion of the ursine-remains found in the brick-earths of the Thames Valley have, however, been assigned to the Grizzly Bear (*Ursus horribilis*) of North America; but as this form is distinguished from its European ally merely by slight differences in the form of the skull and teeth, we are by no means assured that this reference is well founded. Markedly distinct, however, is the gigantic Cave-Bear (*U. spelæus*), the skull of which may always be recognised by the sudden rise of the forehead above the eyes, while the crowns of the molar teeth display a more finely puckered structure than is to be seen in those of the existing species. This gigantic Bear was one of the inhabitants of the celebrated Kirkdale Cave in Yorkshire, of which Spotted Hyænas were, however, by far the most numerous carnivorous denizens. Much rarer than those of either Bears and Hyænas, are the remains of the Glutton (*Gulo luscus*), which have been obtained only among the deposits now under consideration, from the caves of Banwell, Bleadon, Cresswell Crags, the Vale of Clwyd, and Yealm Bridge. The Glutton is now unknown further south than Scandinavia, and in drawing any conclusions as to climate from its occurrence in Britain, we must always bear in mind the comparative scarcity of the remains both of this species, the Arctic Fox, and the Musk-Ox. It is true that the rarity of these forms is discounted by the abundance of the remains of the Reindeer ; but the latter are somewhat local in their distribution, being unknown to the east of London, and if the assertion that this animal still lingered in Caithness till a few centuries ago be true, no great change of climate would be necessary in order to admit of its existence in England. The other Carnivores of the Cavern Period are not of much importance, including species like the Pine-Marten, Stoat, Weasel, Polecat, and Otter, which still exist among us ; although it has been thought that some bones from the Ightham fissure indicate an extinct type intermediate between the Polecat and the Marten.

Turning to the Hoofed Order, we find remains of the Horse common in all the Pleistocene deposits pertaining to the Cavern Epoch, and from the rude yet characteristic portraits of the animal engraved by our pre-historic ancestors it would appear that the Horse of this period was very similar to the Wild or feral Tarpan of the Russian steppes. Since the latter race, together with all the Horses that have reverted to a wild condition, are inhabitants of open plains, it may be reasonably inferred that similar tracts of country formed a prominent feature in Pleistocene Britain. Although Tapirs were wanting, Rhinoceroses were abundant during the period in question, no less than three species having left their remains in the caverns and l rick earths, all of which resembled the existing African representatives of the genus in having two horns and no front teeth. By far the best known of these is the Woolly Rhinoceros (*Rhinoceros antiquitatis*), which, while closely allied to the living Burchell's Rhinoceros of Africa, differed in having its body protected from the cold by a thick coat of wool and hair. Ranging to the cold "tundras" of Siberia, where its frozen carcases are met with, imbedded in the icy soil like those of the Mammoth, there can be no doubt that this species was capable of withstanding a considerable degree of cold, although we may perhaps admit that the climate of Siberia during the time that these animals flourished there may have been somewhat less rigorous than at the present day. As to the difficult question of how the carcases of these Rhinoceroses and Mammoths became preserved in their frozen sepulchres, we prefer to leave this to those fonder of argument than ourselves. If we admit that the Woolly Rhinoceros could withstand a cold climate, there is no difficulty with regard to the other contemporary species, at least one of which has been met with in Siberia, although it does not appear that either was furnished with a woolly coat. Both the Leptorhine (*R. leptorhinus*) and Megarhine (*R. megarhinus*) Rhinoceroses, as these species are termed, differ essentially from the woolly kind by the simpler structure of their molar teeth, which are more like those of the prehensile-lipped, or so-called Black Rhinoceros of Africa ; and the skulls and teeth of the two are so much alike that it requires an expert to distinguish between them. Teeth of both species are found in the brick-earths of the Thames Valley, but while those of the former are common in most of the English caves, those of the latter appear to be only known as cavern-fossils from Gower, in Glamorganshire, and from a rock-fissure near Plymouth.

One of the finest of the Pleistocene Mammals was the great Aurochs or Wild Ox (*Bos taurus*), the ancestor of our domestic breeds of cattle, which was living in the Black Forest in the time of Cæsar. Even then it was described as but little inferior in bulk to an Elephant, and those who have seen the gigantic skulls from the Ilford brick-earths, preserved in the British Museum, and have compared them with ordinary Oxen, will have some idea of the magnificent proportions of the Aurochs. Side-by-side with the latter lived Bison (*Bos bison*) of equally gigantic size as compared with their living Lithuanian and Caucasian representatives (to whom the name of Aurochs is persistently misapplied). Although the Bison was very abundant in Britain during the Cavern Period, it disappeared at an earlier date than its cousin the Aurochs, its remains being unknown from the fens and turbaries, where those of the latter are so abundant. If we except certain remains assigned to Sheep and Goats, the only other Hollow-horned Ruminants that occur in the deposits under consideration are the Musk-Ox (*Ovibos moschatus*), and the Saiga Antelope (*Saiga tartarica*), both of which are of extreme importance as pointing out the nature of the climate then prevailing. Remains of both these animals have hitherto been obtained only from the south-east of England, those of the former occurring as far east as Maidenhead, as well as in the brick-earths of several places in Kent, and on the Dogger Bank, while those of the latter are known only from Twickenham. It is thus very remarkable that these species occur exactly where the Reindeer is unknown, and the suggestion naturally arises that conditions suitable for their existence may have occurred there and been wanting elsewhere. The Musk-Ox, which is now restricted to Arctic America, is such an essentially Arctic animal that it is hard to believe that it could have inhabited a country with a temperature suitable to the existence of the Hippopotamus; while the Saiga is equally characteristic of the open steppes of Russia.

Equally marked as the superiority of the fossil Bison over its living representative, was the excess in size of the Pleistocene Red Deer (*Cervus elaphus*) over its existing Scottish descendants, some of the antlers from the caverns and brick-earths being of enormous length and girth, and likewise notable for the number of points they carry. The Fallow Deer was certainly unknown from both the deposits last mentioned, although it has been said to occur in a bed on the Norfolk coast; but the superficial deposits of the same coast yield remains of the closely-allied Brown's Fallow Deer (*C. browni*). In cavern-deposits the place of the Fallow Deer was more than filled by the splendid Irish Deer (*C. giganteus*), generally known by the incorrect name of the Irish "Elk," and the splendid antlers of which are larger and more massive than those of any other member of the Family. Although deriving its name from the abundance in which it occurs in Ireland, remains of this Deer is met with in most of the cavern-deposits, brick-earths, and river-gravels of England; and it should be mentioned that although in Ireland its remains are commonly stated to come from the peat-bogs, they really occur in the shell-marl underlying the peat. In the outward direction of its widely palmated antlers, the Irish Deer differs considerably from the Fallow Deer, but an extinct species recently described from the superficial deposits of Germany, under the name of Ruff's Deer, so closely connects the two as to show that they constitute but a single group. The Roe Deer (*Capreolus caprea*), which is more a southern than a northern form, is found in many of the caverns, but is rare in the brick-earths; while the Reindeer (*Rangifer tarandus*), although common in the caverns and superficial deposits both of England and Scotland, is, as already mentioned, quite unknown to the east of London. The Wild Boar, which is one of the most recently exterminated British Mammals, requires a mere mention; but the Hippopotamus of the British Pleistocene deposits, which is specifically inseparable from the common African species, is one of the most important of the whole Fauna, so far as climatic conditions are concerned. Occurring commonly in the river-gravels and brick-earths of the south and midland districts of England, its remains are less frequent in caverns, although found as far north as Yorkshire. In our opinion, more importance is attached to the occurrence of the remains of this animal in a deposit than those of any other Mammal, since we cannot conceive it possible that the creature could have existed except where the rivers were more or less open throughout the year.

Elephants were represented by the Mammoth (*Elephas primigenius*), which may be considered merely as a northern hairy representative of the existing Indian species, and the so-called Straight-tusked Elephant (*E. antiquus*), which approximated in the structure of its teeth more or less markedly to the African Elephant. Bounded to the south-west by the Pyrenees, and found but sparingly to the south of the Alps, the Mammoth ranged northwards to Siberia, where, as already said, its frozen carcases are from time to time discovered, and where it must have existed in vast herds. It has recently been attempted to show that the Mammoth lived and died before the Glacial Epoch; but although its remains undoubtedly occur on the old land-surfaces upon which the post-glacial deposits were laid down, the opinion of many geologists is hostile to the new view, and it is probable that the Mammoth saw both the incoming and the waning of glacial conditions.

The Rodents, or Gnawing animals, need not detain us long, more especially since the burrowing habits of some of them render the occurrence of their remains by no means trust-worthy evidence that they are contemporaneous with the other contents of the deposits where they are found. The Beaver, although very rare in caves, occurs in the brick-earths of the Thames Valley; while the Siberian and South Russian Picas (*Lagomys pusillus*) have been found in three caves and the Ightham fissure. The northern Vole (*Microtus ratticeps*), and the Siberian Vole (*M. gregalis*), both of which have been identified from the last-named deposit, are animals essentially characteristic of desert or steppe regions; and much the same is true of the Susliks (*Spermophilus*), several species of which inhabited England during the Cavern Period.

It will thus be seen that the problems presented by the later Pleistocene Mammalian Fauna of Britain are so complex, and apparently so contradictory, that at present it is quite hopeless to arrive at any satisfactory conclusion. That so far as the larger Mammals are concerned, we live in an impoverished age, is perfectly true; but whether, as Mr. Wallace supposes, this is due to the effects of the Glacial Period seems more than doubt-ful, if geologists are right (and we believe they are) in assigning a Post-Glacial date to our brick-earths, river-gravels, and cavern-deposits.

II. The Forest-bed and Crag Periods.

The fresh-water deposit on the eastern coast of England known as the Forest-bed, of which the age is Pre-Glacial, occupies a somewhat intermediate position in regard to its Mammalian Fauna between the Cavern and Crag Periods; some of the species characterising the former epoch extending downwards to the Forest-bed, while others are replaced by those of the Crag. Still, however, the percentage of existing species is high, and as but few of the genera appear to be extinct, we prefer to assign the formation in question to the Pleistocene rather than to the Pliocene Epoch.

Commencing with the Carnivores, we have evidence that the Forest-bed possesses a Sabre-toothed Tiger apparently specifically distinct from the Cavern species, and not improbably identical with one (*Machærodus cultridens*) from the upper Pliocene beds of the Val d'Arno in Tuscany; while the Hyæna is identical with the Cavern form, that is to say, the existing South African species. The Wolf, and probably the Fox, as well as the Marten and the Glutton, are likewise existing species ranging as far down as the Forest-bed; and the occurrence of the last-named is somewhat notable, as showing that even at this early epoch, northern types were capable of existing in England before we have any evidence of the incoming of strongly-marked Glacial conditions. The other land Carnivores of the Forest-bed are Otter and the Cave-Bear; while the teeth of a smaller Bear have been tentatively assigned to the American Grizzly, although we should think it more probable that they pertained to the Brown species. Of marine forms, a Walrus which has been regarded as specifically distinct from the living representative of the genus, and the Bearded Seal (*Phoca barbata*), now inhabiting the North Atlantic, have been recorded from the formation under consideration.

In the Hoofed Order we find the Bison and the Musk-Ox, as well as a large Sheep (*Ovis savini*) apparently allied to the Himalayan Argali, inhabiting East Anglia during the deposition of the Forest-bed; while the Roe Deer, an extinct kind of Elk (*Alces latifrons*), and the Red Deer likewise lived at the same time. There appear also to have been several species of ex-

tinct Deer, among which Savin's Deer (*Cervus savini*) is remarkable for the flattened form of the "brow"-tine, while in the
magnificent species (*C. sedgwicki*) named after the well-known
Professor of Geology at Cambridge the spreading antlers
attained a complexity of structure unknown in any other
member of the genus. Of other Ungulates, the Hippopotamus,
the Wild Boar, and the Horse, date from the Forest-bed ; and
the occurrence in this formation of the former species in
association with the Musk-Ox, Glutton, and Walrus, presents
us with another of the puzzles which almost break the heart of
the palæontologist.   In addition to the Common Horse, there
was an extinct species known as Steno's Horse (*Equus stenonis*),
and distinguished by the small size of the so-called front inner
pillar of the upper molar teeth, or the portion occupying the

Fig. 1.   Right upper molar tooth of Steno's Horse.

middle of the lower border of the annexed figure. In this
respect the species in question was less specialised than the
modern Horse, and makes a step in the direction of the under-
mentioned Hipparion. On the Continent Steno's Horse occurs
in beds of upper Pliocene age, where it was accompanied by
the Etruscan Rhinoceros (*Rhinoceros etuscus*), as was also
the case in the Forest-bed.   This Etruscan Rhinoceros
differs from the Leptorhine and Megarhine Cavern species
in the much lower crowns of its molar teeth, and is likewise, therefore, a more generalised type. So far as can be

determined, the Mammoth does not appear to have come into existence at the period of the Forest-bed; but the so-called Straight-tusked Elephant (*Elephas antiquus*) was abundant, as well as a third species (*E. meridionalis*), unknown in the higher deposits. This southern Elephant, which takes its name from its occurrence in the upper Pliocene strata of the Val d'Arno, attained enormous dimensions, and is characterised by the smallness of the height of the crowns of the molar teeth in comparison with their width, as well as by the large size and lozenge-like form of the discs of ivory enclosed by the enamel-plates on their grinding surface, and the width of the intervening spaces of cement. The enamel-plates themselves are very thick and smooth, being almost completely devoid of the puckerings characterising those of the Mammoth. Although anyone can see the difference between a typical molar of the southern Elephant and one of the Mammoth, some teeth of the former are very like certain of those of the Straight-toothed Elephant, while some of the latter come very close to those of the Mammoth. It is, therefore, advisable in determining the teeth of fossil Elephants to seek the aid of a specialist. It may be added that remains of the southern Elephant have been met with in a remarkable deposit at Dewlish, in Dorsetshire, which must consequently be correlated either with the Forest-bed or the upper Crags.

Among the smaller Mammals we find the Rodents well represented in the Forest-bed, some of the species still existing in Britain, while others are now confined to the Continent, and a few are extinct. In the former class we have the Squirrel, the Wood-Mouse (*Mus sylvaticus*), and the Bank-Vole (*Microtus glareolus*); and in the second the Beaver, the continental Field-Vole (*M. arvalis*), and the Siberian Vole (*M. gregalis*); while of the extinct forms the Giant Beaver (*Trogontherium cuvieri*) indicates a genus characteristic of this formation and the upper

Pliocene, and a Vole (*M. intermedius*) intermediate in size between the Water-Vole and Field-Vole differs from both in having distinct roots to the molar teeth. In the Insectivorous Order we have the Mole, and the Common and Pigmy Shrews, as representatives of the existing British Fauna ; while the Russian Desman (*Myogale moschata*) is now found only in the districts between the rivers Don and Volga, where it leads an aquatic life, not unlike that of our Water-Vole, save that its habits are insectivorous instead of herbivorous.

The few Cetacean remains from the Forest-bed appear all referable to existing forms, and indicate the same mixture of southern and northern forms as characterises the land Fauna. Among these are the southern Right Whale (*Balæna australis*), a large Fin-Whale (*Balænoptera*), the Sperm-Whale—which still occasionally straggles as far north as Britain—the Killer, or Grampus (*Orca gladiator*), the False Killer (*Pseudorca crassidens*)—originally described from a skull from the fens near Stamford, but subsequently found living in the North Sea,— the Arctic Narwhal (*Monodon monoceros*), and White Whale (*Delphinapterus leucas*), the Common Dolphin, the Bottle-nosed Dolphin, and the Porpoise.

We now come to the shelly deposits of the east coast, locally known by the term of " Crags," a name which has been adopted into geological nomenclature. These beds admit of a three-fold division, namely, the Norwich, Fluvio-Marine, or Mammaliferous Crag, the Red Crag, and the Coralline, or White Crag. The former, which is partly of fresh-water and partly of marine origin, shows a Molluscan Fauna of a decidedly northern type, and has at its base a bone-bed in which Mammalian remains occur in considerable quantities. The Red Crag takes its name from the colour of its sandy beds, and likewise contains a bone-bed in which the fossils are mainly converted into phosphate of lime, and are thus valuable as a source of artificial manure. Although its Molluscs are generally of a northern type, this feature is less marked than in the Norwich Crag. The lowest, or Coralline Crag, which is generally of a light colour, takes its name from the number of species of Polyzoa found in these beds; its Molluscan Fauna indicating warmer conditions than those prevailing during the deposition of the upper members of the series.

One of the features of the Mammalian Fauna of the crags is the occurrence of remains of Mastodons, which are quite unknown in the higher beds, and the comparative rarity of true Elephants; while still more noticeable is the abundance of the remains of Cetaceans, referable to many species and genera. Although some of the Crag Mammals belong to existing species, the great majority are extinct, and a small proportion belong to genera no longer existing. It is probable that the greater number of the Mammals found in these beds belong to species which were living during the time of their deposition, although a few may have been derived from antecedent Miocene beds. Certain specimens are, however, met with which have clearly been washed out from the London clay or other older Tertiary formations; and these, which may generally be recognised by their water-worn condition, will be omitted from our survey. Although the Mammals obtained from the different crags are by no means always the same, it will be convenient to treat of the whole series collectively.

Among the most difficult fossils to determine specifically are detached teeth of the Cats, and certain such specimens from the Red Crag, which have been regarded as indicating an extinct species, are so like the corresponding teeth of the Leopard that it would be hazardous to say they do not belong to that animal, although, on the other hand, it would be equally rash to say positively that such was the case. Whether a Sabre-tooth occurs in these deposits is uncertain; but there is no doubt as to the existence in that epoch of the Striped Hyæna (*Hyæna striata*), of Northern Africa and India, as several well-preserved teeth have been obtained from the Red Crag. The occurrence of this species in the Crag, and its replacement in the Forest-bed and Cavern Period by the Spotted Hyæna, is one of those remarkable facts in distribution which we have at present no means of explaining. Both the Wolf and the Fox appear to date from the period of the Red Crag, while the Polecat apparently occurs in the still earlier Coralline Crag. The Common Otter seems, however, to be of more modern origin, since a member of the same genus from the Norwich Crag, and a second from the Red Crag seem to be both extinct. By far the most remarkable of the Red Crag Carnivores is the Giant Panda (*Ælurus anglicus*), at present known only by an upper molar and a fragment of the lower jaw with the last tooth, since the genus to which it belongs is represented elsewhere solely by the Panda or Cat-Bear (*Æ. fulgens*) of the South-eastern Himalaya. The existing Panda, which is an animal about the size of a Fox, with a bright red coat and long bushy tail, is of especial interest as being the sole Old World representative of the Raccoons, and is characterised by the peculiarly complex structure of the upper molar teeth and the remarkably curved form of the lower jaw. Since the Crag fossils present precisely the same character, there can be no doubt of their having belonged to an animal of the same genus, which was, however, double the size of its existing representative. That a creature so isolated and peculiar as the Himalayan Panda should be represented by a closely-allied but gigantic species which lived in Britain in company with the Wolf and the Fox, is one of the most unexpected facts revealed by palæontological investigation.

So far as can be determined, there is no evidence of the existence of true Bears in the Crag, and it is probable that both the Cave-Bear and the Brown Bear do not antedate the Forest bed, although an extinct species occurs in the Upper Pliocene of the Continent. In the Red Crag the place of these animals is taken by a huge Carnivore known as the *Hyænarctus*, which was in many respects intermediate between Bears and Dogs, the upper molar teeth, as shown in the accompanying cut, being shorter and squarer than those of the former, while the carnassial or flesh-teeth were of a cutting type more like those of the latter. Species of the same genus occur in the Pliocene and Miocene formations of the Continent, as well as in the Indian Pliocene. A Walrus (*Trichechus huxleyi*), apparently identical with the Forest-bed form, as well as two species of Seals, one of which is assigned to an extinct genus (*Phocanella*),

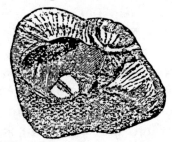

Fig. 2. Last upper molar tooth of the *Hyænarctus*.

complete the list of the Carnivores of the Red Crag ; and it may be added that the occurrence of the former is not out of harmony with the climatic condition indicated by the Molluscs.

Neither Oxen, Musk-Ox, Sheep, or Goats are known from the Crag ; but a Gazelle, apparently extinct, from the Norwich Crag is of considerable interest as indicating the probable existence in England at that period of open, more or less desert plains like those frequented by the majority of the existing members of that group. In contrast to this paucity of Hollow-horned Ruminants is the abundance of Stags, which are especially common in the Norwich Crag, and for the most part belong to types unlike any now existing, although Falconer's Deer (*C. falconeri*) was near akin to the Fallow Deer. Among

the most peculiar is a species named *C. verticornis*, characterised by its short and thick antlers, in which the cylindrical
"brow"-tine curves downwards over the forehead, while above
it are two oval tines, and superiorly the beam becomes flattened
and expanded into a crown of two points. The Pigs were
represented by two extinct species, one of which was nearly
allied to, if not identical with, the gigantic *Sus erymanthius*
from the Pliocene deposits of Attica; while the smaller one
has been identified with another continental species known as
S. palæochærus.

Among the Odd-toed Ungulates, true Horses seem very
rare, although Steno's Horse, alluded to above as characteristic of the Forest-bed, has been recorded from the
Norwich Crag. Three-toed Horses of the genus *Hipparion*
were, however, common in the Red Crag; their upper
molar teeth, as shown in the accompanying figure, being

Fig. 3.   Left upper molar tooth of Three-toed Horse (*Hipparion*).

always distinguishable at a glance by the isolation of the
antero-internal from the enamel-folds of the centre of the
crown. The Red Crag Rhinoceroses are quite distinct from
those of the overlying beds, one being identical with the Hornless *Rhinoceros incisivus* of the continental Pliocene, while it is
possible that a second may be the same as a Two-horned form
(*R. schleiermacheri*), which is apparently nearly allied to the
living Sumatran species, having, like the Hornless forms, large
tusks in the lower jaw. The occurrence of a Tapir in the Red

Crag assists in explaining the present anomalous distribution of these animals; one species of which is Malayan, while all the rest are South American. Although the Straight-tusked Elephant occurs in the Norwich Crag, while the southern Elephant dates from the subjacent Red Crag, the commonest Prosboscideans of the period under consideration were Mastodons, which, it is scarcely necessary to mention, differ from Elephants in the much lower crowns of their molar teeth, which are surmounted by low tubercles, frequently arranged in a small number of transverse ridges, separated from one another by more or less completely open valleys, this type of tooth being much more generalised than that of the Elephants. In one of the Crag Mastodons (*M. arvernensis*) the tubercles of the molars were arranged alternately, and the lower jaw was short and devoid of tusks; in a second (*M. longirostris*) the same tubercles were arranged in transverse ridges, with their worn summits showing a trefoil pattern like those of the Hippopotamus, the lower jaw being at the same time greatly produced and armed with a large pair of tusks; while in the third (*M. borsoni*) the ridges in most of the teeth were three, instead of four, in number, and retained much less distinct evidence of their constituent tubercles.

The Rodents need not detain us long, but the Giant Beaver of the Forest-bed was sparingly represented in the Norwich Crag, while a smaller member of the same genus (*Trogontherium minus*) is found in the subjacent beds; the only other named Rodent being the extinct Vole referred to above, which ranges downwards from the Forest-bed to the Norwich Crag.

The Whales and Dolphins of the Crag are so interesting that they would afford ample material for an article by themselves, and can, therefore, receive but scant notice in the limits of space available. Among the Whale-bone group there appear to have been no less than four species of Right Whales, one of

which (*Balæna affinis*) resembled the Greenland Whale, while a
second (*B. primigenia*) was more nearly allied to the southern
Right Whale, and a third (*B. balænopsis*) was characterised by
its small dimensions.   Hump-backs (*Megaptera*) were likewise
well represented, as were also the Finners (*Balænoptera*) ; while
an extinct genus (*Cetotherium*) allied to the last, contains
several species from the Crag.   It may be mentioned here that
all these Whales are represented by the shell-like tympanic
bones of the inner ear, which differ remarkably in form in the
various genera, and thus prove unerring guides both for generic
and specific determination.   Another type of these bones, remarkable for its egg-like form, serves to differentiate yet
another extinct genus (*Herpetocetus*) of Whale-bone Whales.
Turning to the Toothed Whales, a remarkable feature in the
Red Crag is the number of teeth indicating the occurrence of
large forms more or less closely allied to the Sperm-Whale,
but mostly distinguished by the presence of small caps of
enamel.   There were likewise smaller forms, one of which has
long been known under the name of *Physodon*, although it was
only recently that the writer was able to determine from the
evidence of a Patagonian specimen that it differed from the
Sperm-Whale in having teeth in the upper as well as in the
lower jaw, and thus indicates a distinct and more primitive
Family connecting the Sperm-Whale with the Dolphins.   That
a Bottle-nosed Whale nearly allied to the existing *Hyperoodon
rostratus* inhabited British water during the Red Crag Period, is
proved by an ear-bone in the Ipswich Museum ; and the number of Beaked Whales living at the same time must have been
extraordinarily great, from the profusion in which their dense
bony beaks occur in these deposits.   Most of them belong to
the same genus (*Mesoplodon*) as that rare visitor to the English
shores, Sowerby's Whale ; although a few pertain to an extinct
genus (*Choneziphius*) characterised by the presence of an un-

ossified tubular perforation running through the centre of the beak. A species of the extinct Shark-toothed Dolphins (*Squalodon*), together with a Killer (*Orca*), Black-Fish (*Globiceph-alus*), Dolphin (*Delphinus*), and Bottle-nosed Dolphin (*Tur-siops*), completes the list of Crag Cetaceans. It may be added that the Sirenians, that is to say the Order to which belong the living Manati and Dugong, are represented by a skull of the extinct genus *Halitherium* from the Red Crag, but it is quite possible that this specimen may have been washed out of the Miocene beds.

Although the Fauna of the Crag would have appeared strange and foreign even to an inhabitant of Britain during the early historic period, when the Wolf, Bear, Aurochs, and Beaver still lingered in our islands, could a cave-man have seen Britain as it existed during the period of the Crags, he would not have found the Fauna very different to the one with which he was acquainted, Mastodons taking the place of Elephants, and the Hornless Rhinoceros representing the Two-horned Woolly species, which he had probably been accustomed to hunt.

III. THE LOWER TERTIARY PERIOD.

Between the Coralline Crag and the Hempsted beds of the Isle of Wight, which belong to the middle portion of the Oligocene Period, and are the next Tertiary deposits met with in Britain, is a long gap, owing to the complete absence of all representatives of the Miocene and Upper Oligocene strata of the Continent. In consequence of this imperfection of the record, instead of finding a gradual transition from the Mammals of the Crag Period as we pass downwards through the Miocene bed till we reach the Oligocene, we notice that the Mammalian Fauna of the lower Tertiaries of Britain is utterly unlike that of the upper beds, and shows not the

faintest trace of a connection therewith.   In place of Deer,
Rhinoceroses, Horses, and Pigs, we have, even in the highest
beds of the lower Tertiaries, Ungulate Mammals of strange and
unknown types, all of which belong to genera long since
extinct, and differ widely in the structure of their low-crowned
cheek-teeth from all modern Mammals, although some appear
to have approximated in external form to the Tapirs and others
to the Pigs.   Elephants and Mastodons were entirely unknown,
and the place of Monkeys was filled by primitive Lemur-like
creatures.   All the indications afforded by the Flora and the
Molluscan Flora of the Oligocene and Eocene beds point to
the conclusion that during those epochs Britain enjoyed a
tropical or sub-tropical climate ; and, in some respects, its
Fauna may be compared to that of Madagascar at the present
day, although, of course, the genera of the Mammals, and in
many cases even the families, were different.   Indeed, of the
land Mammals inhabiting Oligocene and Eocene England,
only two groups can be referred to genera that still exist, one
of these being now relegated to the New World.

Lest the reader should begin to think that the whole of the
strata whose Fauna we have to consider in this part of our
subject belong to nearly the same geological period, we hasten
to point out the various groups into which they are divided,
preparatory to the consideration of their Fauna.   The highest
of the Oligocene beds in Britain are those forming the steep
clay cliffs on the western side of the Isle of Wight, in the
neighbourhood of Yarmouth, and termed the Hempsted beds,
from a village of that name which is situated upon them.
These belong to the middle portion of the Oligocene period,
and have a Fauna similar to that of certain beds at Ronzon,
near Puy-en-Velay, in the Haute Loire.   Next in descending
order are the Bembridge beds of the Hampshire basin, whose
Fauna corresponds with that of the gypsum beds on which

Paris stands, and which are consequently assigned to the lower part of the Oligocene; the beds of Hordwell, in Hampshire, and Headon, in the Isle of Wight, likewise belonging to the same great division. The clays of Barton, in Hampshire, which, like those next mentioned, unfortunately yield scarcely any Mammalian remains, bring us to the upper portion of the Eocene Period; while the older clays of Bracklesham, in Sussex, are assigned to the middle division of the same epoch. Better known than these is the London clay, forming the upper portion of the Lower Eocene, and yielding several types of Mammals; beneath which are the unfossiliferous Woolwich and Reading beds, resting on the chalk. Before proceeding to the consideration of the Fauna of these various beds, it may be observed that Mammalian remains are for the most part rare and fragmentary, and that for a full knowledge of the extent of the Fauna of the period, and the structure of its component items, we have to depend largely upon the discoveries made on the Continent or in the United States, both of which are more favoured than Britain in regard to the preservation of early Tertiary Mammals. In our survey of the Fauna of all these beds, it will be more convenient to treat of the animals according to their zoological position, indicating the different horizons in which they severally occur.

At the present day Lemurs are chiefly characteristic of Madagascar, although likewise occurring in Africa, and also represented in south-eastern Asia, but in the Oligocene Period they were abundant in Europe. One of these early Lemurs was described from the Hordwell beds as far back as the year 1844 under the name of *Microchœrus*, but it is only recently that its true affinities have been recognised. Not much larger than a Squirrel, this creature approximated in the structure of its skull to the African Lemurs known as Galagos, but differed from all the existing members of the group in that the lower tusk was formed by the canine tooth and not by the first tooth of the premolar series. Still more different from any living Lemur was the Oligocene *Adapis*, first described from France, and regarded as an Ungulate, but subsequently recognised from the Hordwell beds. It differs from all modern Lemurs in the presence of four pairs of pre-molar teeth in each jaw, and one of the species attained a comparatively large size, its skull measuring upwards of 4 inches in length.

In Madagascar, Lemurs are now accompanied by many kinds of Insectivores, and it is, therefore, not surprising to find a member of that order in the Hordwell beds. This animal (*Necrogymnura*), instead of being allied to the Malagasy Insectivores, appears, however, to have been related to the Gymnura of Borneo, which may be described as a long-tailed Hedgehog without spines, and therefore somewhat Rat-like in general appearance. Civets likewise form an important element in the modern Malagasy Fauna, and the Hordwell Lemurs were accompanied by a member of that group assigned to the existing African and Oriental genus *Viverra*, which includes the true Civets. With the exception of the Opossums, this Civet is the only terrestrial Mammal from the earlier British Tertiaries which can be referred to a still living genus. The other early British Carnivores belong to an extinct group known as the Creodonts, which disappeared with the close of the Oligocene Period. They differ from modern Carnivores in that all their molar teeth were furnished with sharp cutting blades, instead of a single pair of cheek-teeth in each jaw being specially modified for cutting with a scissor-like action. In their dentition these primitive Carnivores approximate, indeed, both to the Insectivores and the Marsupials, and they are undoubtedly far more generalised types than the existing members of the order to which they belong. While some were not larger than a Fox, others fully equalled the dimensions of the largest Bears. In Britain they are represented by one genus (*Hyæno-*

don) from the Hordwell beds, by a second (*Pterodon*) from the Bembridge limestone, and a third (*Argillotherium*) from the London clay. The last is, however, only known by an imperfect skull without the teeth, and may prove to be identical with one of the foreign genera.

Passing on to the Hoofed Order, one of the most interesting of the Even-toed section is the *Dichodon* of the Hordwell and Headon beds, as being the only early British Ungulate having the upper molar teeth with the four crescentic columns characterising the true Ruminants, to the ancestors of which group it was probably more or less closely allied. Connecting these early Ruminant-like forms with the ancestors of the Pigs is the *Hyopotamus* of the Hempsted beds, in which the upper molars were of the same general type as those of the Anoplothere (represented in Fig. *A* of our illustration, p. 324), although the whole form of the creature was more Pig-like, the skull being long and narrow, with large tusks, separated by an interval both from the incisor teeth in front and the pre-molars behind. The *Hyopotamus* was doubtless a four-toed animal like the Hippopotamus, but an apparently allied form from the Headon beds takes its name of *Diplopus* from the reduction of the toes to two in each limb. In the allied *Anthracotherium*, of both the Hempsted and Headon beds, the molars lose to a great extent the crescentic structure of those of the *Hyopotamus ;* and in the gigantic *Elotherium* from Hempsted, and the smaller *Chœropotamus* of the Bembridge series, we come to Ungulates, having tubercular molars of the same general type as those of the Pigs, although in the upper jaw they retain the five-columned arrangement characterising the *Hyopotamus*, and have much squarer crowns than those of the Pigs. There can, however, be little doubt that in this group we are very close to the ancestral stock from which the modern Pigs and Ruminants have alike originated.

On the other hand, the Anoplotheres (*Anoplotherium*), which

Y 2

occur in the Lower Oligocene of the Isle of Wight, and the upper molars of which are shown in figure *A* of the accompanying illustration, belong to what is called an inadaptive type—that is, one which has died out without leaving descendants. These long-tailed animals, some of which reached the dimensions of an average-sized Mule, were remarkable for the

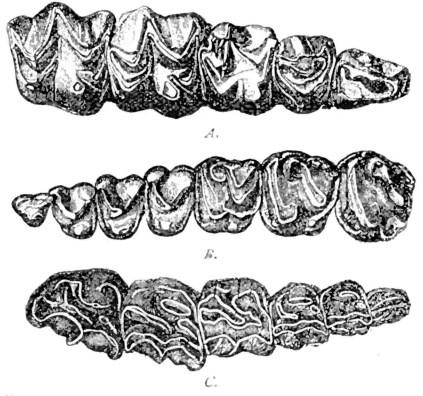

A.

B.

C.

Upper check-teeth of (*A*) Anoplothere, (*B*) Palæothere, and (*C*) Coryphodon. *A* is from the right, while *B* and *C* are from the left side.

circumstance that the teeth formed a continuous series round the jaws, without any interruption by large tusks; and they were further peculiar among the group to which they belong in that in some cases there were three toes to each foot, although in others they conformed to the more normal type in having but two. In these animals the pre-molar teeth (two of which are shown on the right side of the figure) were only slightly compressed, but the nearly allied small and delicately-built Xiphodons take their name from the extreme compression and secant form of the teeth in question, in which respect they recall the modern Chevrotains, or Mouse-Deer. Whether the Xiphodons are really British it is not clear, although a skull from the Red Crag, evidently derived from an older structure, has been assigned to them. The large size of the "tear-pit," or lachrymal fossa in front of the eye, has suggested for another member of this group, having teeth of the Anoplothere type, the name of *Dacrytherium*, the English representative of the genus having been originally described from the Hordwell and Headon beds under the name of *Dichobune*.

This completes our list of the Even-toed Ungulates, and we proceed to notice the few early Tertiary British representatives of the Odd-toed group, or those in which the toe corresponding to the human middle finger is symmetrical in itself and larger than either of the others. To this group belong the well-known Palæotheres (*Palæotherium*), so abundant in the gypsum of the Paris basin, and more sparingly represented in the Headon and Bembridge beds of Hampshire and the Isle of Wight. The structure of the cheek-teeth of a medium-sized representative of this genus is exhibited in figure *B* of the illustration; and in general form these animals somewhat resembled Tapirs, although the neck was relatively longer, and there were but three toes to each foot. It was long considered that the Palæotheres were on the ancestral line of the Horse, but this view is now discarded, and they are considered, like the Anoplotheres, to represent an inadaptive type. A much smaller animal, described as *Anchilophus*, of which teeth have been found in the Bembridge limestone, is, however, either very close to, or ac-

tually on the ancestral line in question.   Its upper molar teeth
are not very unlike those of the Palæotheres, but have the
oblique cross-crests narrower, less inclined, and separated by a
more open valley. Although very common in the Middle and
Lower Eocene beds of the Continent, the large genus of Odd-
toed Ungulates known as *Lophiodon* are represented in Britain
only by a single species from the Bracklesham beds.   While
their teeth are of the same general type as those of the Palæotheres and *Anchilophus*, the upper molars differ in having the
outer wall formed by sub-conical columns instead of flattened
lobes, thereby resembling the corresponding teeth of the modern
Tapirs.   Although most, if not all of these Lophiodons died out
without giving origin to any posterity, the case is very different
with the nearly allied little *Hyracotherium*, originally described
upon the evidence of an imperfect skull from the London clay
at Herne Bay, since this genus is one of the earliest to which
the ancestry of the Horse can be traced.   Thanks to the perfect preservation of specimens discovered in the United States,
where they were long known under a totally different name, we
now know that the Hyracothere was a small four-toed animal,
intimately connected with a still earlier five-toed type, while
superiorly it leads on to the *Anchilophus* and certain allied
Miocene continental forms, and thus to the modern Horse.
The Hyracothere received its name from an idea that it was related to the existing Hyrax; and it is a curious comment on the
early history of palæontology to notice that the lower teeth of
a second species obtained from the Lower Eocene sand of
Kyson, in Suffolk, were at first supposed to pertain to a
Monkey.

If the palæontological riches of the United States have
helped in the elucidation of the true affinities of the Hyracothere, still more markedly is this the case with regard to the
much larger Ungulate originally described on the evidence of

detached teeth from the London clay under the name of *Coryphodon*, in allusion to the strongly marked oblique crest surmounting their crowns. From nearly complete skeletons discovered in America, we know that the Coryphodons, which were animals with somewhat the proportions of a Bear, although furnished with a well-developed tail, differed from both the Odd-toed and Even-toed Ungulates in having five toes to each of the very short and wide feet, and likewise in the structure of the feet themselves. The molar teeth, too, as shown in figure *C* of the illustration (p. 324), are likewise quite different from those of any living member of the Order, and are remarkable for the extreme shortness of their crowns. The nearest allies of these animals were the Uintatheres of North America, distinguished by the presence of a large pair of tusks in the upper jaw, and the two groups collectively constitute the order of Short-footed Ungulates.

One remarkable palate of a skull from the London clay of Herne Bay, preserved in the museum at York, and described under the name of *Platychærops*, has given rise to some amount of discussion as to its serial position. It has been suggested, however, that it belongs to a peculiar group of Mammals from the North American Eocene, which combine many of the characteristics of the Ungulates, Carnivores, and Rodents. Of the latter order there are but small traces in the lower British Tertiaries; but some lower jaws from the Hordwell and Headon beds have been referred to the genus *Theridomys*, which is of common occurrence in the corresponding continental strata, and indicates an extinct Family of the Order Whales are likewise rare, but from the Barton beds there has been obtained a skull belonging to the peculiar group of Zeuglodonts, which are not improbably the ancestral types whence the modern toothed Whales have been evolved. Unlike all existing members of the Order, these extinct Cetaceans had double-fanged molar teeth, whose compressed crowns had the edges surmounted by well-marked serrations; and, what is more remarkable, their bodies appear to have been invested with a bony armour comparable to that of Crocodiles.

The last of the Tertiary Mammals that we have to notice are Opossums (*Didelphys*), remains of which have been detected both in the Hordwell beds and in the Lower Eocene sand of Kyson. It is almost superfluous to add that Opossums, which in Oligocene and Eocene times were widely spread over Europe, are now confined to America, where they attain their greatest development in that half of the continent lying to the south of the isthmus of Darien. The relegation of the originally European genus to the New World is somewhat analagous to the banishment of the nearest living allies of the British Jurassic Mammals to Australia, and is a well-marked instance of that gradual disappearance of the lower types of Mammalian life from the western regions of the Old World, with the development of higher forms, which seems to have been such a characteristic feature in the evolution of the present Faunas of the globe.

ALPHABETICAL INDEX.

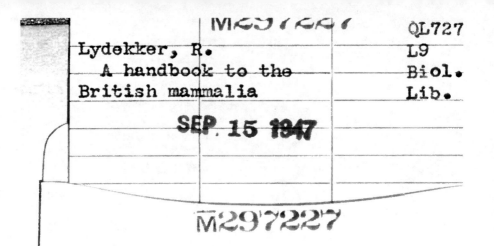

CPSIA information can be obtained at www.ICGtesting.com
Printed in the USA
BVOW04s0958100215

387119BV00024B/420/P